Related Books of Interest

The New Language of Marketing 2.0
Carter
ISBN: 978-0-13-714249-1

Audience, Relevance, and Search
Mathewson, Donatone, Fishel
ISBN: 978-0-13-700420-1

Web 2.0 and Social Networking for the Enterprise
Bernal
ISBN: 978-0-13-700489-8

The Social Factor
Azua
ISBN: 978-0-13-701890-1

Search Engine Marketing, Inc.
Moran, Hunt
ISBN: 978-0-13-606868-6

Do It Wrong Quickly
Moran
ISBN: 978-0-13-225596-7

Praise for *Get Bold*

"For crying out loud, IBM 'gets' social media. Don't you think it's about time that you do? This is the book to get you started."

—**Guy Kawasaki**, author of *Enchantment: The Art of Changing Hearts, Minds, and Actions*

"Sandy Carter has not just written a book, she has set a standard. *Get Bold* is NOT an option, it's an imperative. It's a book to be embraced, studied, and implemented."

—**Jeffrey Gitomer**, author of *The Little Red Book of Selling* and *Social BOOM!*

"Sandy Carter is spot-on in *Get Bold*. IBM has understood for years that this social networking thing meant more than sharing pictures of funny cats. *Get Bold* speaks in a language that will satisfy the stodgiest of CEOs but with a passion that belies the importance of these tools for these times."

—**Chris Brogan**, president, Human Business Works

"Looking for unparalleled innovation and improvements to the way your organization operates? In *Get Bold*, Sandy Carter demonstrates how leveraging powerful collaborative tools will transform your business into a vibrant Social Business."

—**Marcia Conner**, Social Business Industry Analyst and coauthor of *The New Social Learning*

"Sandy gets it. It is all about Social Business and social media, the transformational forces in the world today! Her examples are global and applicable with lessons to help you get started fast!"

—**Loic Le Meur**, founder of LeWeb, #1 social media and technology event in Europe

"Outstanding!!!! Sandy Carter, Women in Technology Hall of Famer, writes about Social Business in a way that you can just 'get it.' Sandy is a talented social media expert—who really understands the business side of technology."

—**Carolyn Leighton**, founder/chairwoman, WITI (Women in Technology International)

"This breakthrough book gives marketers a path to making the entire organization customer-centric using social media with real case studies and strategies for significant ROI. Most importantly, it provides the arguments you need to convince senior management that all departments in the organization must ride the wave together or your company risks getting lost out at sea."

—**Roy Young**, president of MarketingProfs, coauthor of *Marketing Champions*

"*Get Bold* is not another book full of buzz words that describe social media. It provides a clear blueprint for developing strategies that leverage social media to deliver tangible business results. If you want to create a social enterprise, you need to read this book!"

—**Tony O'Driscoll**, executive director, Center for Technology Entertainment and Media, Fuqua School of Business, Duke University

"For years now, companies have been watching the growing popularity of social networking and asking themselves whether this is something they should pay attention to. In *Get Bold*, Sandy Carter urges companies to leverage social media to unlock the intellectual capital within their organizations, paving the way for unprecedented innovation and becoming a new type of Social Business. Her book is based on her experiences helping IBM become a world-class Social Business and working with clients around the world and across industries to help them do so as well. Sandy offers the readers of *Get Bold* an action-oriented Social Business agenda to help them get started today."

—**Irving Wladawsky-Berger**, strategic advisor, IBM and Citigroup; and visiting faculty, MIT and Imperial College

"At this moment, we are on the verge of the largest shift in the communications landscape in the history of mankind. For the first time ever, companies can communicate with their constituents in ways never before possible. This more connected and engaged way of doing business, Social Business, will transform the way business gets done well into the next century. In Sandy Carter's new book, *Get Bold*, Sandy illustrates what leading companies are doing to transform their business around a framework to chart their own path to Social Business success. As a core partner of IBM's on Social Business, we'd encourage you to pick up this must-read!"

—**Jeff Dachis**, CEO of Dachis Group, who coined the phrase "Social Business"

Get Bold

Using Social Media to Create a New Type of Social Business

SANDY CARTER

IBM Press
Pearson plc
Upper Saddle River, NJ • Boston • Indianapolis • San Francisco
New York • Toronto • Montreal • London • Munich • Paris • Madrid
Cape Town • Sydney • Tokyo • Singapore • Mexico City

ibmpressbooks.com

IBM Press Program Managers: Steven M. Stansel, Ellice Uffer
Cover design: IBM Corporation
Associate Publisher: Dave Dusthimer
Marketing Manager: Dan Powell
Executive Editor: Mary Beth Ray
Publicist: Lisa Jacobson-Brown
Senior Development Editor: Christopher Cleveland
Managing Editor: Kristy Hart
Designer: Alan Clements
Senior Project Editor: Betsy Harris
Copy Editor: Cheri Clark
Indexer: Lisa Stumpf
Compositor: Nonie Ratcliff
Proofreader: Williams Woods Publishing
Manufacturing Buyer: Dan Uhrig

Published by Pearson plc

Publishing as IBM Press

IBM Press offers excellent discounts on this book when ordered in quantity for bulk purchases or special sales, which may include electronic versions and/or custom covers and content particular to your business, training goals, marketing focus, and branding interests. For more information, please contact

U.S. Corporate and Government Sales
1-800-382-3419
corpsales@pearsontechgroup.com

For sales outside the U.S., please contact

International Sales
international@pearson.com

The following terms are trademarks or registered trademarks of International Business Machines Corporation in the United States, other countries, or both: IBM, IBM Press, InnovationJam, developerWorks, Watson, Lotusphere, WebSphere, Smarter Planet, and Cognos. Coremetrics is a registered trademark of Coremetrics, Inc., an IBM Company.

Intel is a registered trademark of Intel Corporation or its subsidiaries in the United States and other countries. Microsoft, PowerPoint, and Xbox LIVE are trademarks of Microsoft Corporation in the United States, other countries, or both. Agent 209 is a trademark of DeepMile in the United States, other countries, or both. Other company, product, or service names may be trademarks or service marks of others.

Library of Congress Cataloging-in-Publication Data

Carter, Sandy, 1963-
  Get bold : using social media to create a new type of social business / Sandy Carter.
     p. cm.
  ISBN-13: 978-0-13-261831-1 (pbk.)
  ISBN-10: 0-13-261831-1
  1. Business networks--Computer network resources. 2. Social media--Economic aspects. 3. Business enterprises--Computer network resources. 4. Online social networks. I. Title.
  HD69.S8C37 2011
  658.8'72--dc23
                        2011027924

   Pearson Education, Inc.
   Rights and Contracts Department
   501 Boylston Street, Suite 900
   Boston, MA 02116
   Fax (617) 671-3447

ISBN-13: 978-0-13-261831-1
ISBN-10: 0-13-261831-1

Text printed on recycled paper in the United States at R.R. Donnelley in Crawfordsville, Indiana.
Second printing October 2011

To my bold family.

Personally, I could not have done this without my husband, Todd, and my two angel daughters Cassie and Maria. I dedicate this book to them!

In addition, I dedicate this book to:
My parents, who have inspired me my whole life—
this book reflects them!

My brother, who is my protector!

My in-laws, who have become my cheer squad!

My business family, including IBM and my clients
and partners—the best in the world!

"Other things may change us, but we start and end with family." –Anthony Brandt

Contents

Bonus case studies are available online at www.ibmpressbooks.com/title/9780132618311. Create an account and register your book to gain access to the material. (After you register your book, a link to the additional content will be listed on your Account page, under Registered Products.)

Foreword— Business Is Personal

"Business is personal." That's one of the first things I learned as a freshly scrubbed college graduate with no real working experience. Develop relationships with people, both inside and outside of the company. To get work done, you also have to get to know the people you work with. Remember important details, but more than just the superficial facts of birthdays and spouse's name—get to know them as people.

But I have a confession to make: I'm lousy at remembering these kinds of details. So I was an early user of "personal data assistants" (PDAs) and clicked my heels the first time I laid eyes on a CRM system.

But that is nothing compared to the transformation of what social networks have done for my business life. When I receive an email from someone, I automatically see the person's LinkedIn or Facebook profile, and if available, their latest tweets. This information provides me with the lifeblood of business data: context.

In fact, each time I visit a site or store, I run a good chance of running into someone I "know" because that site has enabled services like Facebook Connect to import my friends into the experience. Rather than reading every review on Amazon, or seeing comments from every person on Huffington Post, I can filter to see only reviews and comments from people I know, namely, my friends. Even search is changing—Google and Microsoft's Bing integrate social signals into search results from around the world.

In a nutshell, social networks and your friends on them are becoming like air. These personal relationships appear where and when you need them, rather than being locked away only on social sites like Facebook, Twitter, LinkedIn, and YouTube.

The impact for business is that you have to be like air as well, and be anywhere, anytime your customers, employees, and partners need and want you to be. I'm talking about you personally as a businessperson, and also "you" as a company entity.

This is the foundation for why it's important to transform you and your organization into a Social Business—because this is what will be required of you to be competitive and successful in the future. More than anything else, businesses that can harness being social and being personal, and that can extend that to every corner and person of the organization, will have a significant advantage. That's because they will make business personal in a way that traditional organizations will struggle with.

If you have picked up this book and are already reading this Foreword, you tend to fall into one of two groups. Either you are a believer and want to get on with it, or you are still trying to figure out if, when, and how you will get started being a Social Business. If you are in the first group, a believer, skip the rest of this Foreword and get going with Sandy's great content! But if you are in the second, let me give you an inkling of the road ahead of you.

The title of this book is *Get Bold*. You will need to be bold for the journey ahead of you because you are moving into unchartered territory. There are no easy answers to crucial questions like the ROI of Social Business or the road map of how to get started. But you could not be in better hands than those of Sandy Carter, who has been at the front lines working with hundreds of companies big and small, all around the world. You won't get all of your questions answered—no book could ever do that. But you will find this book a crucial resource as you embark on your journey.

Bon voyage, and get bold!

—**Charlene Li**, Author of *Open Leadership* and Founder of Altimeter Group

Foreword—
The New Transformation:
Social Business

As we entered the twenty-first century, the business world found itself facing significant change. The introduction of the Internet had ushered in a new era of opportunity and productivity—in fact, the magnitude of this shift was not unlike the changes that spurred the Industrial Revolution a century earlier. And while the Industrial Revolution was bringing big change to business—like unprecedented gains in manufacturing capability, new factory technology, and automation—it was having a similar impact on society, bringing prosperity to an emerging middle class in developing nations such as the United States. The "Information Revolution" of the twenty-first century is also bringing a new middle class forward, this time in places such as China and India. However, this time around, it's enabling work to move seamlessly around the globe, integrating people, processes, and content in new ways. The technologies of the Internet have fundamentally changed how business works and the speed at which it operates.

This wasn't completely clear in the late 90s, however, when many businesses were struggling with the confusion of the dot.com boom (and bust). What would the lasting effects of the Internet be? It was obviously on the scene for good, but by then we'd already seen that by itself it wasn't necessarily a guarantee of business success. Companies created websites just for the sake of getting on the Web, when they needed to question how the new technology could make their businesses more efficient, without destroying them. How would intellectual property be contained, and would employees spend their days surfing the Net? In many cases, the Internet-led business transformation ended up remaking many industries—such as publishing and advertising, to name a couple.

Today, we've seen the Internet evolve from a vehicle for simple content publishing, to a platform for commerce, to a way to connect people, and now finally to an "Internet of things" as mobile devices, electronics, and even appliances become connected to the Web. The concept of researching information and buying goods and services over the Web has now become second nature. In a relatively short period of time, the rise of social media has evolved from a way to share music and files to a fundamentally new way for people to interact with one another. Recent events have shown the power of the technology to play a key role in fundamentally remaking entire governments, thus changing the course of history. So once again, the Internet has issued business with a new challenge. As with the confusion we faced a decade ago, we need to understand how to harness these technologies to become more efficient, transforming both our business processes and our mind set.

Social networking has the potential to unlock the intellectual capital within organizations, to connect experts and expertise, and to pave the way for unprecedented innovation. For example, organizations that have tapped into the power of social tools are able to link their developers or researchers, no matter where they're located, to enable collaborative development that spans the boundaries of geographic borders or time zones. Developers then have the ability to easily exchange ideas and share input, sparking new innovation and allowing development to happen at a faster pace—speeding time to market.

Beyond facilitating collaboration, applying "social" technologies to business processes has the potential to radically improve the way organizations operate. For example, social tools enable human resource teams to identify and catalogue talent and expertise, linking people with the right skills with the right opportunities, when and where they're needed. Plus, HR teams could tap into these social networks to "sense" employee morale or target potential climate problems, proactively responding before issues escalate. This fundamentally changes the way the function works within an organization.

It also reveals the untapped power of the "data" generated by these connections. Organizations are no strangers to data; it's exploding at an incredible pace. And 80% of this data is unstructured—like the data from social networks, which could take the form of a conversation among customers on a message board. This represents a daunting challenge for any organization trying to learn from it or use it to make decisions. Fortunately, new types of analytics engines are helping companies to make sense of this data, unlocking an invaluable asset. By "instrumenting" the social networks inside and outside of your organization, interconnecting the key data they create, and applying analytics, you're able to gain insight into things such as the general attitude toward your brand and customer preferences, and even gain headlights into their buying behaviors. And using this insight, you can make more intelligent business decisions.

Sandy Carter explores these issues in the following chapters, discussing what it means to truly take advantage of these new technologies to improve the way your business runs. As the Vice President of Social Business and Collaboration Solutions Sales and Evangelism, Sandy has studied this issue very closely for IBM—but more than that, she represents a great, first-hand example of how social technology can be applied in a business setting. Embracing social tools very early on, she is now one of the top bloggers at IBM, as well as one of the most followed people on Twitter. In this book, she shares some best practices so that you and your company can truly take advantage of the monumental opportunity that's at stake.

Social technologies are already causing big changes in business, and companies are already seeing results. This book is a compelling and comprehensive look at the steps you can take to ensure you don't miss out.

—**Mike Rhodin**, Sr Vice President, IBM SWG Solutions

Preface

Of the three books I have written, I believe this is my favorite one. Why? I am passionate about social media and Social Business. It is more personal because of my daily use so I am excited to share my point of view with you!

The bottom line is that this book represents my loves:

- **My love of market transformation:** I seek out transformation. Today we are on the edge of the next "big" one. Companies around the world are now focused on becoming Social Businesses. A Social Business has a first-mover advantage since this transformation is about not technology but people. Relationships take time, not just money, and not just technology.

- **My love of learning:** Because this is a new area, I love working with those companies pushing the edge. Inside these covers are more than 70 client best practices.

- **My love of doing:** I have been "doing social" since 2005 and have experimented with it inside my teams as well as externally. The last six years of leveraging these social tools and techniques have energized me and taught me things I could not have learned without doing. I am not just a student of becoming social but a practitioner. I love sharing the lessons I learned from my successes but also my mistakes.

- **My love of *bold* action:** The title of this book is *Get Bold*. Bold is the ability to take a risk, manage the risk, and be confident in the outcome. People who know me know I have a bent for action. This book is designed for your company to create your own Social Business AGENDA so that you can be BOLD in this new world!

- **My love of the never-ending story:** My favorite quote is from an old Indian Proverb: "Tell me a fact and I'll learn. Tell me a truth and I'll believe. But tell me a story and it will live in my heart forever." This book is just a start. I continue to learn from my colleagues, peers, clients, and partners. Please follow my "living" story on my blog (http://socialmediasandy.wordpress.com/) and my Twitter account (http://twitter.com/sandy_carter).

Organization of This Book

This book is organized around a best-practice-adoption model. It is not about technology but about the way to get started with goals, culture, trust models, and governance structures.

Chapter 1, "The AGENDA for Social Business Success," is about understanding what a Social Business is and its characteristics, as well as expected business outcomes like competitiveness.

Chapters 2 through 7 outline the necessary steps to complete your company's own Social Business AGENDA. Based on working with thousands of clients, the book outlines the steps and process for creating your personalized Social Business AGENDA:

A: Align your goals and culture. You need to take this step to be ready to become more engaging and transparent. Do not underestimate the task ahead of you. Culture eats strategy for lunch. Take a look at IBM's Social Computing Guidelines as a way to get started!

G: Gain social trust. This focuses on finding your fans, friends, and followers, and forming best friends from your tippers or most influential clients or outside parties. It dives into what social trust is all about and how you instill it.

E: Engage through experiences. This part of the process focuses on how a company can engage its clients and employees and dives into gaming; virtual gifting; and location-based, mobile, or other stellar experiences to drive that engagement.

N: "Social" network your processes. Since this is about business, figuring out how to add social techniques to your processes is critical. Think about customer service—adding in Twitter to address your customers' concerns. Or try crowdsourcing for product innovation, or communities for incrementing your marketing processes around loyalty!

D: Design for reputation and risk management! This is the number one area of focus for the C level—managing the risk of having your brand online, your employees being your brand advocates, and even your clients becoming your marketing department! I think the value outweighs the risk . . . but see how to develop a disaster recovery plan as you plan for the worst, and expect the best!

A: Analyze your data! Social analytics are the new black! You need to see the patterns of sentiment, find out who your tippers are, and listen daily!

Chapter 8, "Technology as a Competitive Ingredient," focuses on understanding the basics of the technology and a framework to enable you to use these important tools to drive your success. Technology is definitely a critical part of your success.

Chapter 9, "Draw Up Your AGENDA," provides a showcase of complete Social Business AGENDA case studies with a summary on each workstream your company will need to complete.

Based on feedback from my great reviewers, I added a "Glossary of Social Business Terms." Because this is a new area, it helps to have this information handy. In fact, I use it almost daily now with my teams!

Bonus case studies are available online at www.ibmpressbooks.com/title/9780132618311. Create an account and register your book to gain access to the material. (After you register your book, a link to the additional content will be listed on your Account page, under Registered Products.)

ENJOY!

Sandy

Acknowledgments

This story would not have been possible without the help of many people:

First, God, who blessed me with creativity and a love of all things social!

Second, my family: Todd, Cassie, and Maria, who supported my weekends of writing; my parents, who inspired my bold ideas; my brother Gary's love and support; and my in-laws, who cheered me on!

Third, key members of my review team who were deeply involved through all stages of the book: Liz Markiewicz, Kathy White, Ted Stanton, Jennifer Dubow, Judith Hurwitz, Roy Young, and Patricia Santamaria.

Fourth, a set of mentors to lead the way, including Jeffrey Gitomer, Charlene Li, Irving Wladawsky-Berger, and Guy Kawasaki, who all taught me and shared their experiences freely.

Fifth, my customers for the great sharing of their learnings: 1-800-FLOWERS, Amazon.com, American Eagle Outfitters, Apple, Arrow ECS, Ascendant Technology, AT&T, Austrialian Open, Avery Dennison, BASF, Blendtec, Blue Cross Blue Shield of Massachusetts, Boston Medical Center, Cars.com, Caterpillar, Celestica, CEMEX, China Deaf Association, China Telecom, Coach, The Coca-Cola Company, Colgate-Palmolive, DeepMile, Dell, Deutsche Lufthansa AG, Domino's Pizza, Dr. Pepper Snapple Group, Elegance II Energizer, Fabergé, Farmers Insurance, Farmers Insurance University, Ford Motor Company, Forrester Research, Gap, Gatorade/PepsiCo, gDiapers, Godiva Chocolatier, GoMidjets, Harley-Davidson, History Channel, The Home Depot, Honda, Indium Corporation, Jerry Pozniak@TheDryCleaner, Kenneth Cole, Kinaxis, Kraft Foods, Manulife Financial, Meteor Solutions, Mob4Hire, Moosejaw, Mountain Dew/PepsiCo, National Football League, Newell Rubbermaid, Practising Law Institute, Pratt & Whitney, Price Chopper, ProChile, Procter & Gamble, Quantum Storage Systems, Richard Scott Salon and Day Spa, RobustCloud The Salvation Army, Sennheiser Electronic GmbH & Co. KG, Sogeti, Southern California Edison, Southwest Airlines, Starbucks, Taylor Guitars, Teach for America United Airlines, US Open Tennis, uTest, Virgin Atlantic, Visa, Volkswagen, Volvo, The Walt Disney Company, and Zappos.com.

Sixth, all the IBMers around the world who assisted me on this book: Ted Stanton, Chris Crummey, Scott J Smith, Bill Hassell, Charlie Hill, Graham MacKintosh, Mark Heid, Michael Rhodin, Alistair Rennie, Kristen Lauria, Doug Cox, Bart Lautenbach, Matt Carter, Dawn Herndon, Sergio Loza, Camilo Esteban Rojas Lopez, Jeff Schick, Larry Bowden, Thom Hagen, Guy P. Pacitti, Bob McDonald, Carlos Belak, Nigel Beck, and Bob McDonald.

Finally, my new friends at Pearson Education: Mary Beth Ray, Chris Cleveland, and Betsy Harris. Thanks for all your great advice and support.

About the Author

Sandy Carter is Vice President, Social Business Evangelism, in which capacity she is responsible for helping to set the direction for IBM's Social Business initiative. Social Business is a more than $200 billion marketplace.

Her career history is impressive. She has been a Chief Marketing Officer, Chief Sales Officer, Chief Software Alliance Officer, Business Leader, and Strategist who has successfully leveraged social techniques to drive business success. She and her teams have been awarded more than 25 social media awards for her innovative and successful implementation of Social Business techniques.

In 2011, Women in Technology inducted Ms. Carter into their Hall of Fame for the impact she had on the social media and Social Business marketplace. Fast Company named Ms. Carter one of the most influential women in technology, and Everything Channel's *CRN* magazine named her one of the 100 most powerful women in channels in 2010 and 2009.

Ms. Carter is the best-selling author of two books: *The New Language of Business: SOA & Web 2.0,* which won the Platinum MarCom Award in 2008, and *The New Language of Marketing 2.0: How to Use ANGELS to Energize Your Market,* which won the Silver MarketingSherpa award in 2009. Ms. Carter received MarCom awards for her blogger and Twitter communities and for the 2010 Business Partner Virtual Event. She has also been recognized by World Brand Congress as 2009 Brand Leader of the Year, and by Altimeter Group as one of the top 10 women in social media.

She was honored twice with the AIT United Nations Member of the Year award for helping developing countries in the area of technology. Ms. Carter is listed in Madison's Who's Who and the Cambridge Who's Who. She was named Best Speaker by Baptie & Company for receiving the highest speaker rating at the Baptie 2010 Channel Focus North America/Latin America conference. AlwaysOn named Ms. Carter to the Top 25 Women in Tech to Watch list in 2010.

Ms. Carter holds a Bachelor of Science degree in computer science from Duke University and an MBA from Harvard, and is fluent in eight programming languages. She received a patent for developing a methodology and tool to help customers create a technology deployment path in automation of their IT processes.

Visit her best-rated blog at http://socialmediasandy.wordpress.com/ and her Twitter account at http://twitter.com/sandy_carter.

The AGENDA for Social Business Success

"It is imperative that you have a bold agenda to engage your clients, your partners and your employees. The Social Business AGENDA is the connection to outperforming in the marketplace."

Sandy Carter

"What used to be cigarette breaks could turn into 'social media breaks' as long as there is a clear signal and IT isn't looking."

David Armano, author of Logic+Emotion blog

I am a Vice President at IBM®, mom, wife, and a Social Business evangelist. Since the early 2000s, I've been using social networking, social media, social software, or whatever you prefer to call it. What's powerful about the concepts of micro-blogging, wikis, video sharing, video chats, networks, communities, and more is that I get value just by reading and viewing. I consume far more social media than I contribute. My personal network of friends and family has allowed me to stay connected no matter where in the world I am. My professional network of colleagues, partners, and customers has led me to new career opportunities and new friends that I otherwise would never have encountered.

In 2005, I decided to transition from a viewer to a contributor as I saw a new channel to share my ideas and solicit open and anonymous feedback from my trusted network and followers. I wasn't sure at the time what type of effect this would have on me or my employer—IBM. In 2005, I was the Vice President of IBM's largest software brand when I decided to become an avid blogger and power user of social media. Since then, I have been amazed by the progress over the past few years with the rapid growth of social technology. Social media has overtaken the world. In his 2005 book, author Thomas Friedman talked about the world being flat. I would like to add that the world is now flat and connected.

While this book focuses on the value of becoming a Social Business, I don't want to downplay the importance that social technology has played in my personal life. Social media has become a way of life throughout the world. With more than 500 million people on Facebook, and 200 million blogs being updated daily, the power of numbers and of experience has taken over the world. It is growing faster than anything we have seen in the past. Grandparents are talking to their grandchildren, leveraging social media just as clients are impacting companies' products using the same tools. According to Oxygen Media and Lightspeed Research, women are becoming more and more dependent on social media and check Facebook when they first wake up, even before they get to the bathroom!

A majority of the social concepts that I will be writing about were born from early pioneers in the consumer space. These innovative pioneers opened my eyes to the power of connecting with friends and family. They also opened the door for large and small companies to leverage these social technologies—in essence, becoming a Social Business.

A Social Business is a business that embeds "social" in all of its processes, connecting people to people, people to information, and data to insight. It is a company that engages its employees and clients in a two-way dialogue with social tools, is transparent in sharing its expertise beyond its four walls, and is nimble in its use of insight to change on a dime. It is different from social media, in that social media primarily addresses or focuses on marketing and public relations. (That's where the media comes from.)

Inside each of us is a desire to be social and in return feel connected to other people. With the Internet came the ability to connect computers to computers and computers to networks. Email came along and replaced the need to send around office memos. Instant messaging then emerged with a faster and precious way to communicate in near real time, further reducing the office memo and, in some fashion, reducing email. Neither of these technologies provided that social contact that people seek (albeit instant messaging emoticons did help).

With the 21st century upon us, where everyone is so dispersed from their family, friends, suppliers, partners, and influencers, the Internet has reconnected us, satisfying that social desire. Social media is now connecting people with people and people with information. New collaboration technologies that are focused on simplicity and ease of use have led to a platform to share more than just words, but frame those words around your persona alongside videos, photos, your interests, and what's on your mind. My persona is not just that of an IBM Vice President, but also that of a mother and wife. In some cases, this new wave of disruptive technology replaced the "real-world" connectedness with a virtual one.

This connectedness reemphasizes that people are at the heart and soul of every business and relationship. As Jeffrey Gitomer, author of *Social Boom* and *The Little Red Book of Selling*, wrote,

> "All things being equal, people want to do business with their friends. All things being not so equal, people STILL want to do business with their friends."

Social Business has redefined and opened up the aperture on what a friend is, what role an employee plays in a company, how open processes are to clients, and how fast you can move. These definitions are changing just as fast as new technology is being created. When Facebook or the iPod launched, its creators didn't imagine creating an application ecosystem that would see hundreds of individual developers turn into millionaires. It's technologies like these where new markets are being created and defined every day.

Now, a new transformation has come, as big as when the Internet took over the market imagination. Social Business leverages all the social tools and techniques of social media, but expands the usage and efficiencies beyond "media and marketing" to all of a company's processes, both internal (such as human resources and talent management) and external (such as customer service, supply chain, product development, marketing, communications, and more). Just as in the Internet era, when many companies proclaimed that the tools were only for use by kids and universities, we are seeing a repeat of history. Some company leaders think social is just for kids and universities; however, we know better. We at IBM have lived Social as a Business and know its power.

As a Social Business, you can outperform your competitors. Businesses are evolving and differentiating themselves internally and externally by going back to the future. In other words, they are focusing on relationships with their clients, partners, citizens, and employees by engaging new technologies and platforms that powerfully and easily connect them in trusted and experiential ways.

I have had the pleasure of traveling to more than 60 countries around the world. The most common question I get from the customers, partners, and governments (and some of my IBM peers) is this:

> "How can I become a Social Business, and what is the value that it will bring to me, my department, and my company?"

My response:

> "At its core, a Social Business is a company that is engaged, transparent, and nimble. A Social Business is one that understands how to embrace social technology, use it, get value from it, and manage the risk around it. A Social Business embeds social tools in all its processes, and for both employees and clients—the entire ecosystem. In my experience, a leadership company explores the social techniques that really matter to its business with a systematic approach, by creating a bold, unique Social Business AGENDA."

These three characteristics—engaged, transparent, and nimble—showcase the value of applying social tools beyond just your marketing process into the business processes that drive your company's competitiveness. What do they mean?

- **Engaged:** A Social Business connects people to expertise. It connects individuals—whether customers, partners, or employees—as networks of people to generate new sources of innovation, foster creativity, and establish greater reach and exposure to new business opportunities. It establishes a foundational level of trust across these business networks and thus a willingness to openly share information, developing a deeper sense of loyalty among customers and employees. It empowers these networks with the collaborative, gaming, and analytical tools needed to engage each other and creatively solve business challenges.

- **Transparent:** A Social Business is always learning and therefore believes that there should be no boundaries between experts inside the company and experts in the marketplace. It embraces the tools and leadership models that support capturing knowledge and insight from many sources, allowing it to quickly sense changes in customer mood, employee sentiment, or process efficiencies. It utilizes analytics and social connections inside and outside the company to solve business problems and capture new business opportunities.

- **Nimble:** A Social Business leverages these social networks to speed up business, gaining real-time insight to make quicker and better decisions. It gets information to customers and partners in new ways—faster. Supported by ubiquitous access on mobile devices, new ways of connecting and working together, a Social Business turns time and location from constraints into advantages. Business is free to occur when and where it delivers the greatest value, allowing the organization to adapt quickly to the changing marketplace.

The Social Business AGENDA provides a consultative framework across horizontal roles and vertical industries to help individuals and companies understand how they can become a Social Business. Over the past couple of years, my team has been working with customers on developing strategies around techniques to help them optimize their workforce and better communicate with customers and partners through the use of social technologies. The Social Business AGENDA reduces the complexity of becoming a Social Business by narrowing the scope into six workstreams as illustrated in Figure 1.1.

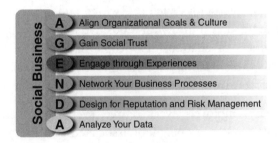

Figure 1.1   The bold Social Business AGENDA

Not every customer will need a strategy across all the six workstreams; however, my team has seen our best results when all six are completed, creating a 360-degree view of the Social Business strategy. My principal approach is to leverage best practices across industries and roles to effectively steer companies and governments down the right workstream(s) to maximize the value they can achieve by becoming a Social Business. Within each workstream, there are five questions to drive the overall outcome:

1. **Value Alignment:** What could or should we do with a Social Business solution?

2. **Role Mapping:** How will different roles use Social Business in their job?

3. **Vision Setting:** What does the Social Business experience look like for us?

4. **Business Case/ROI:** How can we financially justify our Social Business solution?

5. **Solution Review:** Can you show some part of the solution in my environment?

Through the use of the AGENDA framework depicted in Figure 1.1, we will answer these questions and more.

The sections that follow take a closer look at the six workstreams that make up the Social Business AGENDA while the book itself will guide you through the creation of your own Social Business AGENDA customized for your company.

Align Organizational Goals and Culture

This workstream is focused on uncovering organizational and departmental goals to understand what organizational transformation might be required to become a Social Business. Employees play an important role in the Social Business. Just ask Jon Iwata, IBM Vice President of Marketing, who unleashed IBM's employees into the blogosphere (the Internet with all its blogs, microblogs such as Twitter, and interconnected communities such as Facebook, LinkedIn, and more) with a positive impact on the IBM brand. Social capital is the connectedness of relationships people have with others, companies, and societies and the benefits these relationships bring to the individual. Employees represent who your brand is to the world and that connectedness. While at the Yale Club, Iwata said,

> "One day soon, every employee, every retiree, every customer, every business partner, every investor, and every neighbor associated with every company will be able to share an opinion about that company with everyone in the world, based on firsthand experience. The only way we can be comfortable in that world is if every employee of the company is truly grounded in what their company values and stands for. This may sound to some like external and internal messaging coming together—employee as brand ambassador."

Those relationships become connections embedded into the fabric of your or your company's culture. As Karie Willyerd and Jeanne C. Meister wrote on www.HarvardBusiness.org:

> "More companies are discovering that an über-connected workplace is not just about implementing a new set of tools—it is also about embracing a cultural shift to create an open environment where employees are encouraged to share, innovate, and collaborate virtually."

I've always thought of myself as an unselfish person who likes to share my knowledge and findings. On a trip to California to be inducted into the Women in Technology International Hall of Fame, my family and I traveled the weekend before to visit the area. While planning for the visit, I had found a great deal on a hotel that I had always wanted to stay in and passed on the tip to my best friend who was joining us.

After a wonderful weekend at a hotel that exceeded my dreams, we went to check out and noticed a discrepancy on room rates. My friend received the quote on the room as the offer that had been presented; however, for my stay, the rate was double. I approached the woman at the front desk but she had no "authority" to change the rate. I asked for her manager but was told that unless noted in the computer, the rate would remain. The woman at the front desk offered me the option of filing a complaint at a computer they had set up a little bit away from the other guests trying to check out.

I was not a happy customer and wanted to vent. On my iPhone, I use an app called Foursquare, a location-based tool that enables you to let your friends know where you are and post tips on that place. I decided to check-in my location on Foursquare, placed a tip for the hotel that read, "Always get your quote in writing!" and connected with thousands of people. Moments later, a young woman came out of the back office and said to me, "We will adjust your rate if you quit providing information about us in a 'negative tone' on Foursquare." I took the discount on the room and took my family out for a nice dinner.

The old complaint box outside the lobby had now been replaced with social means. I don't need to have permission or be told where to place my comments. I have the freedom to enter a comment in real time with millions of readers worldwide viewing my experiences— both positive and negative. The power shift from process to people had begun as the onsite management team handled a situation that truly would have been bumped up to corporate in the past. If this company's organizational culture had picked up on this change, the hotel manager's passion could have scaled throughout the corporation. A company with no interest or guidelines for social technique usage will be antiquated.

The learning experience for this hotel and hotel chain is the value that social tools can provide for customer satisfaction and customer service. There is also an element of corporate culture that needs to be reviewed to understand the appropriate process and guidelines. While the receptionist's company didn't have a Social Business strategy or policy for this particular hotel, she as the employee had started to monitor what guests were saying about their brand and had just logged in to Foursquare when I placed my post.

Whether you choose to embrace Social Business techniques or restrict them, the worst thing you can do is not have a policy in place to protect your company and the individuals who work for the company. IBM first introduced a social media guideline in 2005 that informs employees what is expected if they choose to participate in social media inside and outside the firewall. I have an internal blog accessible only to my IBM colleagues, but also have an external blog open to everyone. The IBM guidelines define what is appropriate content and where it should be posted.

The NetProspex Social Business Report showed that more than two million contact records of people are within the largest companies in the nation. It reported confirmation that marketing decision makers had the heaviest use of social media. Interestingly, it presented human resources professionals ranking second for social network usage. Meanwhile, CEOs were number 11 on the list, outpaced by office managers and customer service reps.

For Social Business to take off, the top of the organization will need to understand its value and enable the employees to play the role of brand ambassadors. The corporate culture is defined at the top of the hierarchy and executed at the bottom. For instance, one of my friends confided in me that his manager thought he was "goofing off" because he was watching YouTube videos on cloud computing and "looking for a job" because he was on LinkedIn. Overcoming those perceptions is a huge part of becoming a Social Business and changing the culture.

In order to successfully become a Social Business, a Governance Model must be formed that fits your goals and your culture. This Social Business Governance Model is about establishing decision rights within a framework, and monitoring those decisions and their impact. Our experience working with many clients to implement the Social Business AGENDA has found that a critical success factor for success is a right-sized Governance approach. Because this could be a cultural or organizational change, it requires understanding and managing the risks.

Gain Trust

This workstream is focused on reviewing existing networks both inside and outside your organization and understanding how you can better utilize them, expand them, and create new connections. Companies across the world are leveraging social techniques to grow their businesses by selling to their "friends," and friendship, as we know, requires the deepest of trust.

A study conducted by Burson-Marsteller, a global leading firm focused on digital reputation management, and marketing, found that 79% of the companies on the Fortune 500 use

Twitter, Facebook, YouTube, or corporate blogs to communicate with customers and other stakeholders. Eighty percent of companies are using LinkedIn as a primary tool to identify and recruit employees. It's clear we are now in the midst of a revolution. People are using these connections as a primary means of communication, in many cases replacing other more traditional interactions.

Think about the implications of this story. In preparation for a business trip to India, I tweeted about my excitement and energy to spend some time in India as I've seen it grow as an emerging and innovative country. I have visited India before, meeting with customers and being the keynote speaker at industry leading events. I arrived in India after a long flight and nightmare experience in baggage claim. The hotel seemed like a reprise and all thoughts were focused on collapsing into sleep.

When I arrived at the hotel around 11 p.m., the hotel general manager told me that he had put the "group" waiting for me in a conference room, because it had become too large for the lobby. I was not expecting any group and made sure I told the IBMers from the region to greet me in the morning as to not take them away from their families so late at night. After completing the check-in process, I turned to the conference room where the hotel had directed me, not realizing that my "tweet" had become a connection point.

Here in Mumbai, thousands of miles away from my home in the United States, was a group of people who knew me only by my blogs, LinkedIn groups, and tweets. They trusted my expertise and were anxiously waiting to greet and talk to me about Social Business. Through that one tweet, some of the most dedicated followers in India had determined which conference I was speaking at, and therefore at which hotel I would be staying. They had also determined the flight by asking the front desk for the "expected time of arrival," so they gathered and hoped for some time with me, which I gladly gave to my new "friends."

I was amazed that this tweet had truly been heard across the world, and trusted by thousands of people. My connectedness had engaged this group. While social media's growth in India will be largely dependent on the penetration of broadband, this "group" was proof that the global connectedness had extended to the Indian people from one person to another and one business to another.

This experience is like one of many that I have had while traveling to more than 60 countries. What is often overlooked in my story is that while I am gaining "friends" through social trust, so is my company. Remember that my social persona is a mom, a wife, a Vice President at IBM, and a social media evangelist. In India, my "friends" did not meet me at my hotel because of my personal life; they came to meet me because of my professional life and respect they have for the work I do on behalf of IBM. As a Vice President at IBM and Social Business evangelist, I represent not only myself, but also IBM. Thus, when colleagues, customers, partners, and peers come to greet me on a business trip, they are also acknowledging, respecting, and building trust with the company I represent.

Engage Through Experiences

This workstream is focused on helping you understand how to engage through the three I's of exceptional experiences. The engagement is created by exceptional experiences that are integrated, interactive, and identifying. Providing an *integrated* cockpit provides a single view across the channels for a Social Business. Being *interactive* is the heart of engagement. In today's world, you must allow an experience to be playful and the client to be part of it. That's one reason gaming techniques are used by all of the Fortune 500 companies today. Giving a sense of purpose is one of the ways to create the level of emotional response that creates engagement. *Identifying* is all about personalization. It revolves around making the experience special to me and may include location-based services and portable reputation.

Today is about the "conversation," but in reality it is about taking that socially trusted conversation to a new engagement level. To really engage an audience requires a Social Business to leverage exceptional experiences that the new generation has come to expect. A Social Business requires both exceptional work experiences for its employees and exceptional customer experiences for its clients and partners.

With your employee workforce, creating these exceptional work experiences often requires easy-to-use integrated solutions aimed at helping them get their work done faster, and their voices heard more loudly! The exceptional customer experience will focus on attracting and retaining customers, partners, and/or citizens by providing a personalized and interactive experience from a browser or mobile device—reinventing relationships.

Take Apple as an example. I heard an IBMer comment on Apple's style: "They don't just advertise, they teach. They don't just sell; they create learning experiences in their stores." Apple wants you to learn everything their product can do, so then you will teach others. In the process, Apple recruits new and loyal customers who become advocates and evangelists through interactive experience. For instance, online gaming (the average age of a gamer is 35!) has great focus on random rewards, teachable moments, and leader boards that engages and identifies the person through the focused experience. Experience will be king (and queen) in the coming years.

Take, for instance, this engagement through a fabulous experience. Costa Rica has a tradition that has spanned hundreds of years. Since 1781, the people of Costa Rica have participated in a pilgrimage. In fact, half the country, almost two million people, walk the Annual Pilgrimage to Cartago. Due to the H1N1 outbreak, the pilgrimage was canceled in 2009. Many people, like Radio Files, didn't want the country's tradition broken. The town leveraged social media to create a "virtual pilgrimage" by allowing people across the country (and world) to create a virtual image of themselves with their own picture and "shoes" selected from the site. They gave back to the country the ability of the people to walk, confess, and socialize along their journey. More than 300,000 people took the virtual walk with Catholic blogs writing favorably about the nation's will to continue through a tragedy, leveraging social techniques as an alternative.

As I describe engagement, it's important to emphasize that this is more than just connecting. People are motivated by creating passion, emotion, and "happiness." Joshua Porter, author of *Designing for the Social Web,* was an early thought leader who described moving people from being simple "consumers" to becoming "passionate" participants through exceptional experiences. That's the goal of a Social Business.

(Social) Network Your Business Processes

This workstream is focused on reviewing existing business processes to determine how social techniques can streamline certain processes, open certain processes for reuse, redesign inefficient processes, and provide a better collaborative experience inside of certain processes. This means interacting with your customers, clients, and employees by integrating social tools into your processes.

When I refer to "processes," I'm talking about more than just marketing processes here. At IBM, we have socially enabled our HR processes. Most IBM employees would pitch a fit if we tried to take away their access to w3.ibm.com. W3 is our intranet filled with communities of subject matter experts. It's been a central element in our social transformation. With three out of four of our employees firing it up every day, it unites us. We wouldn't be socially enabling our HR processes if it didn't increase our employee retention rate and increase their overall job satisfaction. To share just one statistic: Every 1% improvement in top contributor retention in our software division saves over $50 million.

As a Social Business, IBM believes in leveraging Social Business in enabling our employees to become public subject matter experts. IBM was one of the first companies to have its bloggers develop Social Computing Guidelines for the whole company. Our employees have become active brand ambassadors.

Furthermore, we socially enabled our product development. Many of you have participated in an IBM Jam. If you haven't, you should. The energy, the creativity, and the volume of input from people with different experiences and different roles enable us to produce award-winning products. In the process, ideas get shaped, formed, and tested for viability. The end result is products that you've asked for and that meet your needs. Some of you might follow the blogs of some of our developers. That's just a hint of the productive product development ferment that goes on inside IBM. The speed of our engineers is dramatically accelerated by their ability to build with code and components built by their colleagues.

IBM isn't the only company that's social networking its processes, however.

Working to link clients in more innovative ways, Moosejaw (www.moosejaw.com) uses Social Business to better connect its clients. Moosejaw is a fast-growing retailer specializing in outdoor, surf, skate, and snowboard equipment and apparel. To thrive in a highly competitive market, Moosejaw needed to create an exceptional web experience that would engage a customer community whose appetite for extreme sports is matched by a hunger for communication and collaboration. Moosejaw sought to embed rich Social Business community features into its online commerce experience, thus becoming one of the first retailers to make "multi-channel, social commerce" the cornerstone of its growth strategy.

Moosejaw added social commerce features such as product-level blogging, public-facing customer profiles with photos, videos, adventure stories, and gear lists for upcoming trips (see Figure 1.2). Customers can interact with staff and with other customers on their site. They can continue to connect those threads on their mobile phones when they come into Moosejaw retail stores. This instance provides Moosejaw with a ready-made platform for integrating these social networking capabilities deeply into its commerce platform, which in turn generates amazing results. Moosejaw has increased its revenue from an expected increase in conversion rate (based on an initial increase to 50%) and increased its customer loyalty.

Leveraging the wisdom of the crowd (crowdsourcing) and co-creation to drive differences in your processes will make your Social Business outcomes only stronger in the marketplace. A Social Business's key cultural transformations must support the key global processes, and enabling your processes with social techniques like networking will facilitate the needed transformation.

Moosejaw's social commerce tools

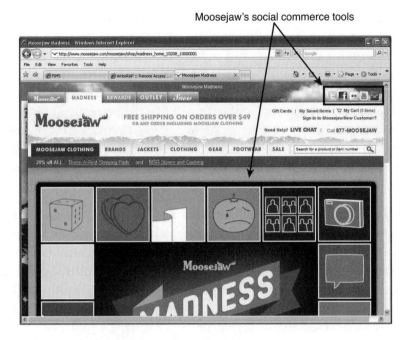

Figure 1.2   Moosejaw: Engaging customers with social media

Design for Reputation and Risk Management

This workstream is focused on helping you understand how your customers view your brand, company, products, and service. It helps to answer the questions of how we are doing, why we are doing well or poorly, what would happen if we changed, and what we should be doing to be more competitive.

In all my discussions with the C suite, the number one challenge is the concern about risk in opening up their business to the blogosphere. The biggest benefit is all about being connected to the clients and allowing them and your employees to express themselves instead of working in a controlled environment. You can't always count on that loyal friend base saying just what you want them to. There are several actionable parts of the Social Business AGENDA to help you avoid and in some cases circumvent a negative "PR storm" about your company and brand.

For example, Domino's Pizza had an interesting experience dealing with a disaster. In a small franchise in my home state of North Carolina, two employees took their flip camera and posted a video that showed very bad and unsanitary food practices at this pizza hub. Soon there were millions of YouTube hits and a Twitter feeding frenzy. Domino's took too long to respond with their YouTube apology and a traditional marketing 1.0 press release. An online research firm called YouGov confirmed that the perception of Domino's brand quality went from positive to negative in approximately 48 hours. This incident outlines how important it is for businesses to "listen" to what people (customers, competitors, or employees) say, write, or in any other way communicate online about their firms, brands, products, or people.

This incident was a catalyst for Domino's to now become a Social Business that manages their reputation. They not only are prepared with a risk migration plan but actively manage their digital reputation by listening. I am sure you've seen their latest focus on listening to what people want—not just in marketing but also in the products they produce. They now have truly personified their image through text-based offers, Facebook, Twitter, and Foursquare usage in the U.K. Their experience truly changed their overall approach to designing for reputation and risk management!

The lessons learned should be applied to all Social Businesses. Actively work your reputation management. Have a risk management plan just in case. And remember, responding in 48 hours in the "old world" would have been impressive. But in the new world of Social Business, it is just too slow. This workstream of the Social Business AGENDA will equip you with the tools to move quickly and systematically so that you are proactively prepared for any issue. In other words, your Social Business AGENDA will put into place a strategy for your team to be on top of the sites all the time (as in the hotel example) and respond quickly using social media communications platforms.

Analyze Your Data

This workstream is focused on reviewing how you can analyze and socialize your corporate data and public data to better organize data for information discovery. Analytics is the new black. If there is one thing that I think will differentiate the winners from the losers, it will be their ability to understand what is happening and to predict what trends are lurking. In the highly competitive arena we have today, Social Business's biggest advantage will be in your data and analytics. To improve and grow, a Social Business has to have insight into as much information as it can.

A friend of mine, Jeremiah Owyang, defined social analytics as "the practice of being able to understand customers and predict trends using data from the social web." The majority of companies are still looking at things like page views or visits; however, Social Businesses of the future such as IBM, Facebook, Pepsi, and others are spending a lot of their time on the next-generational listening, sentiment, and other analytics tools that can propel a company forward. Sentiment is understanding how people feel about your company, brand, or category by analyzing phrases, "tone," and comments online.

Take, for instance, Harley-Davidson. Harley needed to connect 1,363 Harley-Davidson dealers, 786 Buell dealers, 228 retail locations, and 1.1 million riders in the Harley-Davidson Membership Directory. Social media with enhanced analytics gave Harley not only the connected points, but targeted content by role (dealer or client) and a way to increase the focus on that connection.

Let's take another look at IBM and an example that I experienced. The IBM HR department is looking to leverage analytical tools on the employee intranet given that 90% of IBM's internal content is now from social media solutions behind the firewall. We also use advanced analytical tools to gain insight into product launches and key events. This allows IBM to make changes on the fly and shift marketing messages and deliver information as our customers request it.

To understand the effects this can have, in January 2011 we had a large conference in Florida. With many technical people and longtime IBM customers in the audience, they were expecting to see some new demonstrations. About 45 minutes into the opening session, our event team backstage was picking up some negative sentiment from Twitter that people were getting anxious to see demos. After 60 minutes, the audience was getting frustrated.

I was one of the speakers during the opening session, and I can assure you that we prepared and rehearsed the flow for days in advance. That didn't matter. We were losing our audience. When my team showed me live feedback from the audience, it was clear we needed to make a change and do so fast. We altered the remaining 60 minutes of the opening session and went straight into demos. Within 5 minutes my team showed me the live feedback from the audience and the sentiment had turned from negative to positive.

The intense competition has resulted in many new and innovative ways to track and analyze data. The Social Business AGENDA ensures that you are not data rich but insight poor. Social analytics will play a huge role in how you learn to make experiences more and more personal and rewarding for both your client and your company.

Technology as a Competitive Ingredient

Today every business is dependent on technology. It is a driver of competitive advantage. For your Social Business AGENDA, technology will lace all the workstreams. For example, engaging your clients will involve some use of technology, whether mobile, gaming, or basic social media.

The value of this continuous alignment of business and IT is shown in financial results. According to a study at the London School of Economics, continuously aligning business and IT increases overall productivity by around 20%, double individual contributions. It's this kind of synergy that is your goal.

Given that this business and technology alignment is such a critical part of the equation for success, I will share our Social Business Technology Framework as well. It complements the AGENDA and ensures continuous alignment between the underpinning of technology and the Social Business goals.

IBM holds an annual Social Business Jam (a giant, global virtual chat focused on a set of topics by experts and interested parties, typically lasting two to three days). In 2011, the participants of this Jam viewed the social evolution as an opportunity for IT to develop innovative new approaches toward supporting the growth of the enterprise. These could take many forms, such as enabling a remote workforce to easily collaborate with different offices. Creating a smart, flexible strategy for mobile devices that balances the security that the business demands with the mobile tools and applications that users want is one way to spark innovation. Providing analytical tools is another way IT can play a part in Social Business. Analytics can help identify influencers and leaders, create taxonomies to provide a better context for incoming information, and enable users to mine data from blogs, wikis, and tweets, helping determine patterns and better quantify—in real time—brand perception.

The Bold AGENDA Is Globally Applicable

The examples I've provided thus far and many more in the upcoming chapters are happening globally in both businesses and personal settings. Social Business is the new global platform. According to the Global Web Index, the United States is being outpaced by several countries, such as India, Brazil, and the U.K., on those using a Social Networking profile. As you can see from the Global Web Index statistics in Figure 1.3, countries all around the world have embraced these new communication tools.

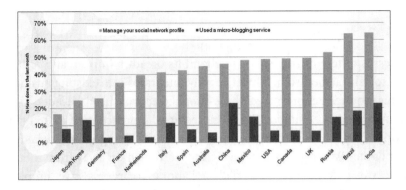

Excerpt reprinted with permission of TrendstreamLimited/GlobalWebIndex

Figure 1.3   Social Networking is the global platform.

Countries have embraced social tools for a variety of purposes. I had the great fortune of meeting with Óscar Arias Sánchez, the president of Costa Rica and recipient of the Nobel Peace Prize for his Central American peace plan. He had planted the seeds of IT and technology in the fabric of Costa Rica. When he became President, his mission was to invest in the people of the country. What Costa Rica needed the most was improvement of education, especially technical education. Costa Rica is reaping the fruits of that goal with companies like IBM, Intel, and now Cisco investing in communities and businesses in the region. In fact, Cisco just created a Cisco Entrepreneur Institute to help small and medium-size business entrepreneurs improve their business skills and learn how to use collaboration and social media technologies.

Clearly, all nations have embraced this new form of communication and information. Regardless of where you are doing business, or setting up your own personal brand, or even learning about how to deal with a life issue, social techniques are now an essential element: Much like air is required to continue to live, social is becoming an essential element for countries, companies, and people.

The examples discussed so far are of companies, groups, and individuals that have taken the lead on Social Business because of their plan, people, process, and passion. How you build your own bold AGENDA and what you create will differentiate you in the future. The chapters that follow dive deep with examples into the Social Business AGENDA and help you and your company or government develop a road map for your journey.

Conclusion

Social Business is different from social media in its breadth, impact, and returns. To truly capitalize on social collaboration, it must be fully integrated into existing business processes and tools. This requires a coordinated, three-pronged approach, with leadership driving the initiative, human resources supporting the necessary cultural change, and IT providing the necessary tools. This will result in a new kind of process. During IBM's Social Business Jam, a participant wrote, "We're going to see a significant transition away from more-structured business processes to a much more socially collaborative process style. Employees will be much more aware of their processes via the communities in which they're involved and will work in a much more dynamic and collaborative fashion."

In this chapter, the bold AGENDA for Social Business came alive. First movers truly have a competitive advantage because social is about relationships, and the strongest relationships are built over time. Social networking tools are dramatically changing the way we communicate and collaborate—both at home and on the job. Many businesses have reached a tipping point, a moment of critical mass, with this new approach to collaboration. They are effectively using social networking as a channel; however, in many cases, they are still attempting to discover how to internalize it and take advantage of the collaborative aspects and cost benefits that becoming a Social Business can bring.

Whether your company is focused on attracting and engaging customers with exceptional brand experiences and personalized interactions across touch points, or improving customer insight and establishing a single view of customers, becoming a Social Business is a requirement in today's world. Social-enabling your business processes while transforming your culture is not an easy task but one that must be conquered.

The bold AGENDA is a comprehensive set of workstreams that covers goals, culture, governance, listening, trust, engagement and experience, processes, risk management, and analytics that will help shape your journey This journey is a global one—think bigger than your regional area!

Let's continue to see how the Social Business AGENDA can help you!

Align Organizational Goals and Culture

"Culture eats strategy
for lunch."
Sandy Carter

"A successful social media strategy is best achieved when there is a corporate culture that balances tops-down direction with bottoms-up initiative with external (customer) facing communication."

Peggy Dau, Managing Partner at MAD Perspectives LLC

A Social Business's Goals and Culture

As you learned in Chapter 1, "The AGENDA for Social Business Success," a Social Business is one that is engaging, transparent, and nimble because of its integration of social techniques throughout its processes and interactions with clients, employees, and suppliers. It is different from just social media in that it is applying social features and characteristics to more than just marketing and communications but extends into the heart of the business, with no business process left behind in the competitive advantages that social brings to the table. The result is a company that is more competitive and effective in the marketplace.

In a Social Business, your company's goals act as a guide through the magical and interesting world of the blogosphere. In essence, the goals drive the AGENDA workstreams.

Your company's culture and beliefs matter more in your effectiveness in this new world than in the past. Consider Frank Eliason, a client service employee at Comcast. His engagement allowed him to observe Comcast customers who were on Twitter posting their concerns. He decided to converse with them and started that conversation with a question: "How can I help you?" Frank then listened and responded to each and every tweet he received. Frank's star power on Twitter had a direct effect on his organization. Since Comcast was supportive of Frank's @comcastcares Twitter page, which has more than 42,000 followers, Comcast has received positive feedback from customers and press. Articles have been posted about Comcast's success with customer support via Twitter in the journals *Businessweek, NY Times, CIO Magazine,* and many others. Comcast is continuing to support social techniques and is creating more defined customer support pages on Twitter such as @comcastbill and @comcast. While Frank is no longer at Comcast, he helped to shape the culture there permanently, from an individual working in isolation to an environment where social techniques were used to reach the goals of the customer service plan.

But setting the goals is only half of the mission. If a company simply copies another company's strategy, but doesn't pay attention to the culture variable, it will not have the same success. This corporate culture variable (which will inevitably be different between the two companies) will play a critical role.

While both goals and culture are important, culture is the essential swing vote. Before moving on, let's ensure we have a common understanding of culture.

What is culture? Culture is about individuals in a group sharing patterns of behavior. It is at its core the collective way in which things operate in a business. There are learned behaviors that are common to all employees. Typically these are driven by a set of shared values. Sun Tzu, a Chinese military general from 3000 B.C., indicated that culture forms an integral part of any organizational strategy. It consists of created and shared beliefs, values, and glue that holds an organization together, and it also involves the very nature of the organization.

Adam Christensen, who is a former colleague of mine at IBM and now a great partner at Juniper, commented on many occasions:

> "Culture is the most overlooked, underestimated factor determining whether social media succeeds or fails in a company. And when corporate culture and social media are pitted against each other, Social Business will always fail. Always."

Because a Social Business is engaged, transparent, and nimble, the way it sets its goals and shapes its culture matters. Why?

To engage with peers, clients, and partners, a company must leverage its employees to be subject matter experts and to have the right conversations. Now, if the culture of the organization is not open, these goals would be difficult to reach.

In addition, a Social Business is always learning and believes that there should be no boundaries between experts, whether those experts exist in the company or exist in the marketplace. Because a Social Business learns from how customers respond, it will tweak its goals based on results; however, if the culture doesn't support giving lots of individuals a voice, or even doesn't allocate funds for a networked platform, the culture won't support those goals.

A Social Business is also transparent. With transparency as a means to a goal, this changes the way that decisions are made. In an organization where hierarchy is the norm for the culture, this decision making that is now more transparent, democratic, and consensus-based may not survive if the culture is not modified.

For a Social Business, being nimble applies to all businesses processes, whether marketing, customer service, supply chain, and so forth. Being nimble is the ability of a company to leverage social networks to speed up business and to gain real-time insights so they can make better and quicker decisions. Culturally, I have seen that those companies that adopt experimentation as a way of life succeed more readily. Again, the culture matters.

Let's take an example. A Social Business gets information to customers, partners, and the entire ecosystems in new ways and new channels based on profiling, geo-location, subscription, and recommendations based on analytics. Experimentation with these new tools would enable a retailer to leverage geo-location tools in which discount coupons could be applied based on a client's location and vicinity to a particular store. Experimentation as part of a cultural norm gives businesses the freedom to interact when and where it delivers the greatest value, allowing the organization to adapt quickly to the changing marketplace.

So, the culture to support Social Business goals does not restrict collaboration and communication between employees and customers, but instead embraces it. While it's important to have a business-to-business (B2B), business-to-consumer (B2C), and business-to-employee (B2E) set of goals, an overall encompassing strategy will ensure that you don't end up creating different silos of social activity when it's not necessary. A Social Business really becomes not a B2B or B2C company, but a P2P—people-to-people company.

If you think about this new Social Business, the one that will be most competitive in the future, the one that most CEOs are hoping to become, the next question is, how do you begin that journey or perhaps how do you increase your speed along that journey to have the right set of goals and alignment of culture?

Social techniques are now widespread, and if your company's goals and culture don't take into account the new collaborative world, you are already behind. But don't worry! There is still time to catch up. Now is the time to really think about competitive and innovative companies that are already successfully leveraging these new techniques. If you have already started, there is still much to learn, beginning with your goals and culture.

The expected outcomes of a Social Business culture are as follows:

- Greater employee engagement for innovation in product, service, and beyond (consider the aforementioned Comcast example)
- Tapping into subject matter expertise
- Enabling your employees to solve problems more quickly
- Experimentation as a cultural norm
- Decision making done in a more transparent, democratic, and consensus-based manner

This chapter is an important one. Please don't skip this Social Business AGENDA workstream. You cannot be bold in the marketplace and win competitively without looking at your goals and culture. Let's begin your formation of the Social Business AGENDA by working through the following:

1. Your company's core business goals (what are you in the business of doing and with whom?)
2. Corporate culture norms required to succeed

When item #2 is an impediment, take the smart approach and find ways to change the culture to create a more collaborative environment.

Goals First. Period.

My dad used to tell me that if you didn't have a destination in mind, any road will get you there! One of the first mistakes people make in their pursuit of Social Business is starting without a goal in mind. I cannot tell you how many C-level executives have said to me, "I need a Facebook page, or a community, or <insert the tool of the moment here>." When I ask why, their answer is always because they read an article on a plane or heard from a competitor that this was the right goal.

Goals could be as simple as gaining more new clients or increasing client loyalty; conversely, they could be as grand and bold as creating a new product in a new category in the industry. The goals should guide everything that you do, including choosing social techniques throughout your company. Some examples include the way Visa set a goal of having more "relevant advertising" and therefore leveraged YouTube for a campaign that encourages consumers to upload their own videos, or the way Boston Medical Center set a goal of expanding their client base by increased referrals and reduced no-show rates with execution through embedding social techniques.

Because a Social Business is about people, some of the goals that my clients have leveraged for great financial gain for their corporations are to do the following:

- **Enable an effective workforce:** Operations, human resources, and other departments can increase overall employee productivity and job satisfaction through improved knowledge capture, expertise location, and collaboration. Travel, training, and teleconferencing expenses also can be reduced.

- **Accelerate innovation:** Product research and development teams can quicken internal idea sharing and discovery, as well as transform how they generate ideas, share strategies, and gather feedback from key customers and partners.

- **Deepen customer relationships:** With more immediate access to content and expertise, customer service representatives can work more efficiently and provide higher-quality service. Marketing and sales teams can have more time to spend with customers and to dedicate to customer-focused initiatives.

For example, a large global consumer products company with more than 10,000 employees in global research and development (R & D) approached me about defining their current goals and challenges. As one executive explained, "After one of our once-a-month teleconference meetings, I spent four to five hours answering questions through email; often it is the same question over and over." In addition, experts were isolated, slowing projects and preventing the reuse of best practices and equipment. With the Senior Team, we agreed that the major goals would be threefold: shortening the development cycle, optimizing the workforce, and fostering innovation. (By the way, these goals will entail a cultural shift as there were difficulties in collaboration among far-flung staff and work sites.)

Every single thing we do in life has an end goal. The difference with life is that we have no choice in our very end goal. But in business, you do. Set out your end goals and work strategically toward them. Be prepared that your goals may shift over time and that you need to be nimble to be able to quickly change your strategy to reflect redefined or new goals.

It is important to determine the difference between in-process goals and end goals. While both are important to track, the end goal is usually the one with the financial model tied to it. For example, "great engagement with clients" is an intermediary goal with a purpose of "new product development," the end business goal. Understanding the difference is important in any consideration of goals.

Social Businesses set meaningful business goals with metrics. Lots of companies (including IBM) expect ROI (Return on Investment) and revenue results from things that don't lend themselves to it, like engagement or market research. In fact, I joke that IBM is a company that measures ROE—Return on Everything. So it is equally important when you set your goals to establish a way to measure them. Otherwise, there will be endless debate on the success of your Social Business initiatives if there are no agreed-to metrics of success. Chapter 5, "(Social) Network Your Business Processes," presents sample metrics to frame to your goals based on your approach and chosen business process.

Culture Matters

Yes, "culture matters" seems like a given; however, in my experience, most people push culture and change off to the side in importance. As one of my clients, who is the CIO at Caterpillar, said during a keynote at IBM's IMPACT conference, "Culture eats strategy for lunch!" So since culture will dictate the best path or even create an insurmountable obstacle, the remainder of this chapter outlines five steps for Social Business cultural alignment.

Culture is a combination of shared values, attitudes, assumptions, beliefs, and behaviors. Culture is grounded in the assumptions about how people interact. If a company's culture is not supportive of collaboration outside their four walls, and in some cases, even restricts the use of things like social networking sites, this culture will block reaching the company's goals. Thomas Knoll, Zappos Community manager, once said,

"Success or failure of a company's use of social techniques is dependent on its culture and goals."

Culture is king (or queen!).

Culture begins with a set of shared beliefs because what people believe drives what they think about value. For example, global consumption of bottled water quadrupled between 1990 and 2005. Despite the fact that bottled water is 10,000 times more expensive than tap water (source: Earth Policy Institute, Wikipedia, www.researchwikis.com), by 2011, the market will have grown 42% since 1999. It started because people believed that bottled water was healthier than tap water. Now I am sure not all of you are selling water, but the premise works regardless of industry. Bottom line: What you believe (remember, culture is a set of shared beliefs) drives what you value.

Corporate culture is how you shape your ecosystem (all your stakeholders) to believe in a set of norms for the organization. Predominantly, it is defined by the behavior and actions of senior-level executives. To get people to buy into your beliefs, they need to hear it from people they trust, see evidence, and experience it for themselves.

How do you get a culture that is ready to maximize the power of a Social Business?

1. Define the role of management and the employees, typically with a solid Governance process, beginning with a set of Social Computing Guidelines and a Social Business Digital Council.
2. Empower everyone to participate.
3. Educate and enable.
4. Build a culture for participation started inside first and top down as well as bottom up. (While not everyone needs to be a contributor, everyone, especially senior executives, needs to understand the importance and value of becoming a Social Business. As a senior leader at IBM, I make the time for all things social because of the value they bring my business. While I do have to schedule and prioritize the engagement into my calendar, it is well worth the time.)
5. Experiment and have a structured approach to learn from mistakes.

Define the Role of Management and the Employees

Telling people what we want them to do and believe isn't enough; it has to be shown. This is why it is critical to have executives show the way, not just talk the way. You need to have a senior leader who is the Social Business Champion. Not every senior executive needs to be active in the blogosphere; however, you need a visible leader.

At IBM, Alistair Rennie, an IBM General Manager in Software Group, personally participates in IBM's Social Business activities. He models the way for the entire division, by speaking at town hall meetings and web conferences, and sharing the IBM story with virtually everyone he meets. Not everyone, and certainly not every executive, is going to become an avid contributor by posting blogs, updating their status, and posting comments in communities. But you need that senior executive to showcase the way.

Executives play another critical role in that they need to support and encourage their departments to leverage social techniques when appropriate. Our IBM CMO, Jon Iwata, a great forward thinker, supports IBM's overall infrastructure and the people to participate in Social Business. In fact, he hired a Vice President of Digital Eminence to signal the importance of the concept to IBM.

One of my responsibilities as a Vice President at IBM is to ensure that I reflect the mission and goals of my company to my peers and teams of people around the world who report to me. I'm a strong believer that employees often look to senior leaders to take guidance as to acceptable behavior. I am very vocal to my peers and team that becoming a Social Business is an imperative for sustaining IBM's competitive advantage as the largest technology company in the world. I recently sponsored and hosted an internal web conference open to all IBMers on "Living Social as a Seller." The goal of this web conference was to share some success stories from me and other IBMers about increased sales result from engaging transparently with customers using social media internally and externally. This action showcased my support of Social Business and the employees who had followed my lead. Once you have the right level of support or buy-in, a Social Business Champion of Champions, there needs to be structure.

Social Business Governance

Governance is the structure of relationships and processes to direct and guide the use of social techniques in order to achieve the goal of the company. The **Social Business Governance** model defines what has to be done to reach the goals, how it is done, who has the authority to do it, and the metrics of success that will be used. Without proper governance, Social Business best practices can be implemented in departmental silos which limit the opportunity for sharing across the entire corporation (see Figure 2.1).

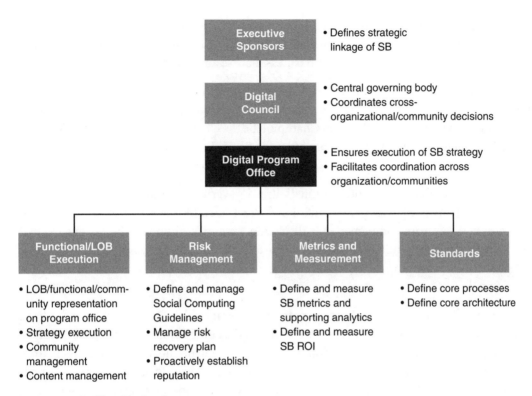

Figure 2.1 Building blocks of governance structure

Achieving the transformative value of becoming a Social Business involves connecting all parts of the organization (including employees, partners, and customers) in new ways. It often requires quite new ways of managing people, flatter organizations, and significant cultural change. While becoming social provides individual flexibility, it's important that the change achieves the *unifying* value for the company of the new goals and culture.

A strong governance program facilitates coordinated change. The governance is led by two complementary leadership groups whose members include the major "organizational structures" (for example, line of business (LOB), Finance, Supply Chain, Marketing, IT, HR, Channel Management, and so on).

The first group, the Executive Sponsor Group, defines the strategic linkage and goals of becoming a Social Business. Members are leaders across the organization and are true believers. They do not have to be the CEO, but they need to be people who are influencers in the organization. This role is very important because an evangelist is someone who showcases the true value of being a Social Business. The ideal situation is where you have a business leader and the leader of the IT business that are joined together in being champions.

The second group is a Social Business Digital Council. This includes executives who are responsible for the organization-wide, execution creation of the Social Business plan. I recommend that your Social Business Champion be the Chairperson of your Social Business Digital Council. The representatives are often the Social Business leaders in their respective LOBs and functional areas, which ensures focus on the vertical and horizontal needs.

What is a Social Business Digital Council? It is a governance body established to ensure that the company is analyzing the reputational effect of employee use of social techniques. The Council—a cross-company, cross-discipline executive council—should ensure that the company is taking full advantage of social techniques to drive business benefit, while simultaneously managing the potential risks associated with employee use of social outside the firewall.

The Council's goal is to seek to foster greater operational collaboration, standardized approaches, and consistent best practice sharing as the company embraces Social Business. You might also want to consider adding an independent member to your council from outside your company. For example, I sit on a couple of Social Business Digital Councils for other organizations as they look to me to provide outside-in feedback, strategy, and guidance.

This Social Business Digital Council is an important step in ensuring success through the organization. In my first experience of becoming a Social Business inside one of the IBM divisions, this was an invaluable part of my governance structure.

The Social Business Digital Council focuses on the key areas of a Social Business culture:

- **Community & Content Management:** Provides a common approach to drive change and adoption at and across the LOB and functional level of internal communities throughout your organization. In addition, this part of the Council drives the formation of a content management strategy,. This focus would be on both internal use and external use of information to spread the word in a consistent and integrated fashion. Chapter 4, "Engage Through Experiences," discusses in detail the role of a community manager and the keys of a content activation strategy.

- **Center of Excellence:** Shares best practices to create a common social voice and approach across and outside the organization.

- **Reputation and Risk Management:** Focuses on regulatory risk and compliance (if relevant), social record retention for general discovery, and other legal and financial risks. In addition, this area proactively manages the organization's reputation and has a defined plan to respond to various levels of negative media or emergencies. Chapter 6, "Design for Reputation and Risk Management," discusses this area in detail.

- **Metrics and Measurement:** Covers all elements of data and measurement. This group starts with proactive listening to guide the engagement strategy and metric setting. This includes internal analytics of social networks, expertise, and projects, as well as the external listening and analytics. This group also is responsible for creating and automating the overall program measurements to track success, progress on the plan, and social return. Chapter 7, "Analyze Your Data," discusses this area in detail.

- **Guidelines & Standards:** This group focuses on process and technical standards for a Social Business. While Lines of Business (LOBs), major business functions, and so on require the freedom to build their social programs tailored to their needs, the Standards group ensures that the overall company can be nimble in connecting across boundaries in ways not always anticipated. Standards for brand and ways of connecting with partners, channels, clients, and so on ensure that the company is viewed as coordinated and focused on needs versus a "collection of parts." Setting policies, guidelines, and processes for the organization and associates to participate in social tools externally will be a key part of the mission. This process is discussed in detail in the text that follows. On the technical side, a common Social Business framework enables the new ways of working, as discussed in greater detail in Chapter 8, "Technology as a Competitive Ingredient."

I was the Social Business Champion for one of IBM's divisions and led our Social Business Digital Council. My Social Business Digital Council was made up of influential participants from all functional areas of our division, for instance, development, human resources, marketing, sales, customer service, and even more of our key areas. We met on a monthly basis, but in the start-up period, we dedicated two days to set out our charter, set our rules of engagement with each other, and define our Social Computing Guidelines. The typical agenda for the meeting included best practices from other companies that were not like us. For instance, we explored some of Nordstrom's best practices, and studied how Zappos was gaining traction in the marketplace in their approach. We also discussed incentives for use, and published our own Social Business Heroes, those who leveraged social inside and outside our four walls for business success. By setting up a Social Business Center of Excellence with a few people (and a few smart interns!), we created a go-to place for answers and sharing.

Finally, we developed our risk management and reputation management plan (see Chapter 6). A big portion of our time was spent planning how to evangelize more IBM employees, partners, and alumni to be brand advocates for us. A brand advocate is a person who is passionate about your brand and references you as a normal course of business. Defining new roles to have in our organization—such as a Social Business Manager or Community Manager—also became important tasks.

If you are a large corporation, I would encourage you to form a Social Business Digital Council, and if you are a small business, I would encourage you to incorporate these items into your business management meetings. In that Council, ensure that you have the right people from all the critical functions, and outside your organization, ensure that you have a charter and set of measurable goals that are linked to the bigger company goals, and that you focus on the needs you have internally to be successful, such as new roles, incentive structure, and your risk management plan.

Part of the employees' role is to develop an interest to be a brand advocate for their company, participate in the education, select the tools from the choices supplied by the top leadership (or suggest others!), and participate on an active, engaged basis.

A great way to shape this interaction at all levels of the organization and ecosystem is to create a set of guidelines and values that shape what the company will and won't allow. It showcases support of its goals and brand values. It provides a way that Social Business can reduce the risk of unleashing its employees into the blogosphere and help to ensure that everyone works together to bring about success.

The Social Business Guidelines

The **Social Business Guidelines** for your company should be based on your values. Consider the following ten best practices:

1. Guidelines should be written by your employees in a social group setting. Those guidelines developed in a participatory fashion will last.

2. Guidelines should state why the guidelines exist; for example, to innovate in a responsible way.

3. Guidelines should be short and to the point.

4. Guidelines should state your position on open dialogue—what's fair game and what's not (confidential information).

5. Guidelines should state consequences.

6. Guidelines should encourage transparency.

7. Guidelines should state privacy and rights of your company's partners and clients.

8. Guidelines should guide in adding value and learning from mistakes.

9. Guidelines should discuss time spent in social media.

10. Guidelines should encourage your company's goals in social techniques.

On www.SocialMediaGovernance.com, you can find a collection of company social guidelines. Read through them and define your guidelines in sync with your culture and goals. For example, in sync with its corporate culture, Zappos's Social Media Policy is "be real and use your best judgment." This Social Policy showcases Zappos's trust in their employees! Intel®'s Social Media Guidelines have a few best practices as well. Examples include "be transparent" and "if it gives you pause, pause." I also love their advice that "perception is reality and it's a conversation." I think the key is defining these with a collaborative group of digital citizens throughout your company.

For large global organizations, corporate culture sometimes needs to make way for local culture. For example, at IBM we have a very open-minded culture supported by our senior leadership team. We have sponsorship from the very top of IBM supporting our movement into end-user-generated content to become a Social Business. However, we do understand that there are also cultural differences across the globe. As such, we make sure to understand these cultural differences and embrace them in our Social Business AGENDA. With IBM operating in more than 170 countries, our team reviews privacy acts around the globe to ensure that we keep the interest of the employees at the center of focus, as shown in Figure 2.2.

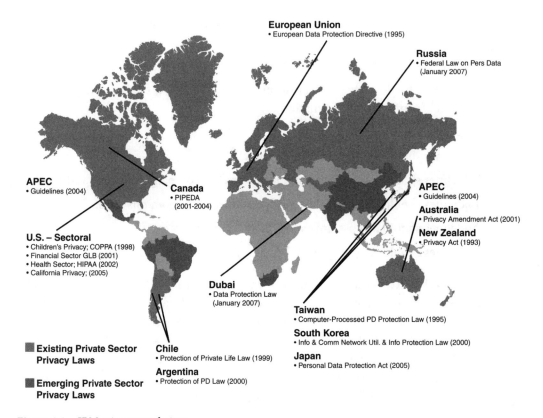

European Union
• European Data Protection Directive (1995)

Russia
• Federal Law on Pers Data
(January 2007)

APEC
• Guidelines (2004)

Canada
• PIPEDA
(2001-2004)

APEC
• Guidelines (2004)

Australia
• Privacy Amendment Act (2001)

New Zealand
• Privacy Act (1993)

U.S. – Sectoral
• Children's Privacy; COPPA (1998)
• Financial Sector GLB (2001)
• Health Sector; HIPAA (2002)
• California Privacy; (2005)

Dubai
• Data Protection Law
(January 2007)

Taiwan
• Computer-Processed PD Protection Law (1995)

South Korea
• Info & Comm Network Util. & Info Protection Law (2000)

Japan
• Personal Data Protection Act (2005)

■ Existing Private Sector
Privacy Laws

Chile
• Protection of Private Life Law (1999)

Argentina
• Protection of PD Law (2000)

■ Emerging Private Sector
Privacy Laws

Figure 2.2   IBM privacy regulations

Social Business Governance is a step in reaching your goals by shaping your culture.

CASE STUDY: CELESTICA—ALIGNING CORPORATE GOALS AND CULTURE

Celestica is a Toronto, Canada–based global electronics manufacturer and end-to-end product life cycle services provider with over $6.5 billion in revenue and 35,000 employees around the world. It provides design, manufacturing, logistics, supply chain, and after-market services to a wide range of customers in enterprise computing, communications, aerospace and defense, industrial and green technology, communications, and healthcare. Celestica started its Social Business journey in 2009.

Celestica is highly regarded for its engineering and supply-chain excellence, and its business strategy is to become the undisputed leader in the electronics manufacturing services industry. To achieve its goal, the company must effectively leverage innovation and best practices created at each of its 30-plus locations and share them across a vast global operating network. To do this, Celestica realized that it needed to provide employees with the right collaborative tools to communicate with each other and drive innovation across multiple locations, functions, and businesses.

In support of this goal, Celestica launched Operations Central in 2009, which enables shop-floor employees with self-service capability to exchange ideas and connect with experts to share solutions and ideas. In early 2010, Celestica established a Collaboration Council, with the goal of driving more collaborative behaviors across the organization, realizing that effective collaboration tools need to be supported by processes that also encourage a collaborative culture. Inspired by the success of Operations Central, Celestica then launched Connections in 2011, which links employees across the entire organization to drive collaboration from within.

Sometimes referred to internally as the "Facebook for business," Connections is a collaboration tool that allows employees to more easily connect with each other across the company's 30-plus locations in 14 countries. Employees use Connections to collaborate on global projects by using wikis to share requirements and project plans, greatly reducing the need for lengthy conference calls across time zones. Connections is also credited with speeding up development cycles and increasing product release frequencies.

Empower Everyone to Participate

Why would you want everyone to participate in your Social Business? Because empowering your employees, partners, and even customers to be proactive in solving problems through social tools makes your company more competitive.

Your employees are in the best position to engage customers, partners, and suppliers. The result is to increase the power of your brand, improve your customer satisfaction, innovate new ideas, and try new sales. For example, the book *Empowered*, by Josh Bernoff and Ted Schadler, features a story about Leonard Bonacci, who developed GuestAssist, a text messaging system to manage disruptive Philadelphia Eagles fans, to highlight a major client satisfaction idea. Fans with a problem send a text to a short code that matches their seat so that a rep can arrive to discreetly resolve the issue. Now, the National Football League has taken the best practice and is implementing it throughout the league.

The Social Computing Guidelines should empower all to participate. With web content publishing of the past, only select people were empowered to post content. Today, social techniques and policy lay the groundwork for those your company selects to contribute content. However, mistakes will be made, and the way that you respond to them will set a tone with your employees and impact their participation, as Peggy Dau wrote in her blog:

> "So, HP empowers its employees with guidelines of expected behavior. Is that really empowerment? I check on various HP blogs from time to time and follow several Twitter feeds. I find them interesting but cautious."

While the guidelines are the start, a true trust relationship must exist with your employees. People will know if you really don't believe in them or in social techniques. You must live and practice what you talk about. Your employees will need positive reinforcement; they need to see peers and role models doing the same thing.

There is a difference between the "participation" of your CEO and your entry-level financial analyst. Yes, social may mean democratic, but certainly the business value varies by whose voice is used. Take Bill Marriott as an example. His goals are new clients and crisis management. As the CEO of Marriott Corporation, he writes his own blog from the heart. He not only drives sales through his blogging strategy but also uses this tool to address any falsehoods in the press. His attitude extends throughout the culture. In fact, in one of his blog posts, the 77-year-old CEO wrote, "What's the big deal? This is simply another medium for me to listen to my customers and talk to my customers."

November 26, 2008, marks one of the biggest spikes in IBM's internal blogging system. That was the day that Sam Palmisano, IBM CEO, posted his first entry in the blogging system. What surprised everyone was that he did not post a blog, but instead commented on someone else's blog entry. His comment was not on another executive's blog, but instead on a blog entry posted by a programmer in Data Integration Services. While his comment was very important, his actions were even more important as it sent a clear message to all IBMers that our CEO believes in transparency and is openly willing to engage with all employees.

Think about the empowerment of having your CEO blogging! The age of the social CEO is coming, but few CEOs today are actively participating. To have a social CEO, he or she must want to participate and have the right audience to interface and to interact with and prioritize the time. Forrester's CEO, George Colony, in his blog interview, projected that in five years 20% of CEOs will be socially active, and in ten years it will be closer to 50%. He continued by saying that corporate boards will begin looking for people who can be social for CEO positions.

Empowerment is the process of enabling or authorizing an individual to think, behave, take action, control work, and make decisions in autonomous ways. Ensure that your movement into Social Business takes this very important factor into account!

Consider Social Business awards as well as a way to reinforce the practice. At a recent Women in Technology Conference, we gave away "virtual" Social Business merit badges to put on participants' email footer, blog, and so forth if they had mastered certain elements of social techniques. Inside IBM, colleagues can reward each other through a program we call BlueThx (see Figure 2.3). Employees can choose to have their BlueThx rewards and recognitions show up on their corporate Profile page.

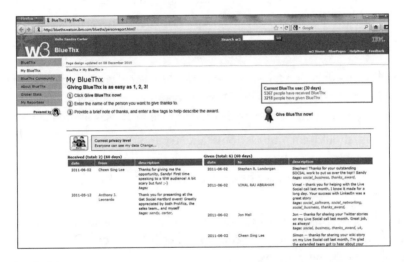

Figure 2.3   The BlueThx page.

Educate and Enable

Just empowering and sharing your goals are not enough. To get your employees to take the next step, you need to inspire them to do so. You need to provoke them into action. So what causes people to act? They need an easy way to get started.

To help people get started, make sure you provide them with the appropriate education. Think about the tools that you think fit your goals and then set up training for your employees. This training should include easy ways to start. For instance, one company set up a "paint your face (book) day." I was at Farmers Insurance University to share best practices on Social Business and they had a session of best practice speakers from all over the industry.

Peer-to-peer training is often the most effective. What I mean by peer-to-peer training is focusing your training efforts around educating a couple of people in a specific job role. You might have to spend some additional time with them so they fully understand how to use the technology. The goal is for these people to become your advocates and build specific use cases on how some or all of these tools can help them do their job better. Now you have some advocates in a certain job role, and you want them to go educate their peers with similar roles and responsibilities. For example, if I'm in corporate communications, I want someone in corporate communications to educate me on how this is going to help me in my job. The same holds true for other job roles.

A couple of things to ensure you are successful and engaging:

- Make sure your education takes into account the level of your employees. If you have some employees who are already active, it could be as simple as these employees training others through lunch-and-learns, or formal classes offered at your facility.

- The training should encompass tools and technology, how to leverage them as well as best practices and case studies. Tools that assist internal communications increase efficiency and reduce costs by applying them in the right way, engaging the employees.

- Because there is a divide between those who leverage social techniques and those who do not, you will find that the education needs to be continuous and in waves to make room for the new believers.

- Training should be customized by job role, as it assists in people understanding how this can help their role.

- Reverse mentoring programs can help—such as a junior employee being paired up with an executive who is scared or just not savvy about social techniques. At IBM, we have a program called BlueIQ that is basically a program that recruits volunteers to do just that: reverse mentor. BlueIQ Ambassadors are social software experts who help IBM employees, teams, and communities with using social tools, such as blogging, Dogear, and communities.

- Make sure that the education is hands on. There is nothing that sinks in faster than active learning. For instance, I was recently at a conference where they had a "community building" booth for those companies that wanted to set up a community right then and there! It was so effective because you didn't learn about how to do it; you did it!

At IBM, our training is done in person for the C suite and key influencers, and, for the empowered employees who are located in hundreds of countries, via online tools. For example, we have videos posted in communities on best practices, and our Social Business Heroes—those who have seen great returns from their use—share simple how-to videos and stories with everyone. In addition, we have set up an "I Live Social" section in our discussion threads. This enables all our employees to see how to leverage social techniques in sales, customer service, marketing, and beyond. In addition, we set up a series of seminars for our IBM Business Partners so that they can also effectively leverage the new tools in their small businesses, and even present an esteemed award—called the Beacon—for the best usage of social.

We are not the only company that has internal programs. I was recently at Manulife in Canada for their Global IT meeting. With their leaders from throughout the world, their conference focused on innovation and featured three outside speakers to share best practices from across the industry on becoming a Social Business. Training should include case studies—to prove it works—and don't be shy about asking others to share. After all, a Social Business is all about sharing its expertise!

Building a Culture for Participation Started Inside First

The best way to learn is through doing. Start your team out by participating inside your four walls. There are a lot of great benefits to taking this approach. You can learn quickly from mistakes and generate value for your company. IBM first started experimenting with internal communities back in the early 2000s. We learned some valuable lessons around building and maintaining a healthy community. During this time, we also were building out our guidelines and starting to measure the business value of communities. It wasn't until 2008 that IBM started to allow communities to be established externally on www.ibm.com. In 2010, IBM won a Forrester Groundswell Award for excellence in support via social media with an estimated ROI of $100 million savings in support annually.

There are many tools that are built or can be set up for internal-only use—for instance, wikis to enable you to share information dynamically, or blip.tv that features private RSS feeds. There are micro-blogging tools like Twitter that enable an internal-only view of communities, and even video tools like Ustream with private channels for inside corporations. Starting inside first gives you insight into how your employees will leverage the tools and provides a way to reduce the risk of how they will respond once outside the firewall.

For example, a building manufacturer had a business model that needed to be more engaged with its clients. However, they decided to first use social inside their four walls to learn the lay of the land before they took their involvement external. The goal of the internal use was to reduce the risk of a social disaster outside the four walls given that the employees would learn the ins and outs of social first in a safe environment.

The ultimate goal was to create an agile, efficient culture of open collaboration that would lower cycle times, drive innovation, and speed product time to market.

They set up communities of interest internally to tackle challenges common across locations, marketplaces, and skill sets, and leveraged wikis and blogs to facilitate the sharing of knowledge and expertise, as well as feedback and comments. They had more than 10,000 employees working in 400 communities on regional initiatives. After this internal project, they now have more than 1,600 employees who are collaborating in external communities to drive product innovation. And most important, they now have 10,000 "trained" advocates for their brand ready to go!

Deloitte Consulting also focused first internally. With a project called Deloitte D Street, they set up a community to ensure that they had the collaboration inside their company first. With a set of social tools to help them form virtual teams, educate employees, and even provide flexible work options, they reached their employees and trained them while raising their employee satisfaction rate. Because the average age of their employees was 27, the use of social tools for Millennials turned out to be a big satisfier! As David Boland, the leader of the Deloitte D Street project, commented,

> "Deloitte created an interactive decision tree to help users think through who they're trying to collaborate with—internally at Deloitte, or with contractors, clients, or vendors. For example, the decision tree leads users to better understand the best ways to use the tool, and get the information they're seeking."

You can set up an internal community to share new ideas or brainstorm that next big product. At IBM, we formed ThinkForward. It is a community of almost 5,000 marketing and communications experts to share and collaborate on our IBM brand while learning about communities and their value. In addition, IBM has SocialBlue, an opt-in social networking site for IBMers. On SocialBlue, you can customize your profile page with information about yourself; upload and share photos; share your ideas, thoughts, and opinions through top-five lists, which we call "hive fives;" and organize events with other IBMers. There were 38,000 members in nine months. All of these activities help IBMers learn how to behave and optimize in the Social Business world.

Deloitte and IBM are not alone. Coca-Cola, Sprint, Eddie Bauer, and Johnson & Johnson not only have tried out the techniques internally but have now externally launched their social projects more successfully.

The goal of launching first internally is to provide your employees a practice ground in which to learn how to be effective with the tools in an internal setting first, to reduce the risk when you move your engagement outside your four walls. Lessons learned typically include how to communicate in 140 or fewer characters, how to effectively use the tools, and how to interact online!

CASE STUDY: SOGETI—ALIGNING CORPORATE GOALS AND CULTURE

Sogeti is an IT service provider with more than 20,000 people in 15 countries. They embraced Social Business in many small steps, with local initiatives going back as far as the late 1990s.

In 2007, the Sogeti board of directors instituted a broad initiative to stimulate bottom-up innovation, the exchange of ideas and increased bonding between employees. For Sogeti as a service provider with many employees spending their days working from clients' offices, bonding and knowledge exchange are both important and challenging. Responding quickly to clients' requests is part of Sogeti's core business.

After starting with strategic discussions, an InnovationJam® was held—a massive brainstorm where all employees were invited to share their ideas and opinions. Not surprisingly, many of the ideas revolved around applying social media inside Sogeti. The InnovationJam kicked off broader discussions about culture, innovation, and the balance between top-down and bottom-up initiatives. Also, a Sogeti internal social collaborative space was launched.

The whole initiative was one of transparency: All workshops, activities, and progress were made visible and open for discussion. Once the social collaborative space was made available, the people who were already most active in the public social media space were invited to become VIP early adopters. They served as the catalysts for change, bringing content, ideas, and, through networking, broader adoption. The corporate social space was one where private topics were explicitly allowed—the content was in no way restricted or steered and anyone had total freedom to create. Besides the business communities, more personal communities were started on topics ranging from "Japanese language" to "diving" and "vacations."

There were almost no straightforward training sessions to teach these new tools, but instead there were "life hacking" workshops, where participants were encouraged to look for ways to optimize their workday. How to move activities out of email to a more productive and engaging environment. How to save time by finding the right resource/person quickly. What new ways you can use to deliver something to a client. A lot of experimentation was encouraged. The support team highlighted initiatives that had good potential and helped to make connections where they weren't made organically.

Employees have defined new services and created new communities. Also through experimentation, blogs are starting to share the hard-to-capture knowledge of the professionals (see Figure 2.4). Without a doubt, the results are positive, though in many discussions it still proves extremely hard to translate this back into dollars: A culture of bottom-up innovation and knowledge exchange? Priceless!

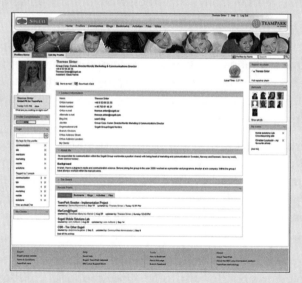

Figure 2.4   A profile page on Sogeti's website.

Experiment: Have a Way to Learn from Mistakes and Others

The definition of experimentation is to "try something new, in order to gain experience." The goal of experimentation is to see what works for your company and your clients and employees. Social techniques provide a great way to experiment. Trying something in the morning can yield results by noon so that changes can be made. It is important that your employees and others experiment with the usage as you cannot understand the value of social without having experienced it for yourself.

Social Businesses pilot innovations. They stimulate the extended management team to break the mold of existing business models. Think "green field"—what would you do if you were a new entrant with no legacy burden or the freedom to question the obvious? When you think you have the answer, ask "why" again.

Neal Schaffer, the author of *Windmill Networking: Maximizing LinkedIn,* wrote, "It's about finding what sparks engagement, spread of word, new fans, and action in what you do in social. And guess what? You won't know what works until you try it, analyze the results, and incorporate your findings in how you refine your social strategy going forward."

Frame your experiment carefully and determine what you are testing. It is important to understand "what you know" and test "what you think." For instance, you could be testing the best use of your employees in brainstorming on video or blogs. You know that involving employees in brainstorming the next product feature is a best practice, but you "think" that video is a better way to get the results. This experiment is about the most effective tools. Experiments could be focused on best use of social techniques, best use of a tool, new engagement methodologies, cultural differences in different parts of the world, and the list goes on. Be careful about the experiment.

Unfortunately, there is a misconception that most of the effort required in successful experimentation occurs during the actual conduction of the experiment. In fact, the bulk of the effort in successful experiments is invested before the experiment itself is conducted, in the preexperiment phase. Moreover, substantial effort is also required after the experiment is conducted, when the results are analyzed, understood, extrapolated, documented, and disseminated.

Social Businesses have a mechanism to learn from the experimentation. Make sure when you experiment that you are sharing the learnings through the Social Business Digital Council discussed earlier in the chapter.

CASE STUDY: IBM

IBM is a great case study of leveraging culture plus social to increase its value. Adam C. Christensen described IBM's approach. First, IBM is a B2B company. In fact, we would call it a company of more than 300,000 experts across 170 countries. The goals that IBM set are to drive growth, especially in the white space areas and growth markets. The culture is one of being intensely diverse, progressive, and highly collaborative but risk adverse.

Going into Social Business in a big way was a big move for IBM. The following are the key ways that IBM aligned our goals and our culture. They have become best practices for many companies.

1. **Role and Guidelines.** IBM set Social Computing Guidelines back in 2005 for blogs with a group of IBMers who were some of the first bloggers (I was in that group!). The guidelines were a set of boundaries that supported our business conduct guidelines that were already in place for interactions at parties, or in events. This was one of the most significant starting blocks that IBM did to set a standard of expectation for its employees. You can find the guidelines at www.ibm.com/blogs/zz/en/guidelines.html.

2. **Empower.** IBM encouraged everyone to participate and, given our risk-adverse nature, actually did a study with MIT to prove the value of social connections to the senior team! This study truly empowered the employees through the trust now bestowed upon them. Many senior IBMers are avid Tweeters, LinkedIn users, bloggers, and Foursquarers and set a great example. The bottom line is that IBM views its employees as its best brand ambassadors.

3. **Educate and enable.** IBM has numerous internal online education and in-person education on best practices and tools and techniques in the social realm. It is considered best-in-class in the leveraging industry. In addition, for its ecosystem, IBM offers free "Getting Started Guides" and webinars. In addition, they feature classes on "Best Practices for Social Media Marketing & Lead Generation."

4. **Build a culture for participation started inside first.** IBM has more than 16,000 bloggers in BlogCentral, more than 53,000 members on Beehive sharing photos, and more than one million viewed wikis, and hosts multiple Innovation-Jams to get employees involved in shaping IBM's future. It tracks the positive ROI and expense reduction that it sees from its internal Social Business focus. For example, matching the right experts has seen a productivity-driven savings of $4.5 million per year and $700,000 savings *per month* in reduced travel.

5. **Experiment and have a way to learn from mistakes.** IBM has set up social Business Digital Councils in its divisions. These councils have multiple functions that share ideas, collect best practices, and learn from mistakes. The highly collaborative culture at IBM ensures that there is positive sharing to learn and

take each idea to the next level. In addition, we have a Digital Council for IBM Global that is run by Ben Edwards, our Vice President of Digital Eminence.

IBM, as a Social Business, has truly aligned its culture and goals for success. This is a perpetual process, and as IBM continues to reinvent itself, its employees are trusted and great brand ambassadors for the company. Companies leveraging that ignore culture and their strategy may be derailed irreparably. Social Businesses are those that focus on culture, the right people, acting on the right set of goals. It is this set of priorities that makes Social Businesses outperform in the marketplace.

Conclusion

In this chapter, we went deeper into the bold AGENDA for Social Business around aligning your company's goals and culture. Social Businesses need to have solid goals and to consider culture before beginning on the social journey. Projects without regard to culture fail. If the current culture doesn't align, Social Businesses need to change it, and create a culture of engagement and experimentation. Top-down mandates generally don't work and neither do completely grass-roots efforts. It takes a cultural change. Experiment and learn. This is a continuous process! And don't forget to measure the results. In Chapter 5, I will share some ways to calculate your ROI.

Now that you have completed the Social Business AGENDA workstream on goals and culture, let's take that power to outside the firewall. Let's proceed with how to gain "friends" through social trust!

CHAPTER

3

Gain Social Trust

"Best practice companies focus on their trust plan to protect their reputation. We live in a trust economy where trust is the new currency, and our social ecosystem includes friends and followers."

Sandy Carter

"We want sellers who act more like friends. Companies buy from people they trust."

Judith Hurwitz, President and CEO of Hurwitz and Associates

The Circle of Trust

Every Social Business has to generate trust in its brand, employees, and products. I still remember the movie *Meet the Parents,* in which the father explained the concept of the "circle of trust" to his future son-in-law where trust in his family revolves from person to person. While we can laugh at the situations of this funny movie, the context of the message is one that is very real and very important. Trust, while often overlooked, is crucial in the Social Business world. People want to do business with someone they trust, and with the social tools, all relationships depend on this concept. Our common sense tells us that trust is earned and not easily given. How do we survive in today's business world in relation to trust? "Who do we trust" and "Who trusts our company" become critical questions to answer.

Trust Is a Protector for a Social Business

Trust guards your Social Business digital reputation. That digital reputation is how people view your company from the online content available in the blogosphere. This trust varies with the relationship, whether for employees, customers, and partners. For example:

- Employees build social capital through interactions that can happen naturally through work. The social environment can be provided by the company and built into work processes (hence the power of social enablement of business processes).

- Building trust and a reputation with customers and prospects requires a different kind of thought and focus. There is no shared "platform" (although LinkedIn, Twitter, Facebook, Wikipedia, and so forth, are shared by all) that guarantees interaction. Targeting, use of analytics, and engaging with honesty and value are key. It's not enough to simply focus on the customer's interests, but trust is built by understanding where they spend time and their motivations. Trust and a digital reputation are built by making the customer successful.

- Partners and channels have aspects of customers and employees. A business partner who has more than 50% of their business with your company might be deeply integrated into your core processes and have a social interaction pattern somewhat like a customer. Other partners, however, can also be hybrids—a bit of a competitor and customer. Their business relationship is not integrated into your business processes as deeply, so it takes on a different type of relationship.

Building Social Business relationships is not very different from building relationships in real life. The interactions build trust over time. As you build more positive relationships, you create a positive reputation. In the digital world (both inside and outside the organization), these relationships can connect to people and places previously impossible. Social Business retains shared opinions of friends and trust, resulting in a digital reputation that extends to a personal and even organizational brand. It's establishing this individual and organizational digital reputation that creates an environment to truly "engage" others.

A Social Business is about people and relationships, not about the latest social tool. Because people are at the core, relationships come front and center and all relationships are built on trust. People want to buy from sellers who act more like friends. They want to call someone in product support who really cares about them and wants to help them. They want to trust the advice that you give them on solving a problem. In short, your clients are seeking a relationship with you that is not one-sided.

With time, consistent positive interactions, value, and a demonstration of commitment, your company will be on its way to creating strong digital reputation with trust.

Why Is Trust So Important?

The Edelman Trust Barometer (www.edelman.com/trust/2011/), an 11-year running study that touches more than 5,000 people on five continents, measures the significance of trust. In their recent study, they found that when a company is distrusted, 57% of people will believe negative information about them after hearing it one or two times. When a company is trusted, only 25% of people will believe negative information about them after hearing it one or two times. By contrast, if a company is trusted, more positive messages will be repeated and believed.

In a business setting, above all, trust enables people to do business with each other. Trust is contagious and exponential growth can occur when your loyal customers, partners, and employees are advocates on your behalf to their friends. In return, this will help your company's probability of gaining new clients. Trust among friends helped catapult Facebook to more than 600 million users and LinkedIn to more than 100 million users. Eighty percent of sales for more than $20,000 are impacted by five or more influencers, according to Nick Hayes, President of Influencer50 Inc. Influencer50 is the foremost influencer identification and engagement management firm that serves the Fortune 100 companies. And the data continues on the value of trust.

comScore is a highly regarded Internet marketing research company that tracks Internet data in order to study online behavior. From comScore's report "The Social Media Phenomenon," you can see why trust is so important:

- 81% of people check online comments before purchasing.
- 56.3% of users said they *"got to know"* brands through online channels.
- 58.7% made *purchase decisions* based on user-generated online info.
- 89.9% of users still *pay attention* to online comments even when not making a purchase.

People trust their friends before making purchase decisions and therefore that relationship is a valuable item. With the world being so interconnected, one of the most valuable currencies is your company's trust shown in your reputation both on- and offline. The trust economy is often on a global scale and mostly traded among friends. Compare that to the past. In the past, people outsourced trust to a few people who filtered the news and information. They censored what was important and what was not. In the social era there is a loss of this "blind" trust. The trust economy rewards those who have a personal relationship with their clients. These relationships—or in Social terms, your friends, followers, and fans—are a key success factor in developing trust. Social Business uses social networks and social tools that serve as a new set of eyes and ears to generate trust. Companies will be able to not only deepen their existing trust, but leverage that trust to introduce new products and explore new markets. From seeing comes belief-changing insights, which then spur trust and action.

Developing Your Trust Plan

Part of your Social Business AGENDA is the workstream to develop a plan for actively creating and guarding your social trust. Building social trust is one of the most important things your company will do, and it is achievable when you pay attention to the three components necessary for developing social trust in the Social Business AGENDA:

- Expertise and thought leadership
- Responsiveness and consistency
- Transparent and open conversation

As you develop your trust plan with these three components in mind, you will need to consider your *trust creators* (an ecosystem of friends and followers) and your *tippers,* as illustrated in Figure 3.1. A tipper is a person who influences the rest of the clients and potential clients online and offline; usually about 5%–10% of your product or category's population.

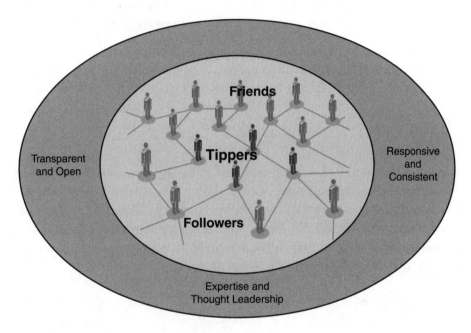

Figure 3.1   Gain social trust

Expertise and Thought Leadership

One of the top keys in trust building is your subject matter expertise. In fact, in the Edelman Trust Barometer study, an "expert" was the number one credible source of information. This year's study showed that trust in experts is higher than ever. In fact, 70% agreed that an expert or a member of the academic community were of the highest valued sources. Sixty-four percent said the same about a technical expert from within the company and 53% vouched for the credibility of a financial or industry analyst. If you provide this access to experts in your company, you give your clients or potential clients the ability to learn and trust your company.

For example, a dry cleaner in a crowded marketplace could differentiate himself by avoiding the temptation of tweeting endlessly about his own specials and values. Instead, if he focused on offering helpful content to those with issues of stains on their clothes, he could become a subject matter expert (SME). This SME creates a sense of trust about the dry cleaner, making them more likely to be enticing to clients. True story or great example? Actually, it is a true story about a dry cleaner in New York (Jerry Pozniak @TheDryCleaner) who leverages Twitter in just this way to generate more business and a great ROI.

SMEs will offer their authoritative opinions on things happening in their area of the business. They are not afraid to take a stand and sometimes create controversy. This aspect of thought leadership is essential in establishing trust. Thought leadership is showcasing a future trend, direction, innovation, or idea. By constantly producing content that is genuine, up-to-date, thoughtful, and insightful, you can develop a leadership base that will follow your lead and generate trust.

For example, at IBM we created a blog on a new technology area. We invited our IBM top SMEs to blog and share their expertise. One of those SMEs is Jerry Cuomo, who discusses and dishes on IBM's vision on public, private, and hybrid cloud computing. He is definitely an expert, earning the title of IBM Fellow, one of the highest technical distinctions, and writes about his vision for the market. The stir of opinions on his videos and original ideas is generating trust in the community on behalf of IBM.

> **NOTE**
>
> Not all forms of communication are created equal. For establishing trust, video is better than audio and audio is better than a chat window. Video provides a way for people to see the personal side of your brand and employees.

Yes, content is important—most people would say it is still king! Your knowledge and content are what provide value and instill trust in your company and brand. There is no substitute! You might be familiar with the popular phrase "knowledge is power." In my opinion, "knowledge is power, only when shared by a trusted person."

Key to Trust: Responsiveness and Consistency

There is a direct correlation between your responsiveness and consistency in dialogue and your trust. If a potential customer asks you a question online, requesting more information, and you either don't get back to the person or you take a week to respond, it is sending the wrong signal to your potential customer. In governments, e-government is used as a way to increase citizen trust by improving interactions with citizens and perceptions of responsiveness. Time is of the essence and lack of responsiveness sends a signal of lack of importance, and lack of trust. I followed the United States presidential elections in 2008 and it came to me as no surprise when I discovered that all of the candidates had started their own LinkedIn page. I decided to send a request to join a candidate's network and within minutes it was accepted. I don't suspect that the presidential candidate was the one who accepted it, but the quick response from the candidate or staff was impressive.

Another recent example is when hackers cracked into Amazon.com and caused all books written by gay, lesbian, bisexual, and transgender (GLBT) authors to disappear, Amazon reacted quickly to assure everyone that they had not done this. While there was a hashtag created on Twitter about the incident, because the company was responsive, most people believed that they did not deliberately remove GLBT materials from their site.

Cordero, a web hosting company, experienced a power outage that affected their servers, leaving their clients' websites down. On Twitter, Cordero directly responded to their clients. While they did get negative comments, there were referrals because of the way the situation was handled so quickly. The bottom line is that you need a great way to listen to the conversation of your friends (clients) so that you are responsive to their needs to build great trust.

Trust results from building and maintaining a relationship. It takes time and dedication as both parties need to mutually benefit over a period of time. Once you finally "get it," you must continue to dedicate the time and energy to keep it. This process is not easy but is well worth the investment.

So, what does this all boil down to as a best practice? Dedicate the time and commit to long-term relationships. I recommend setting standards in terms of a "promise" as to how long it will take your company to respond online to your clients and potential clients. The biggest excuse people make about not wanting to engage in the social world is that they do not have the time. I dedicate a portion of my day to engage with my friends and followers to ensure that I provide them appropriate responses in a timely fashion to sustain my trust with them.

A Social Business will have clarity about who in the organization owns the responsiveness. It does not have to be everyone; however, your goals and strategy should guide your decision on your company's expectations. Google CEO Larry Page believes that Google needs to go "social" to compete. To that end, he sent out a company-wide memo alerting employees that up to 25% of their annual bonus will be tied to the success or failure of Google's social strategy and their contributions to it. If you want to build trust through subject matter expertise, you need to ensure that you have an active and consistent commitment from your experts to blog, tweet, or participate in communities. If your goals are to have the best customer satisfaction, your client service team had better be online listening and participating in the conversation.

When one of IBM's internal data centers went offline due to a networking issue in 2011, email (among other applications) went down and affected thousands of users. Employees heard about the outage through IBM's internal micro-blogging system within minutes and continued to collaborate on their internal social networking solution. This was made possible by IBM's responsiveness to their employees, empowering them with alternative methods of collaboration. Communications on this situation continued until it was resolved.

The bottom line is that Social Business responsiveness should be measured not in days, but in minutes. That responsiveness and consistency is around all constituents—employees, customers, and partners. Businesses must push the leaders and the individual personalities of the company to be accessible and trustworthy. People trust individuals more than a corporate image. At the end of the day, people like to buy from people. Being available and responsive to customer comments, questions, or complaints is an essential element for creating a relevant, authentic online presence, one of the key factors affecting whether your followers trust you and your brand.

Transparent and Open Conversation

Because there is no longer privacy, especially online, everything you do or say is essentially out in the open; every mistake, every decision, every action, every response, every success. To establish trust around your brand, your company needs to be completely transparent. Trust has never been more important than in today's economy.

Openness and transparency will disarm negative news or discussions and enable you to get in front of problems before they grow too large. A couple things that can crush trust in the realm of Social Business is ignoring the voice of the customer, not genuinely wanting to engage and listen but trying to use a social channel like other channels (one-way communication), and using social media only for marketing and sales purposes while turning a deaf ear to customer concerns and conversation. Communication that is deceptive and not transparent will ultimately be turned against your company until they can learn to embrace the broad conversation and use it as an opportunity to listen, engage, and improve.

Remember that this transparency goes beyond your clients into the inward processes in your company. Your employees will embrace the transparency that a Social Business provides.

Sometimes this is a little scary to management when the flow of information and ideas is not hierarchical; however, in the long run, this is part of the positive value of being open.

One Social Business example of transparency in internal processes is CEMEX of Mexico. CEMEX is truly a brick-and-mortar company—they are part of the cement market. Not only are they a highlight of leveraging the Social Business AGENDA, but they won a Forrester Groundswell Award for their focus on driving trust throughout their internal employee networks and driving their business into new markets for their premixed cement product. The leadership and culture came from the very top, Chairman and CEO L. H. Zambrano, who led the effort on becoming a Social Business:

> "A quiet revolution is underway. It started with new ways of creating and sharing information on the Internet. It continued with the emergence of smart phones that enabled anytime, anywhere mobile communications. Now, the revolution is linking people in social networks that enrich how they connect, share, and live. Welcome to the Collaboration Revolution."

CEMEX has worked to leverage the knowledge and dialogue of its people with internal social networking and tools to capture, codify, and quantify this dialogue. CEMEX wanted to set up the community such that the members would build it, populate it, and fine-tune it themselves, with a new level of transparency in sharing of corporate information.

CEMEX deployed an internal social platform called Shift. Shift was created to help the company become more efficient and agile, but also to enable employees with similar objectives to share opinions, thoughts, information, experience, knowledge, and best practices. CEMEX designed Shift as a social network with a business focus. When employees use Shift, ideas, suggestions, and recommendations bubble up across the global network. Communities of interest are formed to tackle challenges common to their locations, markets, and skill sets. Projects can move forward without the barriers posed by traditional hurdles, such as overreliance on email and live meetings. And trust is built and grown through the system.

Shift was ultimately designed for a new kind of workforce, one that is mobile, global, empowered, and very transparent! CEMEX is empowering employees in new and important ways that go beyond traditional titles and roles. The payoff of Shift is lower cycle times, faster time to market, and real-time process improvement. These have driven the company's innovation initiative from five projects to nine in a short time. Because there are no boundaries to this Social Business, Cemex is always learning. There are no boundaries between experts inside the company and experts in the marketplace. The business embraces the tools and leadership models that support capturing knowledge and insight from many sources, allowing it to quickly sense changes in customer mood, employee sentiment, or process efficiencies.

Transparency needs to occur with your entire ecosystem, and it cannot be delegated. You cannot fake it. Your senior team needs to either embrace it or find that Social Business Champion who will do so on behalf of the company. I follow Gini Dietrich's blog on Spin Sucks, a blog dedicated to marketing and public relations professionals. In her blog on transparency, she wrote, "Why is this [social media] different…than writing a speech for the President, ghost-writing a column for your CEO, or writing a review about a product you received, free-of-charge? The difference is this: All of those examples have an approval process. They all have 'canned' PR messages. The person whose name goes on each of the pieces has the opportunity to review, make changes to fit their own voice, and post as their own. Social media is instant. It's immediate and there isn't an approval process. There isn't time. It happens in real-time. That being said, the person (or people) handling social media doesn't necessarily have to be the CEO. But it has to be someone who has the ability to speak on behalf of the organization without having to get approvals."

Make sure that openness and transparency enable your company to learn. This learning spirit that occurs from the transparency and openness will help your company solve business problems and capture new business opportunities.

Your Ecosystem Expands to Include Friends and Followers!

When companies talk about their ecosystem, they often are referring to their partners, contractors, independent consultants, and suppliers who help them deliver new and updated products or services. A Social Business expands the typical definition of a company's ecosystem to now include friends and followers. While your friends and followers might not directly produce a good or service, they act as expanded members of your team! They might or might not be a client of your product, but you do need to earn their trust as well. In essence, these friends and followers become brand advocates for your company, meaning that because of their trust in your company and because they like your brand, they advocate on your behalf.

In the online world, there are differences in friends and followers.

On Facebook, friends connect from other relationships—direct and indirect. If you and I are both friends of Mark or of a company, then there is a higher chance that you and I can become friends.

On LinkedIn, a lot of relationships are more business-to-business related and therefore references and background are very important.

On Twitter, a follower could be added without any thought at all—in fact, there are programs, or as some call them, "robots," that accept followers from anyone who makes a request.

In communities, those who belong to your community, which is an online group of people who share and interact around a common interest area, are considered friends as well.

It is very important to understand how to make a friend or follower in the different tools that are prevalent in your region. The rest of this chapter helps your company develop those friends and followers.

Does a Company Have Friends?

Many people ask me, "How can a company have friends?!" Companies are like people. The actions that make people great friends are the same that make companies great friends. In the social world, friends and followers are your clients and potential clients. In essence, they are a group that has self-segmented and therefore is highly valuable.

Does it matter if your company has friends? Syncapse Corporation is a global leader in the areas of community building, technology solutions, and digital measurement. They published a report on the value of these relationships over a two-year period. For example, 68% of Facebook fans (of a company) are "very likely" to recommend a product to family and friends (as opposed to 28% of nonfans). Eighty-one percent of fans feel a connection to the brand (versus only 39% of nonfans). People can be friends with companies!

As social networks mature, the relationships we forge within each one reflect our interests and aspirations. With this maturity people become friends with companies, objects, and ideas. Trust is earned and its stature is representative of our collaboration and contribution over time. Business success depends on people, people making connections, people sharing ideas, and people building trust. An employee thinks of a new way to streamline a process and tells his or her supervisor. A product developer gathers feedback from customers and passes it on to the design team. A consumer identifies with a brand and purchases the product.

One by one, relationships are established and nurtured, laying the foundation for continued growth and profitability through trust. The bottom line is that friends are advocates for your company. These advocates recommend you to their friends, who buy your products, usually with a lower cost of acquisition to your company.

For example, Larry Carvalho formed RobustCloud as an entrepreneur focused on advisory consulting services in the cloud computing field. Larry started first with evaluating various directions for his business. Once he decided on cloud computing, he put his effort into educating others about this new technology. This gave him an early understanding and feedback from attendees. Attending relevant conferences helped build a network in the field. Working toward this goal, Larry grew his connections on LinkedIn to more than 900 connections by sharing his insights, knowledge, and expertise—not by promoting his company.

Gaining trust depends on how you build contacts. Sharing insightful information is a good way to get contacts to see value in the information you provide. Using contacts you already know as an intermediary to introduce you to new contacts helps remove the risk of the "unknown commodity" syndrome that tends to plague new relationships. Points you make through blogs and tweets need to be fair and relevant to the domain you cover. They need to be posted with a sense of urgency that covers current topics.

Take, for instance, Cars.com. Cars.com is a top destination within the automotive industry that delivers a comprehensive suite of tools and information to help buyers form opinions on what to buy, where to buy, and how much to pay for a car, and to help sellers connect with in-market car shoppers. They are a $400 million business that began their Social Business journey a few years ago.

At Cars.com, they focused on social trust in a few ways with their ecosystem. They focused on understanding their clients and partners. And they turned their attention to friends of the industry—selling cars! They learned that all of them wanted someone to advise them on what to buy through both trusted editorial experts and peer opinions. This understanding led to a focus on a set of expert "friends" who wrote professional reviews, blogs, and consumer vehicle reviews. Because their goal was to engage in the world of word of mouth, which is one of the top influencers of automotive purchase decisions, their trust strategy was built on forming relationships with the entire ecosystem, rather than on promotion. In addition, they listened and responded quickly to their ecosystem by enabling clients to leverage social networks at the same time they're using Cars.com, building trust through every relationship.

The important part of planning will be determining how your company builds their relationships, converts them to friends, and leverages them to become brand advocates:

1. Go where your ecosystem hangs out.

2. Have your friends come to you.

3. Determine who your tippers are.

For example, if your company is selling dog food, you would know that Dogster is the number one online community for dog lovers. Your strategy could be to befriend those in Dogster and determine the tippers in that context. How you build trust with those influencers will be critical for your digital reputation.

If your company is selling biotechnology, you could create a private community and invite those you think are interested to meet you there. This "expert" community could be leveraged as the tippers to drive a point of view in the industry.

Let's go through each of these three approaches as your company determines the best approach for your goals, culture, and trust model.

Go Where Your Ecosystem Hangs Out

Your corporate goal in creating trust online begins with your company finding out where those who are interested in your product, brand, or category hang out online. To think it through, imagine a personal example. Suppose you had moved to a new city and you liked books. To meet new friends, you might join a book club.

The same is true online, where people form communities or participate in blogs. You need to go where your community hangs out and talks. Because you are joining them, not building the community, you want to start out by listening to the conversations and adding value. If your Social Business has friends already there, reach out to them. If you don't, ask the community why. Your participation should be transparent, always keeping your brand promise and overall corporate objectives in mind. Add value from the beginning.

For example, as an author, I wanted to learn from the best. I found a great and active author group in LinkedIn and joined. I then spent time adding value by sharing my experiences on my first two best-selling books. That sharing of expertise and experiences enabled me to ask advice and counsel from the community. If I had just jumped in and started asking questions, I would not have gotten the great support that I received from that community.

So how do you decide whether to jump into an established group or create one? The simple advice I would give is to determine whether your company is sought for its advice and point of view (that is, people seek out the advice). If that is the case, form your own community. However, if you are in the first steps of outreach and have defined your target audience, focus on placing your messages where the target audience will find them—which means that you would join the right communities. Some companies will do both! For instance, Ray Wang is sought after for his knowledge of gamification. His level of expertise is so high in this new area that people approach him and his company, but his company still participates in established communities.

In the B2B world, a great example is IBM. IBM wanted to engage chief financial officers (CFOs). The challenge? How does IBM engage with a senior-level, tightly knit community whose members are highly selective about interacting with peers and other professionals? IBM needed a space where CFOs were comfortable and that they went to naturally. Because the goal was to gain trust of the other CFOs, IBM wanted to share its subject matter expertise and thought leadership but also learn from other best practices.

The choice of community was LinkedIn, as it was a platform familiar to most CFOs (for instance, in India, there are more than 2,500 CFOs on LinkedIn). As a pilot, IBM worked with India and our CFO of IBM India. At the beginning, he had fewer than 10 connections. In the first six months, his connections grew to 385 CFOs, representing firms with over $3 billion in IT spending. As the IBM CFO engaged in more consistent thought-leadership conversations, he grew his connections 30% month on month, and now he hosts the largest single CFO community on LinkedIn. He gets regular requests for peer meetings and business discussions, as well as invitations for public speaking engagements. Also, popular blog topics have yielded immense and surprisingly candid insights on key issues for CFOs in India. A true success for leveraging communities that exist!

Take a look at your core competencies and consider whether your ecosystem views your company as the expert in a given topic area. This will help you understand whether your company should consider creating a community on your domain versus joining a public community like Facebook or LinkedIn.

As an example, the Practicing Law Institute (PLI) is a nonprofit organization and premier provider of continuing legal education in the United States. Its core competency is providing guidance and helping lawyers to grow their professional careers. PLI launched a website called PLI XChange. It is managed by invitation only and is offered to all registrants and faculty of PLI seminars, among others. PLI XChange encourages comfortable collaboration, allowing users to choose how they participate, what they want to display in their profile, whether they want to be contacted via email or instant message, and more.

The top sites on the market (like Facebook and Twitter) are likely places for your friends to go. In February 2011, IBM built a supercomputer called Watson™ to play Jeopardy against the two greatest champions of all time. After the three-day mach concluded and IBM's Watson was the champion, IBM wanted to capitalize on this market opportunity. IBM posted lots of rich media on www.ibm.com, but where they really attracted new markets was in the Watson Facebook and Twitter stream that they created. Watson's Facebook page now has many fans and its Twitter stream has followers.

But you will also determine that the most prevalent social media sites are not the only place your ecosystem hangs out. For example, if you love Java because of your technical work interest and post about it on your wall all day, are you going to drive your friends to tears on Facebook? Finding these like-minded souls will be important to your success but will require some digging to find related online communities. Chapter 7, "Analyze Your Data," covers the right analytic tools to determine where potential communities of interest are.

Finding these communities is a great way to get started. Take, for instance, gDiapers, a company that makes environmentally friendly disposable diapers. Co-founder Jason Graham-Nye did not set a goal to create a community but first went to where his ecosystem was. He discovered a community already discussing his topic in a Yahoo! Group. Then he found ways to add value and help his friends "channel their passion" and become "gMums." Joining communities of interest is a great strategy for companies of all sizes.

A common question that companies striving to be Social Businesses ask is "What are the topics that my company should focus on?" This is an important question because determining these key areas determines where you go. These should be chosen with thought and tweaked through time.

Tools such as the Google Keyword Tool can be helpful for those refinements. The tool is geared toward helping you determine the right words to focus on based on your website, find negative words for tracking, and overall refine the appropriate choices for your comprehensive analysis. If you type in a term, the Google Keyword Tool will show you the other terms that people are using when they are also searching for your term. For instance, if I type in "Sandra Carter," it suggests "Sandy Carter." If I type in "flowers," it suggests "garden" or "fresh cut."

Have Your Friends Come to You

Building a community is a great way to have that engagement with your ecosystem and "friends" coming to you; however, *building* a community is very different from *joining* a community.

Building a community involves getting people to come to your watering hole because of a shared interest in a trusted environment. As such, consider where you want to build your community. Do you want to own the community on your own domain or should you build a community on a consumer site like Yahoo! Groups or Facebook? Consider the pros and cons of these locations.

Just having clients coming into a place (like a blog) to comment isn't a community. A community is one where the members interact with each other. It dialogues. For example, for our Social Business Partner Community, we had a community come together online to brainstorm on key best practices. With our community manager, we began with discussion groups and issues to debate. Our community leveraged videos, case studies, and even virtual gifts of thank-you to community members who greatly helped others. Our community now trusts and interacts with others who could be considered "competitors" because of the value in the shared subject matter expertise.

A great community manager can make all the difference in the world, and in my mind is a requirement of success. A community manager's responsibility is to keep the community members active and engaged. It is one of the fastest-growing professions today and even managed to get a "Community Manager Appreciation Day" dedicated to it! In 2011, more than 2,000 tweets globally celebrated and thanked this new professional. If you are hiring someone to build a community or maintain an existing community, the skills that you would look for are slightly different. I know that building a community is somewhat harder than maintaining a community. To create a community requires unique skills with an emphasis on sharing a vision that your company buys into, and a great relationship builder.

People in this position are working to build, grow, and manage communities around a brand or cause. It fact, you can consider them change agents. They foster communication as an ongoing task. Internally, they help to eliminate the silos, and encourage and enable teams to work together. They are bold, as working cross-functionally across an organization is not for the faint of heart.

Lee Odden, in his TopRank blog covering Social Business topics, outlined an hour of a typical community manager's day:

6:45 am **Check and reply** to company blog(s) comments.

6:55 am **Scan news feeds** for interesting articles, blog posts, media to share. Write tweets, updates, etc., with short URLs. Schedule messages for sharing throughout the day.

7:10 am **Check Twitter, Facebook, LinkedIn** comments, Retweets, messages, and reply as necessary.

7:20 am **Scan persistent search** for topics, keywords, and brand terms to reveal commenting opportunities on industry news websites and blogs. Make comments, take notes for future blog posts.

7:30 am **Revisit company blog comment** management tool for new replies.

7:35 am **Revisit Twitter,** Facebook, and LinkedIn for specific follow-ups.

7:40 am **Scan social media monitoring tool** for mentions, links (alternatively, alerts can be used to surface events as they happen).

7:45 am   Review Social Dashboard and web analytics for the company blog for notable links, trending traffic sources, and relevant conversion metrics (RSS subscribers, email subscribers, downloads, webinar signups, sales inquires).

Your community manager should focus on a few areas for success. First, set the strategy for the community, and define its direction and content activation plan. Next, recruit and be a cheerleader for the community by attracting new members to join but also forming relationships with those in the community. Based on those relationships, they need to encourage a great dialogue, and debate. For instance, the Jimmy Choo community manager often uses polling to get the debates going! These dialogues and debates could be online and maybe offline events, and activities. And finally, they need to be providing feedback from the community in a structured way through the Social Business governance process (outlined in Chapter 2, "Align Organizational Goals and Culture"). In essence, the community manager is the engine of the community who keeps it alive and active.

So, since a community manager is a mandate, what else is important in creating an active and valued community? The following list outlines my top recommendations for creating a community and generating/maintaining activity:

Seven simple rules for building a community:

1. Make your goals clear. Explain what you're trying to achieve when you engage your community.

2. Hire a great community manager who embeds himself or herself into the community.

3. Attract or invite the right members for the group.

4. Encourage and stay close to engaged discussions, and acknowledge the feedback from the participants in your dialogue.

5. Reward contribution in the community to help it grow and thrive. It could even be something as simple as showing a great contributor with a "scoop" of new content!

6. Ensure that you add real value. Focus on the content, not in making sales.

7. Follow the trust rules. Be consistent and responsive, open and transparent. Community members need to know that there is someone at the other end of the online community who's listening, and who will respond and engage with them.

Teach for America enlists the most promising future leaders in the movement to eliminate educational inequality. As the United States' largest provider of teachers for low-income communities, they enlist members to teach for two years in urban and rural public schools.

They have a large alumni community made up of professionals who completed their two-year teaching assignment and moved on to other professions. The vast majority of members are just starting their two-year teaching assignments, and are just out of college or university.

In an effort to connect these new tech-savvy teachers with other new teachers and alumni from around the United States, they have created a community to allow members to easily search, find, evaluate, tag, and recommend teaching tools and resources. The goal is simply the sharing of resources that are valuable to teachers. The community manager actively engages this community to leverage the collective knowledge of alumni, members, and staff experts.

Another great community outside the United States is in Latin America. Camilo Esteban Rojas Lopez, the IBM Spanish South America (SSA) Social Business Leader, started a business partner community in March of 2011. Less than three months later, there are 120 active members from BPs in the following countries: Venezuela, Colombia, Ecuador, Bolivia, Chile, Paraguay, Uruguay, and Brazil. The value of the community is the sharing of subject matter expertise, in particular in a set of reusable tools for the partners. This includes presentations, point of views, whitepapers, and collateral in Spanish.

Currently there are many active discussions in the community (see Figure 3.2).

Figure 3.2   The SSA BP community

The community is shaping the direction of IBM's SSA region. The community requested more video in which a subject matter expert (SME) brings a discussion or a presentation and the community establishes a dialog. The community now hosts two webcasts a month, and participation has gone through the roof! In addition, the community is used to request help from IBM and its partners.

For instance, just last week a partner in Uruguay needed help with a client, and when he was successful, shared all the best practices with the community.

CROWD VS. COMMUNITIES

With 2 billion people connected to the Internet, Social Business is quickly becoming the primary means for communication and collaboration. Young people may have spearheaded the changes, but people of all ages have joined the virtual revolution: 89% of the millennial generation uses social networking sites, but so do 72% of baby boomers. And the gap is closing.

In the new Social Business marketplace, communities are the number-one social tool in use around the world. According to the 2011 GlobalWebIndex Survey of 51,000 web users, Facebook is the dominating community, except in Russia, Netherlands, Japan, and China, where local brands dominate. Communities are also the number-one social tool that Social Businesses are leveraging to socially empower their human relations process. For example, Celestica, Cemex, Sogeti, IBM, and others have leveraged internal communities to change their culture and internal innovation.

Communities are very powerful. They are a group of people interacting in an online space about shared interests, topics, or material. Communities provide an excellent way to connect members of a team and help them stay in touch and share information. Communities can be public or restricted, allowing community owners to control who can join the community and access community content.

But even with this growth in communities, as I talk to companies around the world, the big question that I get is, "What is the difference between just a group of people—a crowd and a community?" Sometimes the question is, "How do I get a group of people to become a community and see value in the community itself?" This question has fascinated me for a while, as I myself have built communities and have learned from others by researching the power of a community, taking classes, reading everything I can get my hands on, and talking to lots of clients who have been successful! In addition, at this year's SXSW, the social festival down in Austin, Texas, I heard a great speaker talk about this subject as well.

My conclusions for building a great community versus just a crowd are as follows:

1. **Leadership vs. equality.** The best communities have strong community managers who provide leadership and direction for the group. They help establish the

goal of the community experience and define the business problems trying to be solved. They help develop and shape the community norm, start conversations, and listen. They attract and build the right content, stories, and subject matter expertise. Crowds have no leadership that is stable. As such, they struggle with a defined direction and so wander and lose focus. CEMEX, the world's largest building materials supplier, has leadership not just from a community manager, but from all the way at the very top, their CEO.

2. **Purpose vs. pride.** A community is motivated by purpose. Its members share a goal. For instance, Dogster, the number-one community for dog lovers, is driven by the love of dogs. The community states, "This vibrant community is a must for any dog enthusiast!" Crowds are run by pride—sometimes pride of ownership, not purpose.

3. **Engaged vs. sporadic.** A community is engaged in active discussions and sharing. They comment, debate, and share expertise. They are consistent and responsive. For example, the DeveloperWorks® community is very engaged even though it has more than four million members. They engage through member-driven topics on technology. The engagement is driven by trust in open and transparent discussion ("this is what works; this doesn't") and by perceived value. IBM has experts who are passionate about providing the best support in the industry. With the right people in the community, the value-based engagement shines through as the members become community champions—internally and externally. Crowds are in and out of discussions in a sporadic way. They are not committed to the discussions but pepper themselves in and out of the discussions.

4. **Belong vs. benefit.** A community is powered by belonging so that its members can influence. The satisfaction that they get from the community is partially that they are part of something bigger. For instance, the China Deaf Association has a community that centers around providing real-time, online sign-language interpretation to improve the lives of deaf and hearing-impaired people. This 200,000-member community is driven by belonging to a community of people like them. Crowds want benefits—or rewards. Crowds like to get; communities like to give.

5. **Collaboration vs. connection.** The best communities collaborate as a normal working style. They feel the value exists with more input and a diversity of debate. For example, Pepsi, a large global consumer products company, has its community focused on accelerating development and project pipelines for

> innovations and new products. Product innovations increase as people collaborate through discovery and expertise. Crowds want connection; communities believe in the collective brain!
>
> The amount of members is not the key metric and does not equal a strong community. A crowd mentality is driven by the broad set of people that you have access to, not a relationship with. A community is about having passionate members who belong. A relationship does exist as a "friend" or subject matter expert.

IBM's developerWorks site is a good example of a B2B community. With more than eight million people registered on developerWorks, IBM has created a set of communities and social networking capabilities to allow people to connect with business, and business to connect with businesses. With a great community manager energizing the members, this community makes it easy for a customer or even a partner to locate technical experts through developerWorks. It also allows partners to work together, bringing together complementary skills to create added solutions based on IBM technology. I didn't realize the true value of this until last year when I was participating in an IBM business partner roundtable and one of the partners informed me that he subcontracted and later hired an eclipse programmer after locating that individual through his developerWorks profile.

Determine Who Your Tippers Are

You could have many friends; however, the key to competitive advantage is not the quantity. It truly is about influencing the influencers. Seth Godwin, the marketing expert who created the concept of permission-based marketing, wrote:

> "Many brands and idea promoters are in a hurry to rack up as many Facebook fans and Twitter followers as they possibly can. Hundreds of thousands if possible. A lot of these fans and followers are faux. Sunny day friends. A better idea defeats a much bigger but disconnected user base every time. The lesson: spend your time coming up with better ideas, not with more (faux) followers."

In essence, what you are looking for are those who will invest time in your brand, product, or category. Those people are the ones who influence others with their point of view and opinions. In his best-selling book *The Tipping Point,* author Malcolm Gladwell described how a small subset of society has a dramatic influence on the beliefs and behaviors of large social networks. He called these people who create "tipping points" "sales-people" and "Mavens." For simplicity, we'll just call them "tippers."

In the analysis of external social networks, a vast majority of the content is created by this very small group of tippers (5% as measured in the IBM Business Value Assessment). They provide the foundation for the casual participants (75%) who occasionally comment or post ideas. The tippers accelerate building friendships and a digital reputation.

Meteor Solutions, a provider of word-of-mouth analytics and optimization, collected data from a cross section of their clients. The analysis showed that the type of ecosystem a brand amasses on social sites matters more than the number. On average, approximately 1% of a site's audience generates 20% of all its traffic through sharing of the brand's content or site links with others. And these "tippers" drive an even higher share of conversion.

The tippers directly impact 30% or more of overall end actions just through their recommendations alone. According to a recent Forrester Research report, "Peer Influence Analysis," by Augie Ray and Josh Bernoff, a minority (about 6% of U.S. online adults) generates 80% of all influence impressions and roughly 14% of online adults generate 80% of the influence posts (source: Forrester Research, Inc., "Peer Influence Analysis: Mass Influencers Are the Key to Achieving Scale in Social Media Marketing," by Augie Ray and Josh Bernoff with Jennifer Wise, April 20, 2010). Knowing your "tippers" will be important for your strategy.

How do you find these influential people? Using social analytics tools helps you to identify who these people are, what type of content they like to share about your company, and where they go to share. Chapter 7 takes a detailed look at the tools themselves. For instance, if your most influential conversations for your company and brand are shared on Facebook, take your email lists and determine who on your company's list has a Facebook account.

For example, Sharpie, a division of Rubbermaid, wanted to build a community of their tippers to dialogue, listen, and learn. How did they find their ecosystem of friends? They identified Sharpie groups on Facebook, YouTube, and Flickr and determined those with the most influence. Some were even celebrities like the Zappos CEO. He tweeted this one day: "**zappos** was just admiring the stainless steel sharpie the other day, someone sent me a pic of it."

Sharpie joined the conversation and learned a lot about their clients and friends. Based on what they heard, they created on their website a section called "Sharpies Uncapped." This section celebrates the different uses of the Sharpie, like drawing Elvis, or honoring moms through a Sharpie Pen.

For the tippers, Sharpie wanted to showcase their innovations so they created the "Sharpie Squad." The Sharpie Squad is a separate place showcasing their tippers' Twitter, Facebook, and other social pages. Sharpie really focuses on their innovation and unique talent. Through many touch points, they form trust relationships with those who then become an influential army for them online.

The most important thing to do, once you find out who your tippers are, is to make them feel special. For instance, at IBM we seek their opinions on new product releases, and preview our announcements to them. We provide them with information that is the root of their becoming even more influential through knowledge and thought leadership. We also treat them as special and make them heroes, sometimes featuring them on our virtual events. And at our conferences like our Social Business Forum, we have a special blogger VIP seating, and a meet and greet with key executives.

The same logic holds true for internal social networking as well. Sogeti, a Capgemini subsidiary that specializes in technology services, needed to connect its more than 20,000 employees spread across 200 offices in 14 countries. When they decided to introduce an internal social networking tool called TeamPark, they wanted to find the right participants to get the environment growing before the official launch. Sogeti turned to Facebook for the answer. They took a look at the organically grown Sogeti Facebook page and found a list of employees. Figuring these users were socially savvy, Sogeti invited all of them into the soft launch of TeamPark to get their feedback and have them prepopulate content and communities.

I build my network as if I were building my own small business. Who would I want on my team? I carefully select those in my inner circle by their interest alignment and shared values. What skills do they bring to the table? Instintively, I want people in my network who have knowledge and skills that I need to learn. I will then leverage this important group to apply their collective knowledge to a particular problem. In a small business, loyalty is very important so I share information that is of value to my network, helping them reach their goals. I focus on the people and my relationship to them, trying to motivate them and help them where I can.

For example, when we were building a community around a new technology area, I sought out experts on the development of the technology and the use of the technology. We leveraged an IBM internal tool called Atlas for advanced social network analysis. Atlas uses automated expertise modeling and network analysis to identify the right people and the shortest paths to reach them—who knows who and who knows what. Visual diagrams help IBM understand who are the most connected hubs among the network, who are the important bridges linking groups, and who are the tippers that can influence your organization.

In addition, as we grew the community of tippers in this area, we wanted to make sure we shared a common interest of helping each company achieve its goals. It was not at all about IBM's products but about building intelligence about our community's common needs. Our community had first insight into directions, and was even opened up to competitors. In the end, the community became the authoritative source on this new technology, all were winners, and the group still continues today as we tackle new challenges in the fast-paced new technology development.

What About Your Enemies?

Keep your friends close, but keep your enemies closer. I was recently presenting at a high-level CMO conference, and I was asked this question: "I fully agree on your friend and trust model. But what do you do about your enemies?"

Chapter 7 discusses social analytics tools. These tools can be used to determine those with negative sentiment about you. It will be as important to keep your eyes on these people as it is to keep your eyes on your "friends."

If your enemies try to lie about you online, they will be found out. The community itself is self-policing and will find out the truth. If the content is incorrect, you can correct the perception. If the statements about your company are truthful but not complimentary, you can fix and apologize. This strategy is part of an overall Risk Mitigation plan, covered in more detail in Chapter 6, "Design for Reputation and Risk Management."

Conclusion

A Social Business AGENDA has a plan for developing social trust with its ecosystem, including friends and followers. This chapter defined the concept of how to develop that trust. Trust is built through subject matter expertise and content but also through transparency and openness. Responsiveness and consistency also play critical roles. Tippers add additional associations that further drive trust in your network. Your focus should be placed on developing a "friending" strategy, and engaging in a social trust plan. Trust is a protective characteristic that leads to tangible benefits. Lack of trust in your company is a barrier to change. Let's now proceed on to Chapter 4, "Engage Through Experiences."

CHAPTER

4

Engage Through Experiences

"The key is to reinvent customer relationships through great engagement not 'fly by' social media."

Sandy Carter

"Engagement—the act of creating meaningful connections—is key to building a vibrant community."

Rachel Happe, cofounder and Principal at The Community Roundtable, a private peer network for community managers and Social Business practitioners

Engagement Is the Energy of Social Business

My family and I just returned from a trip to Costa Rica. From the jungle to the ocean and even the volcanoes, the country engages you with activities, unique foods, and friendly people. Costa Rica's government started the tourism focus with a "day of tourism" set up to teach the citizens of the value of tourism for the country. The strategy of tourism has been well thought out for this Central American country, with engagement of its people being at the forefront. Since 1999, tourism has earned more foreign exchange than bananas, pineapples, and coffee combined, according to Intituto Costarricense de Turismo. Costa Rica ranks first among Latin American countries.

What is engagement? Very simply, it is the way that a company or country holds the attention of its ecosystem, client, or potential client. Engagement is personal. It drives businesses to think of being not only business to business (B2B), business to consumer (B2C), or government to citizen (G2C), but also people to people (P2P). Engagement also means that experiences are differentiated, relevant, and valuable. Engagement is always two-way—meaning dialogue, interaction, and interest through both parties. Those parties could be client to company, or company to employee, or employee to client! Questions around engagement include these:

- How will you hold your clients' and employees' attention in new ways that increase interest and loyalty?
- How will you involve the client and employee more effectively and directly?
- How do you use two-way collaboration to sync with your clients and employees?
- Can you hear the voice of your customer through the vast amount of data? How about your employees?
- How can you personalize your engagement with the customer based on their online behaviors, previous experiences, and profile information?

As a leader in a Social Business, you have aligned your goals and culture per the model in Chapter 2, "Align Organizational Goals and Culture," to support your clients and enhance your competitiveness. Your trust model, as described in Chapter 3, "Gain Social Trust," is in place. Now, engaging your clients, employees, and other influencers is your top priority. For example, Apple's genius bar is near-perfect support, real geniuses and scheduled help sessions that overdeliver. The recommendations of Netflix, an online video provider, provide customized user movie recommendations based on previously selected movies to promote itself as more of an entertainment advisor than a transaction site. Build-A-Bear, a business built with both offline and online experiences, adds social content like parties, websites, Facebook pages, and more to turn a product into a full experience.

Why is this a point of focus now? The customers of today and tomorrow have a different level of expectation in terms of engagement. They expect customer service teams to be customer-friendly and knowledgeable about what they tweet. If your company doesn't have a great reputation, customers probably won't consider your brand, and if they do decide to go with your product or offering, your teams need to be available at any time in all channels. Customers expect your company to have an experience that is like none other. On top of all that, they expect you to be able to anticipate needs before they are demanded. With the unprecedented level of focus and heightened customer exposure for every employee, honoring your customer above all else has become a mandate. I call this new client the "social client."

The same has become true of the new employees. They expect to be social and online. They want a leadership team that is open and involves them in the decisions. Brainstorming and ad hoc teams to solve key problems are expected and required in order for this new employee to remain with your company. Millennials, those born between 1977 and 1997, expect you to use the new social tools, and 94% of them in 2011 will use online methods like LinkedIn and Facebook to find a job with your company, according to the new study by Elance, a leader in online employment and millennials. These new employees are networked 24/7 and expect the company to accommodate pervasive connectivity and collaboration. I call this new employee the "social employee."

Throughout this chapter, the Engage workstream will help your company create exceptional experiences to attract and retain customers and employees. Engagement is real and active. The experience needs to set you apart in the marketplace and becomes a long-term competitive weapon, not just a fleeting advantage.

A Social Business has engagement through an experience—the feeling of good friends at a party, the trusted neighbor over the backyard fence, the perfect retail experience, the wisdom of the crowd. In short, this engagement will come from daily experiences with your company. A Social Business's experiences are not a hard sell but a relationship through community activities, events, charity, and more activities that humanize the corporation.

As you continue through this chapter, remember that your customer and employee experience is strongly influenced by other relationship and transaction activities in other industries. So don't skip over ones not in your industry. Those other industries will set the bar for your clients and employees who will want similar experiences in your industry.

Employee and Client Engagement Drives Business Results

Employee engagement drives business results.

If you look at engaged employees, there is a correlation between performance and engagement. Gallup's Q12 (a 12-question survey designed by Gallup to predict employee and workgroup performance) defines this relationship as follows:

> "Engaged employees work with passion and feel a profound connection to their company. They drive innovation and move the organization forward."

In addition, Gallup wrote this:

> "The world's top-performing organizations understand that employee engagement is a force that drives performance outcomes. In the best organizations, engagement is more than a human resources initiative—it is a strategic foundation for the way they do business."

In May 2011, IBM published a paper called "The Essential CIO—Insights from the Global Chief Information Officer Study," which was based on face-to-face conversations with more than 3,000 CIOs worldwide. A key result of that study showed that 66% of CIOs from top-performing organizations see internal communication and collaboration as key to innovation.

According to the Social Workplace, a leading resource for research, best practices and insights on social intranets, and employee engagement, those companies that used social techniques (Web 2.0 tools) with their employees achieved an 18% increase in engagement versus 1% among those that didn't. And the benefits they achieved from that higher engagement with their employees were in four key areas:

- More effective client interaction
- Faster connection with experts
- Greater productivity
- Stronger recruitment and better retention

Client engagement drives strong business results.

If you now look externally at engaged clients, you see similar business results. From that same methodology, Gallup has identified 11 questions—the CE11—that measure customer engagement and link powerfully to financial performance. The 2011 study revealed that customers (both B2B and B2C) who are fully engaged represent an average 23% premium in terms of share of wallet, profitability, revenue, and relationship growth over the ordinary customer. Organizations that have optimized engagement have outperformed their competitors by 26% in gross margin and 85% in sales growth. Their customers buy more, spend more, return more often, and stay longer.

The 5th Annual Customer Engagement Report of more than 1,000 companies, produced by Econsultancy, a company focused on advice and insight on best-practice digital marketing, found that customer-engagement importance is growing by 5% year over year, demonstrating that the best companies are focused on increasing engagement through social techniques. The greatest increase in engagement experimentation was in the use of social networks, video, and mobile.

These are the benefits of a more engaged client:

- Higher loyalty
- Greater advocacy
- More spending
- Stronger satisfaction

At the end of 2010, IBM published a study called "Capitalizing on Complexity." The study was conducted through insights from CEOs worldwide and was the largest CEO study ever completed. A top trend was about reinventing relationships with their customers. The study showed that 95% of standout organizations, those that outperformed on their financial results, will focus more on "getting closer to the customer" over the next 5 years because of the increased shareholder value that it brings. This makes customer engagement the numer one priority to succeed in the new economic enviroment. Standouts are especially determined to put customer engagement front and center, convinced that they must not only stay connected (or reconnect) with their customers, but also keep on learning how to strengthen those bonds.

So regardless of whether we are discussing employee or client engagement, social techniques drive higher engagement, and higher engagement drives a more competitive Social Business.

Employee Engagement with the New Social Employee

Engaged employees are those who know the company's values and are empowered to leverage those values with their partners and clients. They know their role and understand how to reach out to the right expert. These new social employee are about commitment and success. They know that the executive team, at all levels, is open and transparent.

While this is very important, not enough companies have an employee engagement strategy in place yet. In fact, when IBM recently surveyed 700 chief human resource officers and executives, more than three-quarters (78%) said they didn't think their companies were good at fostering collaboration or social networking. Additionally, fewer than one-quarter (21%) had increased how much they invested in the very tools that would make them more successful.

This new social employee is looking for certain things in this engagement. Michael Fauscette, who leads IDC's Software Business Solutions Group, discussed five characteristics of the new social employees in order for companies to engage them in the workforce.

Social employees do the following:

- Look for coaches and mentors, not "bosses."
- Want empowerment to take on business problems without micromanaging but within established guidelines.
- Need the freedom and ability to form ad hoc workgroups as needed to address business issues and problems, including those external.
- Demand open and transparent executives.
- Desire an inclusive decision-making culture.

Your social employee engagement strategy needs to include the capability to provide feedback, have frequent communications, form relationships, share desired experiences, and brainstorm solutions. For example, IBM has a program for new employees called Succeeding@IBM. For the first 6 to 12 months after new hires join the company, they are part of a social networking group where they collaborate on topics and get to know other folks outside of their immediate departments. This engagement experience helps with networking on a worldwide basis, a key skill for today's global workforce. It also gives new employees a broader base of knowledge that they can tap into as they adapt to their new jobs and culture.

For employee engagement, I would measure these factors:

- **Employee sentiment (how your employees feel about issues in real time):** For example, many leading companies are using social analytics tools to pull out of company blogs, wikis, and other social networking forums inside the four walls of a company the insight on how their employees feel about the company, policies, and overall issues. Many leadership companies are now doing this instead of doing yearly company surveys that are dated as soon as they are released.

- **Crowdsourcing (new innovations and ideas from employees):** For example, IBM held a "ThinkFuture" event. ThinkFuture is a four-day, online, collaborative event bringing together IBMers around the world to brainstorm and strategize on the future of leadership and talent development. The first 24 hours were spent web-streaming workshops to participants around the world; the next three days were spent in an online discussion forum that IBM calls a "Jam." There were 2,617 registered participants for the Jam, generating 3,579 posts.

  After IBM's analytics experts helped analyze the results, IBM commissioned five teams of early-career HR professionals from around the world to tackle major areas of insight. The first results from those teams are powerful and very forward-thinking—the first steps in a multistage strategic planning and implementation process that will unfold over the next decade at IBM. Measuring the power of this collective intelligence and the value it brings to tactical and strategic issues is a key metric to consider.

- **Increased productivity:** For example, Konecranes is a company based in Finland that focuses on "lifting" businesses that offers a complete range of advanced lifting solutions to many different industries worldwide. They engaged their employees through an internal community to enable the finding of experts in a more effective manner. Some employees would need to find people who know about lifttrucks and speak Russian, for instance. Using this internal community, they increased their employees' engagement with other experts, which led to double-digit improvement in their productivity.

- **Network density:** Your network consists of your colleagues that you communicate and collaborate with. By measuring the density of someone's network over time, you can understand whether they are expanding their reach and continuing to network with new people. By looking at the density with a 2D view, you can correlate who that individual collaborates with most, as well as get a better understanding of their physical location. The goal is to ensure that your teams have the geographic and organizational structure to enable people to become "connected" beyond their immediate team.

Client Engagement with the New Social Client

An engaged client is one who is attentive, interested, and active in their support for your brand, product, or company. The depth of their conversations online showcases their knowledge and care. They recommend and passionately advocate on your behalf in the blogosphere. This new social client marks the end of the ordinary customer, however. Based on how the social client acts online, you will need to engage them in different ways. Here are three profiles that I typically look at for client engagement:

- **Tippers:** Those who influence the rest of the clients and potential clients; usually about 5% to 10% of your product or category's population (see Chapter 3 for more details). Engagement with your tippers needs to be deep and knowledgeable with a big emphasis on active listening.

- **Active participants:** Those who sometimes comment while acquiring information and knowledge. Engagement with your active participants will be based on how to pull them into more active involvement with your brand.

- **Passive participants:** Those who use social tools only to acquire information and knowledge. They do not comment or share their thoughts and opinions. Some articles call these folks "lurkers." They lurk around the information but do not take an active part in it.

This new social client is looking for certain things in this engagement:

- **Social clients who are tippers:**
  - Look for involvement in new products, messaging, service, and beyond.
  - Want rewards, public sponsorship, recognition of their influence.

- **Social clients who are active participants:**
  - Look for ease in ability to participate, add comments, rank content, "Like" pages, or link to common sites like Facebook and LinkedIn.
  - Want rewards, honors, recognition.

- **Social clients who are passive participants:**
  - Look for relevancy.
  - Want fun, different, compelling experiences.

Your social client engagement strategy needs the ability to customize given the client. For example, at IBM's Lotusphere® 2011 conference, with more than 5,000 attendees, IBM set up engagement for all types of social clients. For instance, for our tippers, we had a blogging VIP area and "check-in" points for location-based service tools like Gowalla where we awarded those clients who checked into the most places. For greater involvement, we offered greater incentives and recognition. We also enabled our active participants to play a role through "TweetUps" (networking events that occur from tweeting the location of the place that everyone comes to around a discussion topic) and ensured that the engagement with colleagues was fast, easy, and fun. For our passive participants, our "Social Media Aggregator," a single integrated social dashboard for all tweets, videos, blogs, Livestream, and more, was a way that they could keep up with all that was happening around the venue with a single view of the event (see Figure 4.1)!

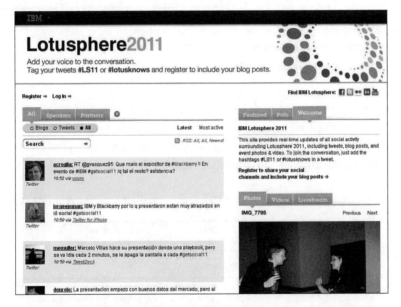

Figure 4.1   IBM Lotusphere 2011 social client engagement

Client engagement is not easy to measure. Altimeter Group's Survey of Corporate Social Strategists, from late 2010, found that social strategists struggle with relying on engagement data, as illustrated in Figure 4.2. Even though 65% of strategists need engagement metrics for evaluating the success of their program, no standard metrics existed.

We asked 140 Corporate Social Strategists: What measurements are most important to evaluating the success of your program?

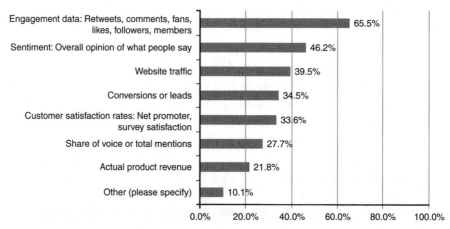

Source: *Survey of Corporate Social Strategists, Altimeter Group, November 2010*

Figure 4.2   Social strategists struggle with relying on engagement data.

Until standard metrics are identified, I would measure and report on different metrics based on the type of reporting I was doing and to what level of the organization. The Altimeter Group's Survey of Corporate Social Strategists shows that speaking to the level of the person with whom you are working, as illustrated in Figure 4.3, really makes a lot of sense.

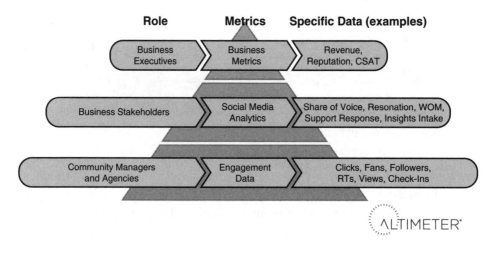

Figure 4.3   The ROI pyramid

For instance, if I were speaking to the business executive team, I would talk about the value of engagement on *revenue or conversion of a potential client into buying their first product, offering, or service with your company.* For example, GoMidjets, a U.S.-based software company, began their engagement strategy as a Social Business by strong participation in technical forums, communities, and Jam sessions. They solicited feedback on their latest software product, and began to see new clients come in from these engagements. In fact, GoMidjets founder Tamir Gefen says that of his new client conversions, over 40% of his leads come from this very "hands on" engagement in communities that lead right to his bottom line.

If you are speaking to the business stakeholders, I would talk about the value of client engagement on the following:

- **Awareness and client sentiment:** Awareness is a measure of a brand being known in the marketplace, and sentiment is the way people view what you are doing either positively or negatively. For example, when Apple released the iPad, 73% of circulated tweets were favorable toward the iPad, but 26% expressed disappointment (or negative sentiment) that the iPad could not replace the iPhone, according to a study from Attensity, a company that focuses on the empowered client. This negative sentiment can be leveraged extensively to improve.

- **Innovation of ideas from outside your four walls:** Given the focus on crowdsourcing, or having the blogosphere collaborate on a problem online to come up with the best solution, one of the top outcomes to look at for business leaders is the number of new ideas that came from the client engagement. For example, IBM launched a new software design and development initiative called The IBM Liquid Challenge Program. The purpose of the program is to find the world's best talent to design and develop innovative software applications for IBM. As a Liquid Player (freelancer), a person is challenged to develop key components of IBM's new applications on a weekly basis. This exciting opportunity rewards designers/developers on successful components and helps Liquid Players to create their digital reputation. The key metric of success for this Liquid Challenge will be the number of new ideas generated from the crowd that are viable, usable, and successful!

If you are speaking to the community managers, I would talk about the value of engagement in terms of the following:

- **Responses (how many comments and responses are you getting to polling, blogs, discussion threads):** A good measure of engagement is the ratios of responses and comments to blogs/polls/discussion items, and the like, to get a true feel for how engaged the community is around a topic.

- **New knowledge acquired:** The best community managers also measure new ideas, thoughts, or opinions that they get through the community. Adam Cranfield, Director/Consultant at Form Digital Consulting and former community manager at a variety of companies, told me he measures "nuggets." A nugget is a new insight gained from the community. For example, Home Depot started a community around home improvement videos on YouTube. One community member showed a video on how to alter a product sold at Home Depot to make it easier to install in a home. Home Depot took that video and set up a meeting with the supplier, who changed the product based on this "nugget" of information from the community!

- **Active participants and tippers in the community:** Community managers want to know if they have a lot of influence in the community or passive participants. Although this is not just a numbers game, the numbers help you gauge new interest and growth in the community.

These are not all the metrics of engagement you will want to explore but some ideas that you will want to shape based on your company's goals and culture. Chapter 7, "Analyze Your Data," covers how many of these items can be measured and compared against your competitors and industry as well.

Principles of Engagement

Before moving on to engagement examples, I wanted to lay out the overall principles of engagement. A big question that I often hear companies struggle with is, who does the *engaging*? Is it the employee, company, or product? Actually, it could be all three or any of the three, depending on your engagement strategy.

For example, products can be the focus of engagement. Pratt & Whitney is a world leader in the design, manufacture, and service of aircraft engines, space propulsion systems, and industrial gas turbines. They decided to have their clients engage with their new engine, the F135, through Facebook and Twitter to effectively lobby the U.S. government to use their engine. To date, they have effectively had more than 300,000 engagements of people with their F135 engine!

Your strategy could be to do all three. For example, IBM has engagement with the following:

- **Employees:** blogs, products of offerings
- **Product or concepts:** Watson, the machine that played on Jeopardy, has his own Facebook and Twitter accounts
- **Company:** IBM has an official Twitter ID

Some basic guidelines I recommend when deciding which of the strategies to implement are these:

- **Employees:** I highly recommend that every company enable their employees to engage with clients and potential clients, as well as with other employees and leadership. If you don't want them engaging with clients in the consumer space (Twitter, Facebook, Google Talk), then consider providing alternative and more secure means that are controlled by your organization. There are a variety of Software as a Service (SaaS) or cloud solutions available.

- **Product or company:** The decision to have engagement at a product or company level to me is dependent on your goals. If you want people to relate to a particular product, then I would consider a strategy to engage the product. But if you have multiple products and limited Social Business Managers, I would consider focusing on the company. If you do decide to go down this path, make sure that the person(s) responsible for the product or company are experts in that subject matter. That is, don't just give the responsibility of a product ID over to a PR person; have that product ID be owned and managed by the team responsible for the product.

For example, Quantum, a storage software company, launched a major new software upgrade for its storage products. While this product was critical, they focused their engagement strategy through Twitter, Facebook, and SlideShare (a location that openly shares PowerPoint® content) on their company, not just the product. They used the launch of the product as the compelling reason to engage with the company. According to the company, it was a success. Quantum mentions on Twitter increased 250% during the announcement, and retweets and recommendations increased in double digits, including links to their new SlideShare presentation.

On the other hand, Procter & Gamble, a world leader in consumer products, decided to have engagement at the product levels for their brands. For example, Pampers directly engages mothers in the Pampers Fit Stop campaign in stores as well as online with their Pampers Village website. Their focus on the "Parenting Network" engages through providing access to subject matter experts like child-development gurus and medical professionals. The "Ask an Expert" section puts visitors directly in touch with the experts, who offer answers to questions about a variety of parenting concerns, such as feeding and sleeping habits.

The difference in engagement tactics reflects as much size as strategy of the company in dialoguing with their clients. While this is an important part of the strategy, the principles of engagement are the same for leveraging a product, a company, or an employee as the cornerstone of the engagement.

The following six principles of engagement are great rules to leverage as you develop your strategy:

1. **Focus on a goal for your engagement:** Define your goals upfront. These goals will drive your overall engagement strategy. Zappos, a company owned by Amazon. com that focuses on being the best shoe provider in the world, published their community goals in terms of their Family Core Values (http://about.zappos.com/ our-unique-culture/zappos-core-values). These values drive their engagement online. For example, the core value "deliver WOW through service" drives an engagement in customer service that differentiates it from any other company in the world. The focus is the value of the WOW play, not cost or efficiency. And Zappos is not the only one. Many companies are doing a "company to customer pact" to write out the social agreement on rules and goals for engagement. Check out www.ccpact.com.

2. **Focus on your subject matter expertise and value to the reader, not on selling:** Your engagement strategy is not your sales strategy, but how you form a relationship. For example, a small dry cleaner in New York started a Twitter account, not on his business, but about his expertise of taking care of clothes like taking stains out. His value proposition as posted on Twitter: "Dry cleaner to the stars. Have been profiled in the NYT, NY Mag, and TimeOutNY. Here to give away free tips and news about garment care, and to learn from you." It worked because it engaged on a subject of value that eventually grew his overall business.

3. **Be consistent in commenting and engaging, driven by a *great* community manager:** To engage and hold someone's interest, you need to be consistent in your comments and dialogues. This is where the community manager becomes so important (see Chapter 3) in maintaining the level of activity. A great

community manager can make all the difference in the world, and, in my mind, is a requirement of success. A community manager's responsibility is to keep the community members active and engaged by setting the strategy, gaining the trust of the members, and ensuring the appropriate content activation plan. While the community manager stimulates conversation, this cannot be the only person from your company who is active in the community. Put your best out there and motivate them to be consistent.

In fact, we have spent quite a bit of time in this book on the importance of community managers. I recommend that you read through the community management report from Rachel Happe to really understand this new type of role and employee in your company. It's available at http://www.slideshare.net/rhappe/the-2011-state-of-community-management.

According to the 4Q 2010 ComBlu report (http://comblu.com/news/social-media/the-state-of-online-branded-communities-2010.aspx), of the 241 communities from 78 enterprise-level companies in the U.S., almost half of all companies had no visible community manager. ComBlu found that those companies that do have a community manager are the most successful. One of my favorite examples is the Jimmy Choo Facebook page (https://www.facebook.com/JimmyChoo) where the active community manager sets up polls and surveys, and stirs up conversation.

4. **Have a content strategy:** Social businesses require a content strategy to truly engage. If your content or information is not fresh, not relevant, or not valuable, then people will go elsewhere. Think of content as the aggregation of voices. Information coming from your employees, marketing, development, and other functions will make the message stronger. I encourage companies to distribute to their tippers and active participants key facts and information that they can then blog/tweet/comment on in their own voice.

Take, for instance, the Indium Corporation, a premier materials supplier to the global electronics, semiconductor, solar, thin film, and thermal management markets. For their engagement strategy for content, they leverage their Point of View content to keep their content fresh and engaging. With the impact of this content strategy, 14 Indium engineers blog consistently about their thoughts on the vision and direction. Just a note, these 14 people are not full-time people but blog as part of their overall thought-leadership agenda as part of their regular jobs. This approach is fairly simple to execute but the payoff is that it enables the clients to get to know Indium as a company, thought leader, and friend. A great Social Business content strategy requires continuous, steady investment to build and manage the network, with eventual value created as the network grows. Many companies have their community manager drive the content strategy.

5. **Focus on relationships, not numbers:** Engagement is about a relationship. The relationship must be established, maintained, and nurtured. The focus shouldn't be on "making the numbers." For example, Melanie Baker, the community manager at PostRank, focuses on forging relationships. She is the Technology Triangle's longest-serving community manager and is much loved. In addition, @PaughGinney from Brazen Careerist (www.brazencareerist.com) focuses on relationships. The site was just named one of Mashable's "top 5 online communities" for starting your career, and the members rave about their personal relationships with him as one of the main reasons. Contrast that with Moonfruit (www.moonfruit.com), a free website builder that ran a Twitter sweepstakes to gain momentum in the market. It seems to have worked because its website had a huge spike in traffic following the promotion. Afterward, the traffic plummeted back down to normal. The mistake Moonfruit made was that they focused on the number of visitors, not the lasting relationships they could have formed with the visitors.

6. **Integrate social techniques:** The linkage between the social tools that you choose matters. So if your Twitter, blog, and Facebook pages are not in sync in terms of message, you will have an issue in portraying your brand in a way that is effective. Yes, this is management 101, but many people forget these rules in the virtual world. The most successful Social Businesses leverage social platforms such as Facebook, Twitter, and YouTube in a unique but consistent way to build off one another.

For example, at the Super Bowl in 2011, Volkswagen, a German car manufacturer, integrated its Twitter hashtag, Facebook game, and YouTube commercials into a comprehensive focus. This integration strategy enabled one of the emerging best practices in the aggregation of the message as a way to grow engagement for Social Businesses. It worked! Sentiment is evaluated by social mention in terms of three basic categories: *positive, negative, and neutral social media comments.* This is shown as a ratio of mentions that are generally positive to those that are not. Volkswagen's Beetle had the highest ratio after the Super Bowl at 69:1—that's 69 good social media comments compared to 1 bad one. They not only engaged, they engaged in an extremely positive fashion!

And this is not just for large businesses. Richard Scott of Richard Scott Salon and Day Spa, a medium-size business in Westchester County in New York, has integrated his Facebook offers and Foursquare into running his overall business, leveraging those great relationship and word-of-mouth skills that occur naturally in his salon and taking those relationships to the next level. He has grown his business and visits by new clients in double digits due to this brilliant integrated strategy.

How Do You Engage?

To leverage these principles of engagement most effectively, there are three essential techniques that we have found have the greatest success rate. I call these the *Three I's*:

- Interact (mobile, gaming, gifting, location-based services, crowdsourcing)
- Integrate (online, offline)
- Identify (content, emotion, personalize)

Note that each of these is a two-way engagement:

- To *interact* means that your clients or employees become active participants. For example, in gaming, they are playing the game, as you are teaching and instructing them in a fun way.
- To *integrate* means that your company will have online and offline engagements that fit together to form a full picture of your company. So you will not see one view in an event online and a different personality of the company in a store. If you are not integrated in your approach, engagement is weakened.
- In *identification,* the key is to identify with your clients or employees and to personalize your approach in engaging with them. Your goal is to provide them an experience that is just for them. They comment on your blog because it speaks in their voice, or about their passion, and gets them involved.

Engagement is a long-term strategy. There are short-term benefits but it is not a strategy that can be done in a typical fast-and-dirty fashion. Social clients and employees are interested not in engagement "drive-bys" (meaning only one dialogue or comment) but in really getting to know your company, product, or employees. This next section highlights the key best practices for Interact, Integrate, and Identify, with a few case studies to really engage you, the reader!

Use the sheet illustrated in Figure 4.4 to track your progress.

What are your goals?
- Target Audience:
  - Segmentation?_____
- Engagement Plan:
  - New? _____
  - What's Top Priority? _____
- Social "Smart" Goals:
  - Specific:
  - Measurable:
  - Achievable:
  - Realistic:
  - Timeframe:

Value Message:
  - Relevancy? _____

Interactive:
  - Facebook
  - Twitter
  - LinkedIn
  - Mobile
  - Virtual Gifting
  - Location-Based
  - Video

Integrated Plan:
  Linkage Points
  Analytics on Connections:
  (i.e., those who comment are more likely to buy)

  _____

  Phased Approach:
           Phase 1:
           Phase 2:
           Phase 3:

Information
  Emotion Hook:
  ___ Humor
  ___ Subject Matter Expertise
  ___ Access
  ___ Loyalty-Building
  ___ Collaboration
  ___ Consistency

Figure 4.4   Action sheet

Interact

Anything becomes engaging when your client or employee plays a role in it. If you provide your clients with an opportunity to make choices about content, process, and product, then you increase their willingness to engage you. Your company needs to create an environment so that your clients, potential clients, and employees can apply their own analysis and evaluation. While there are many ways to interact, this section discusses the most effective methods of interaction with your clients and employees. Those top experiences include mobile, gaming, virtual gifting, location-based services, and video.

The choice of the engagement tool will be based on your company's goal and importance of that tool with your clients and employees. In addition, I will provide you a sneak peek into some of the new engagement tools coming in the future that you may want to start exploring in experimentation mode.

The following case studies illustrate some of these concepts.

Mobile

To interact implies that an engaging experience needs to be convenient. Mobile devices are everywhere, so a strong engagement strategy for employees and clients is mobile, simply based on convenience and availability. Most of the basic social tools leverage mobile as well. For instance, according to Twitter CEO Dick Costolo, over 40% of all tweets come from mobile devices.

MobiThinking, a world leader in mobile research, predicts that mobile device usage is growing with no end in sight (http://mobithinking.com/stats-corner/global-mobile-statistics-2011-all-quality-mobile-marketing-research-mobile-web-stats-su). With 77% of the world's population now having a mobile phone, and more than 5.3 billion mobile subscribers, there is no other medium that offers that reach and interaction. Over 85% of new handsets will have mobile web access in 2011, and there will be more than one billion mobile Internet users worldwide by 2013. Traditional phone sales still outnumber smartphones 4:1, so your mobile strategy needs to target all phone users equally. The interaction a client has with a company over a mobile device impacts the client's overall views about the company. Per MobiThinking, a client who is satisfied with a mobile experience is 30% more likely to buy from that company, recommend it, and be loyal to the brand.

The key elements to consider for the mobile portion of your engagement strategy are these:

- Mobile networking (like Twitter, or your own community)
- Mobile coupons and gift cards
- Mobile website
- Mobile experiences
- Mobile crowdsourcing

CASE STUDY: CREEK WATCH

Citizens of the world are engaging in helping the planet through a mobile application called Creek Watch (http://creekwatch.researchlabs.ibm.com/). Developed by IBM Research, this mobile engagement tool empowers citizens worldwide to monitor their watersheds and report conditions. Every update provides vital data that local water authorities can use to track pollution, manage water resources, and plan environmental programs.

This application enables everyone to contribute to cleaning up our waterways—crowdsourcing, if you would, for the world through great engagement.

Crowdsourcing leverages the "crowds" on the Internet to enhance products or services, provide a point of view, or even better the world. In this example, Creek Watch involves crowdsourcing problems with our waterways through networking people to the government.

The keys to success are that it is an easy download from the Apple App Store, and its low cost—it's free. But the best feature of all is that the app enables and engages you to help the planet. First, you see a waterway—like a creek or lake. You use your iPhone to take a picture and then upload the following information:

- Water level (dry, some, or full)
- Flow rate (still, slow, or fast)
- Trash (none, some, or a lot)

This social application then aggregates the data. You can see what others have uploaded or written—that's the crowdsourcing magic—mobilizing and engaging citizens around the world. As the data is consolidated, it is shipped to the water control boards in the local regions which can take action on this data. The great thing about this application is that it engages citizens to a level to assist government and management of our water systems.

CASE STUDY: AUSTRALIAN OPEN

To engage its fans, Tennis Australia heavily leverages its Australian Open website. This interactive, media-rich online experience allows fans to listen to live radio, review highlights of the day's play, read blogs, and follow the scores from every court as the action happens. Features such as SlamTracker—which lets fans interact in real time with the draws and scores—make visiting www.australianopen.com the next best thing to being there. According to IBM, which hosts the event website, during the two-week tournament the site attracts almost 10 million unique users.

For mobile engagement, the Australian Open (AO) launched a special augmented reality application for iPhone users. This engagement enabled iPhone users to point their phone at the venue to view information on the match. With real-time scores, schedules, draws, and player information all available on smartphones via a purpose-built Australian Open mobile website, fans can stay in touch with every Australian Open 2011 match while they're on the go.

This application also includes AO View, an augmented reality feature that uses the phone's camera and GPS to give fans at the event an enhanced view of the data that is all around them. For the first time ever, fans can access the full Australian Open program on their iPad via the Australian Open iPad application. This new application brings together data from a variety of sources to connect fans with the online mood that the tournament generates. Special features include schedules and draws, fan data, and autograph pages.

The Australian Open is a Social Business that drives loyalty and repeat attendees to the event through buzz and engagement, as well as increased sponsorships for the events. This buzz and engagement provide the stickiness needed for the Australian Open to meet their revenue goals.

Gaming

As business and organizational leaders, we need to consider the role of gaming dynamics for customer and employee engagement. Gaming can spark creativity and new opportunities for both B2B and B2C interaction. Serious gaming is the use of gaming techniques in the business world. Rick Gibson of Games Investor Consulting says "analysts estimate that 50% of companies will have 'gamified' [leveraged serious gaming techniques] by 2015. That's 13.5 million businesses in the U.S. alone." Serious gaming is the process of using game thinking and game mechanics to solve problems and educate via engaging users. By the pure definition, "serious" means they are games designed for a purpose other than pure entertainment.

The goal of these games could be to train, advertise, generate demand, or simply energize the user. Gaming does vary in its business use. It could be a simple game on an iPhone like the Infinite Banking Concept game (http://itunes.apple.com/us/app/infinite-banking-concept-game/id417938367?mt=80), which showcases a contest to span a four-year period of time during which five methods of financing a car are compared, or Barclaycard Waterslide Extreme, a game based on Barclaycard's "iconic" waterslide advertisement, which focuses on the brand image (Barclay's game was been downloaded more than two million times during the first week of introduction). Both of these games were built for the purpose of making the brand more fun.

Research into human behavior demonstrates that people are motivated by challenges that feel inherently worthwhile. Both the scholarly literature on games and the real-world experience of game designers demonstrate that people will compete for extraordinarily low-value prizes, or no prizes at all, when the experience itself is the reward. Companies and governments are beginning to use the elements of games and competitions to motivate employees, customers, and communities. This phenomenon has become known as gamification.

In using gaming for education, a game has about 80% higher recall than traditional education. Consider this for your employees. Because most people today play some form of game, will employees be satisfied solving problems in typical ways or will gaming be demanded? For example, if players organize themselves to successfully complete specific endeavors during their "play" time, will they be content during work hours in organizational structures, with central command and control? Chances are they're more likely to want to work on virtual teams distributed around the world, undertaking multiple endeavors, taking advantage of the thought processes that succeeded for them in online gaming.

Consider gaming concepts to help managers assemble a high-performance team to solve a problem. Most managers look at a pool of candidates and pick the top performers based on résumé, past experience, and interviews. Now consider a similar concept of assembling a high-performance car for an automotive game. The gamer will select different parts of the car (tires, frame, engine, size, etc.) with an overall weighted score so they can easily view how the entire car will perform when all the parts are put together. Now let's apply that concept to high-performance teams. Imagine if the manager could select and unselect certain candidates for his or her team and collectively see a weighted score of how the entire team will function together. That would provide a level of predictive analysis to help assemble a team that has the highest probability of success using gaming techniques.

Gaming could be used in businesses to create an experience that is compelling. Take Groupon. From Groupon's website, their history is interesting. They grew out of a website called The Point that let you start a campaign asking people to give money or do something as a group—but only once a "tipping point" number of people agree to participate. By delaying action until enough people come together to have a real impact, The Point helps consumers, employees, citizens, activists, parents—or anyone—come together and solve problems that they couldn't solve alone. Groupon then took this to the next level for city dwellers because there is so much to do that it is overwhelming. By focusing on one item of goods or service each day, Groupon makes it simple. And by leveraging The Point's framework for collective buying, Groupon is able to offer deals that make it very difficult to say no.

Groupon uses serious gaming as part of its business model. For example, it gives out a "free lunch" by giving steep discounts, it has a time element with the clock ticking on each deal, and it encourages team play by having a "tipping point" before the deal is active. All of these are part of serious gaming strategies. Gap announced that it made $11 million worth of sales in a single day on Groupon!

Overall gaming impacts customer experience, and profits. Using games to engage has a compelling value proposition. When well implemented, a game can virally target people in a specific demographic where they live in a medium they love and understand. The games can then be used to gather information about the player and even generate leads. Almost every company will have to adapt to this new gaming generation as either customers or employees. This new business environment is emerging.

According to The Apply Group, a marketing consultant, at least 100 of the Global Fortune 500 will use gaming to educate their employees by 2012, with the United States, the United Kingdom, and Germany leading the way. The average age of a gamer today is between 25 and 44 years old, with an average income between $35,000 and $75,000. Also, 58% are men and over 42% are women gamers. Games are popular today across the world.

Mobile social gaming is on the rise—and women are leading the way. Social gaming is engaging by nature—using teachable moments and learning from peers to gain the interest of the audience. Many popular games exist today. One popular game on Facebook is called FarmVille, with more than 80 million users, where over 62% of players are female with an average income of between $60,000 and $100,000. The largest demographic group playing FarmVille are actually stay-at-home moms (source: Zynga, the company that produces FarmVille).

The key elements to consider for the gaming portion of your engagement strategy are the following:

- Build or include? Build your own game or include yourself in someone else's game.
- Goal of the game: education, demand generation, awareness.
- Metrics of success.

CASE STUDY: FARMERS INSURANCE

Farmers Insurance Group of companies is the U.S.'s third-largest insurer of both private Personal Lines passenger automobile insurance and homeowner's insurance, and also provides a wide range of other insurance and financial services products. The company has engaged its targeted audience by leveraging the FarmVille game such that players of the game can see and click on the Farmers virtual airship. The virtual airship is available in the FarmVille game free for players for 10 days.

Once you log into FarmVille, you will be greeted with this pop-up, detailing that the Farmers Insurance blimp is going to fly high over your farm. In the game it says,

"The blimp itself is more than just a mere promotional decoration, as it will serve a functional purpose: insurance for your crops against withering! During the promotion's run, you will not have to worry about any of your crops withering for ten days after you place the blimp on your farm, giving you an opportune time to churn out some of the many four-hour crops currently available to plant, including the Limited Edition Candy Corn crop, or the relatively new Columbine crop."

This is a very innovative way to engage your clients by adding value in the game for those who play it, not just making this a promotion! This is an integrated campaign with a Facebook fan page as well. Those who "Like" the Farmers page get an opportunity to actually ride in the airship. From their fan page wall, fans can gain quick access to quotations, locate local dealers, and directly ask a question. Farmers Insurance claims that more than five million users downloaded the airship, and in that time, Farmers' Facebook fan page went from a handful of fans to more than 120,000. Marc Zeitlin, Vice President of eBusiness for Farmers, told me, "We currently have more fans than any insurance entity other than Progressive's Flo. This airship has made it possible for consumers to interact with us digitally through our website and to engage with us on a personal level."

CASE STUDY: IBM INNOV8 AND CITYONE

IBM has two serious games that I'd like to highlight. Innov8 is one near and dear to my heart because I helped to create the vision for this gaming strategy. Innov8 was created with the goal of education. It was rolled out as an IBM academic initiative to explain a new technology to students across the nation. To this day, more than 1,000 universities use it. This engagement strategy with students means that the next generation is familiar with IBM's view of technology. It provides a "brand" name for university graduates who will be future leaders of the world and future potential customers. In addition to education, we took the game to a shortened web-based version, where Innov8 became IBM WebSphere®'s number one web-based lead-generating asset.

Due to the success of Innov8, IBM created its first Smarter Planet™ game called City-One, a city sim that features a city with a certain set of recognizable problems afflicting its energy, water, retail, and banking industries. According to Phaedra Boinodiris, Serious Games Program Manager at IBM, CityOne gives players the opportunity to "discover how to make our Planet smarter, revolutionize industries, and solve real-world business, environmental, and logistical problems."

Per Phaedra, "the ROI for both Innov8 and CityOne revealed that in five months, the games resulted in 100 times the investment put into it." While both games are free to play, registration is required—this is a must in order to track results.

Virtual Gifting

A virtual gift is an online image or picture of an object that your company or an employee might give to someone. It is not a real item or object but exists only in the virtual world. For example, at IBM's IMPACT conference, in the virtual world, we gave away virtual "hex" necklaces that spelled out words using only 0's and 1's. In our internal virtual gifting strategy, we have employees present blue ribbons of "thanks" as a virtual gifting to show appreciation and teaming from other employees.

As part of a Social Business strategy, virtual gifting can supplement your engagement with clients and employees. As you can see from the preceding examples, context plays a major role in type of gift, and placement of gift. In addition, in all cases the ability to showcase the gift is an important item. Promotional value links to the gift's context, use, and perceived value by its recipient. Your virtual gifting strategy will depend on where you are offering the gift and to whom. The goal of virtual gifting is to engage through trial—virtual trial of goods that retailers and manufacturers have been doing for years. It is just as effective in the virtual world as it is in the real world. Think through if and how virtual gifting can be part of your engagement strategy because of the results that it brings.

Virtual gifting is a great way to engage your audience. Fifty-seven percent believe virtual gifting is as meaningful as real gifting, and according to Magid's report "Media Futures 2010 Wireless and Consumers," Americans spent $168 million on mobile virtual goods in the past year, with 45% of smartphone owners playing mobile games and 16% of those spending an average of $41 per year on in-game virtual goods. In 2011, 72% of respondents planned to send virtual goods as a gift on Valentine's Day. And 31% of people who planned to send a virtual gift on Valentine's Day would be purchasing their first virtual good.

Big brands are leveraging virtual gifting not to just build revenue through a strong loyalty strategy. This strategy is leveraged not just by online dating services, but also by big businesses like Pepsi, Coke, IBM, Nordstrom, Volkswagen, Volvo, Toyota, and the list goes on. For example, H&M, a Swedish clothing retailer, launched a virtual-goods campaign in a social game called MyTown (MyTown is a location-based gaming service). While showing off its denim and blue garments (they called it the Blues), they engaged consumers and enticed them to shop in the real store! With more than 700,000 players, they gave away virtual goods throughout to drive real-world sales.

CASE STUDY: GODIVA

Godiva is a leader in premium chocolate, and has been for over 80 years. To engage their Social Client, they launched with Communispace an invite-only all-woman private research community of chocolate lovers called Chocolate Talk (Communispace is the leader in providing Online Consumer Insights Communities for Market Research and helps to create communities for businesses). The goal was to listen to the comments about how chocolate affects their members' lives.

Godiva engaged in learning with the community and listening. They found core "nuggets" that were game changers for the company. The community commented on the accessibility and affordability of the chocolate. Godiva, based on the engagement of the community, decided to address each of these concerns with a new product that was individually wrapped chocolates (and therefore more affordable) and placed them in more outlets, like CVS and airport stores. In addition, they increased their "virtual" channels, and used a Facebook application to give away "virtual chocolates" to friends and families in Facebook. With this focus on "casual gifting" and accessibility, they truly listened their way to a game-changing strategy.

An AdNectar study of Godiva chocolates virtual gifts with two groups of people found that "those exposed to the virtual chocolate were 20% more likely to purchase a real box of Godiva in the next 6 months than the control group that was not exposed." This is particularly notable because most purchase-intent studies of online campaigns barely break 2%.

Also, overall Godiva's wholesale business is up 42% YTD June 2010, driven primarily by their new distribution in grocery and drug stores (Safeway, Publix, Wegmans, Kroger, CVS/pharmacy, etc.). In addition, Godiva was also the number one premium brand of chocolate at CVS/pharmacy (source: IRI Latest 4-Weeks Ending June, 2010) with a share of 19.3, surpassing Lindt's share of 18.9.

CASE STUDY: VOLVO

Volvo wanted to evolve the image of their brand from being one of just safety to being one of "cool" as well. They initiated a campaign on branded virtual goods, leveraged through a game called MyTown, a location-based gaming service. This campaign used several elements of engagement—virtual goods, gaming, and location-based services.

When a player checks into an auto dealership or garage, he or she can receive a virtual sedan, or Volvo steering wheel, or tire. To engage in this way means that a potential client would have to drive into the dealership, raising odds that a real car would actually be purchased. Another outcome was based around customer service. As clients waited for their cars, the game provided a fun way to pass the time.

The results that Volvo measured were 5.3 million Volvo-branded check-ins, 1.3 million Volvo-branded virtual goods (including a steering wheel, a wheel, the Volvo iron mark, and the S60 vehicle), 20,000 clicks to "See the S60 in Action," and a click-through rate (CTR) of 1.5%, which is double the normal rate.

While Volvo won't publicly share the overall business results, the fact that they are leveraging virtual gifting again in their corporate social responsibility campaign leads to the conclusion that this engagement strategy worked. Their next virtual-gifting journey is focused on raising money with Alex's Lemonade Stand Foundation (ALSF), which is trying to find a cure for pediatric cancer. The virtual good is a cup of lemonade that you can purchase for $1, with 100% of the proceeds going to the ALSF.

Location-Based Services

One new area for interaction is location-based services (LBS). An LBS uses the geographic positioning system (GPS) feature of a mobile device to engage at the geographic location where your client or employee is currently located. It provides not only the ability to make interaction fun, but the ability for companies to deliver entertaining and interactive experiences when needed or desired. And, of course, we all know that it is all about location, location, location!

What does an LBS enable you to do? It allows you to find out where your clients or friends are, to learn their favorite places in cities or stores, and to locate others in a common location (I used it at BlogHer, the world's largest women's blogging conference, to locate a group of folks I had never met in person, but wanted to!). From your mobile device, you can "check in" to the LBS to indicate that you are at a certain location and find others who are there, get the top tips for that location, and more.

One of my favorite quotes that I heard at the Austin, Texas–based South by Southwest (SXSW) Social Media festival is "the future of mobile is local." Fifty-five percent of all text messages ask some form of the question "Where are you?" With billions of mobile users globally, location-based services will be the next phase of Social Business engagement strategy.

How are companies using LBS? Today, it is being used in a variety of ways by tying your physical location to your social areas of interests.

These are the primary uses:

- Discounts based on location
- Information based on location
- Recognition for an event

For example, retail and commerce-based customers are leveraging LBS to offer marketing promotions and discounts to shoppers. At SXSW, if you checked in, you could get a free ride in downtown Austin from Chevy as part of their SXSW promotion. Governments, libraries, and cities are using LBS to make it easier to find information or directions when you are in their location. Library usage is so popular now that in February 2011 there was a full conference on leveraging location-based services for libraries in which Joe Murphy, a leading innovator and trend spotter and Science Librarian at Yale University Libraries, spoke on "Location Aware Technology for Libraries." Technology companies (like IBM) are using it at events to direct traffic to particular demos or sessions and to create a SWARM. A SWARM is a badge that proclaims you had more than 50 people checked in at the event or location. And restaurants are leveraging it to draw a crowd on a particular night, hyping up the SWARM badge.

These are the main LBS tools:

- **Foursquare:** Foursquare hit the seven-million-user mark at the time of publishing, with 40% of its users outside the United States. According to Foursquare, they grew 3400% from 2009 to 2010, and had more than 381 million check-ins. Marc Jacobs, Toronto Reference Library, Dominos, Starbucks, IBM, and Intel are all using Foursquare today, according to Foursquare's latest website stats.

- **Gowalla:** Gowalla is an application similar to Foursquare. They have about one million users and have tried to differentiate themselves on new features and functions. They added a check-in facility so that from within Gowalla, a user can also check in with Foursquare. Most recently, they added a "Highlights feature," in which each location would have a set of highlights as a value-add for users. Their vision was to turn the world into a "social atlas."

- **Jiepang:** Jiepang is China's version of Foursquare, with the same functionality, but with a very local flavor and a more plain and simple interface. For instance, restaurants and food are big areas of focus in China so Jiepang focused there for their introduction. They built a directory of restaurants in most major cities in China that made the service usable and valuable instantly. (At press time, China has blocked both Foursquare and Gowalla, favoring Jiepang.)

Make sure you familiarize yourself with these tools as the following case studies showcase real business examples around them.

CASE STUDY: STARBUCKS

Starbucks, a company that made its name with its focus on coffee available everywhere, leverages Foursquare to engage its most loyal clients (in China, they use Jiepang). In addition to awarding badges—the Barista badge—to each client who checks in at a location, Starbucks now has a special offer for the "mayors" of its locations. The mayor of the Starbucks store unlocks the Mayor Offer, which provides them money-off specials. For instance, the deal offers customers a $1 discount on a frappuccino through a message: "As mayor of this store, enjoy $1 off a NEW however-you-want-it Frappuccino blended beverage. Any size, any flavor. Offer valid until 6/28." Mayorship has its financial rewards but also its status. The mayor has "bragging rights" to this particular location. Never underestimate the value of these status rewards!

The value of this engagement is both loyalty of clients and recognitions for your most faithful consumers. On the consumer side of things, getting $1 off a frappuccino is a pretty nice discount, considering that customers routinely pay $4 or more for their favorite blended beverage.

CASE STUDY: HISTORY CHANNEL

Leveraging Foursquare, the History Channel provides great historical factoids when someone checks into a historic location. For instance, they point out the first building in a city, or the first to have an Otis elevator.

They have also tied this to the launch of their TV series, narrated by Liev Schreiber, *America: the Story of Us*. It is the most in-depth television series ever produced by the History Channel. As a reward, the History Channel presented ten randomly selected Foursquare users a prize the week of the TV series debut.

There are no public facts released yet on how this affected their viewer ratings on cable, increased web traffic, or raised any other performance metrics since this is one of the most experimental uses of LBS so far. But I will keep you posted on my blog with any published results!

CASE STUDY: DISNEY

Leveraging Gowalla, Disney's engagement strategy for its theme parks now includes LBS. To have more interactivity while at the parks, Disney created branded stamps and photos to be rewarded once a person completed certain tasks in the Disney parks. My kids go crazy for the Disney pins while at the parks, trading and "social networking" to get the pins from other kids that they need for their collection. Just as with the real pins, guests (and my kids!) can now trade and collect the stamps, but on their smartphones. With hundreds of stamps to earn, everyone who watches fireworks or goes to the Disney Princess castle can earn their place by checking in (go to http://gowalla.com/disneyparks for more information).

In the first four months of execution, there have been more than 10,000 customized trips using Gowalla inside the U.S.-based parks. This location-based program has set the bar high in the industry.

Video

According to YouTube, over 13 million hours of video was uploaded in 2010 and around 35 hours' worth of video is being uploaded every minute! And the amount of video viewed is growing over 56% year over year. YouTube is now the second-largest search engine on the Web, with 50% of YouTube's 300 million users going there at least once a week (source: en.gauge Media 2011 report "The Shift Report").

Video is a power booster to your engagement strategy, with interactivity occurring as users generate content and learn from others. A video hosting service allows individuals to upload video clips to an Internet website. The video host will then store the video on its server, and show the individual different types of code to allow others to view this video.

Some of the interesting tools in this space are YouTube, Ustream, Youku, Tudou, OoVoo, and Chatzppl. For example, 32% of YouTube's viewers watch health videos—more than food or celebrity links. So if you are a healthcare provider or a pharmaceutical company, this tool is truly one way to engage your audience.

As technology continues to advance and networks can better handle large data transfers, some companies are starting to leverage live video streaming or video chats. For example, for all of IBM's Major Technology Events, we livestream the keynote addresses from our Social Media Aggregation page. Unlike uploading an already-recorded video, live video streaming is in real time, allowing participants viewing the stream access to the people, content, and information as it happens.

Video streaming is very popular in announcing new products to market where you can have customers, analyst, and press all attending remotely to see the announcement as it takes place. This method of video collaboration is also more engaging. Since it's real time, remote participants can ask questions and interact with the speaker as required.

Video is a powerful part of your engagement strategy.

CASE STUDY: BLENDTEC

Blendtec, a manufacturer of blenders, has probably the most famous video campaign. Tom Dickson, the CEO of Blendtec, used to test his blenders with wood and other items to ensure that his quality standards were up to the right level. The then-new marketing director George Wright decided to see if sharing this tough quality standard with video could help to showcase their competitive differentiators.

They started with $100 of supplies and a CEO who believed in his product. By leveraging Tom Dickson blending up everything from wood to iPhones, they have earned Blendtec a cultlike following. After 186 videos, Blendtec's retail sales are up a reported 700%, its YouTube site has 200,000-plus subscribers, and it has been featured on major mainstream media outlets like *The Today Show, The Tonight Show, The History Channel,* the *Wall Street Journal,* and others.

Their strategy was to be authentic, with a cross between an infomercial set and a small-time game show. They did purchase advertising with Google and Yahoo, but their success is mostly due to the tagging in YouTube as well as the fun, viral nature of the video! And think about this. It all started from something their CEO and inventors did naturally to ensure their quality!

CASE STUDY: CHILDREN'S HOSPITAL BOSTON

Children's Hospital Boston is a comprehensive center for pediatric health care. It is one of the largest pediatric medical centers in the United States, offering a complete range of health care services for children from birth through 21 years of age.

The Pediatric Intensive Care Unit (PICU) Without Walls is a pilot project intended to bring pediatric intensive care resources to anyone—in anyplace—across the world by creating a web-based video library of notable clinicians speaking on essential topics in the care of critically ill children. The specific objective of the video library is to feature expert physicians from across the globe speaking on the full range of topics essential to pediatric critical care medicine, explaining topics in pediatric respiratory care, utilizing both didactic teaching as well as patient simulation.

In his presentation at the 2011 IBM Impact Conference, Dr. Jeffery Burns, Chair of Critical Care Medicine Program at the Children's Hospital Boston, discussed the need for more engagement with other doctors around the world. Because of the limited amount of space and time, he had to turn down numerous requests from other doctors who asked to observe his techniques in Boston.

Leveraging the understanding of how adults learn, he had his first "aha" moment while watching his son play Xbox LIVE®. He notice that he was playing with people around the world that he had never met before, just like his international team needed to work together to solve problems real time. The second "aha" moment was when he was watching the Masters Golf tournament. He watched the winner give a speech in HD video, while showing his winning putt in a video stream. Featured on the same page was an avatar where the user could experience how to shoot the winning putt.

He called IBM to learn about how the Masters experience could be used to engage doctors from around the world. He is now testing a solution called "PICU Without Walls" that is portable enough to be placed on a USB thumb drive and leverages a social network model to drive "wisdom" of the crowds and engagement globally. He can show a video of how to solve problems in different geographic areas, all having different health issues, and leverage avatars to showcase different procedures in a simulation model. This social learning test is using video, but video with gaming techniques. We will keep our eyes on this social learning experiment progression.

CASE STUDY: SUN LIFE FINANCIAL

At the 2011 IBM Social Business Forum in Orlando, Thomas Anger, Manager, Collaboration Services at Sun Life Financial, described how Sun Life has engaged its employees. Sun Life Financial is a Canadian financial services company.

Sun Life began IdeaShare, a three-month contest to get the best employee ideas around the globe. It was designed to get employees generating and commenting on each others' ideas. But the real challenge was getting Sun Life's far-flung staffers to participate. To better engage their employees, two senior executives—the VP of market development and the SVP for group benefits—created a video with themselves as avatars explaining an idea contest to get people excited. The video spread rapidly and generated an increase in the participation of their employees in the internal community. In fact, it led to more than 250 new ideas!

These ideas included improvements in the way customers get authenticated when calling the company and a new push to enable more online communication and less paperwork in dealings with customers. Another outcome was broader awareness and participation in Sun Life's internal collaboration tools, for which the usage is now growing at 10% per month.

After five months, the pilot has generated more than 330 ideas, 932 comments, and more than 4,300 votes from employees across the Group Benefits and Customer Care Centre. Seven ideas have been implemented enhancing service and product offerings to their clients. As Thomas explained on stage: "We now have examples and stories of information sharing between people who didn't even know each other existed a year ago. And the new people-to-people connections are starting to deliver benefits, like increased collaboration, less reinventing the wheel, and greater speed to market. Our employees are engaged like never before."

Check out their story on Youtube!:
http://www.youtube.com/watch?v=6Wgwn5R3EQQ.

Future Engagement Tool Experimentation

There are three new engagement tools that have not had solid business results to date but that to me show promise of future engagement. I believe that this experimentation will change the way we interact with brands of all kinds.

First, there is now a new way to allow automated or what is known as "hyperpassive" check-ins. An automated check-in means that a store or location has a device to automatically check you into their location to offer you coupons or intrinsic rewards without the client or potential client having to actively check in. The application could be in a bank, where you check in a person who walks through the door, to see what types of clients use the banking office, vs. an ATM to offer the appropriate services based on their patterns of visitation.

Second, there are new services like Assisted Serendipity that will offer companies more information based on location. According to its site, Assisted Serendipity is a free service that notifies you as soon as the male/female ratio turns in your favor at your favorite local hangouts. Using Foursquare's check-in data, they monitor the venues you are interested in, and notify you as soon as the ratio "tips." A business usage of this technology could be if your target market was around mothers and you wanted to offer a particular discount in the store when you had more moms present, or even tailor a demonstration based on who is in a store: a cooking demonstration vs. a demonstration on the latest power tool! Knowing when you will maximize the use of that discount or demo to your targeted audience would be valuable information in your strategy.

Finally, there are RFID bands that people wear that can be used to store your social networking profiles. According to en.gauge media's 2011 The Shift report, more than 96% of people between the ages of 18 and 25 have a social networking profile. With these RFID bands, companies can have a real-world association with the virtual world of Facebook, Communities and beyond. Below are two case studies of companies experimenting with this technology in Europe.

CASE STUDY: COCA-COLA VILLAGE

The Coca-Cola Company engaged teenagers in its Coca-Cola Villages that now embed social aspects into the real-world experience. The Villages are a two- to three-day experience with watersports, sunbathing, and game-playing amusement park–style activity for teenagers. While the Villages are present around the world, the Village in Israel featured a new experimentation RFID bracelet. When the students arrived, they were given an ID bracelet with an RFID signal that is programmed with their Facebook ID.

The students could then venture all throughout the village and "Like" activities that then showed up on their Facebook pages. The teens could also tag photos taken by the roaming photographers and just wave their ID bracelet to tag the picture in Facebook. This RFID-based solution was an experiential event for Coca-Cola Israel that synced everyone who participated, live with their friends on Facebook.

The results that they have measured to date include the community and interaction of the teenagers with Coke as a brand after the experience in the Village. While no public data is available today, they are expanding the experience to other Villages across the world.

CASE STUDY: SALVATION ARMY

The Salvation Army, headquartered in London, has leveraged innovative engagement methods for its market. It held an International Youth Forum for those age 18 to 29. They leveraged a social networking device held by the delegates called a Poken. The Poken was a physical device that contained their contact information, including Facebook connections. When they touched their Poken with those of other delegates, the contact details were automatically exchanged.

According to Mark Calleran, the Chief Information Officer (CIO) at the Salvation Army, more than 31,000 interactions (making friends) took place during the event.

The top three "Pokenauts" managed to make 215, 190, and 170 friends. In addition, they had numerous live streaming video reviews through the Poken as well. Just as in the Coca-Cola example, the engagement strategy was to find a way for the community that came together once to stay connected beyond the event. And so far, this community has continued the engagement.

CASE STUDY: AMERICAN EAGLE

American Eagle Outfitters is an American clothing and accessories retailer based in Pittsburgh. They are currently experimenting with a new kind of engagement with Passive Check-in through an application called Shopkick.

Customers who enter an American Eagle location with the Shopkick application open are immediately recognized via the mobile device. The customer is alerted with a message and points for deals within the location. The application can be used to scan items and earn more points and/or deals. American Eagle kicks off semiautomatic check-ins when you walk into their store or go into a dressing room. You get "kickbucks" for activities in the store that can be used for purchase later.

On one day, for instance, American Eagle advertised 40% off for any Shopkick check-in. This consumer engagement is integrated in with the point of sale (POS) experience. This mobile application did make the Budget Fashionista's Top 10 Mobile Shopping Apps List because of its ease of use, and the mega discount! On the Shopkick Facebook page there are a lot of "Likes" of the use of the application with not only American Eagle, but also Best Buy, Macy's, and Wet Seal.

Integrate

Being able to integrate your client's and employee's experience across different business processes, social tools, and audiences is critical. Imagine watching an ad, being totally engaged in its content, and then when you go onto the Web, you have a completely different experience. Or imagine that you had a customer service experience that was completely different from your engagement in crowdsourcing or in marketing.

The examples that I shared in the preceding section focused on one element of a company's strategy, but trust that all the processes were integrated around tools, goals, and purpose.

As you engage the audience, remember that most people use more than one social tool such as Twitter, LinkedIn, and Facebook, as well as many more, and they talk via the blogosphere with reporters, clients, employees, and beyond. Also know that they engage with you in more than one business process: marketing, client support, product innovation, communications, sales, and more. You need to ensure that your engagement strategy has an integrated message and approach. Imagine that every digital touch point is part of your online brand ecosystem.

The areas of integration to plan for are the following:

- Business processes (more on this in Chapter 5, "[Social] Network Your Business Processes")
- Social tools
- Ecosystem (employees, clients, reporters, influencers, etc.)

The case studies in the sections that follow illustrate some of these concepts.

CASE STUDY: BNY MELLON

BNY Mellon was established in 2007 from the merger of Mellon Financial Corporation and The Bank of New York Company, Inc. BNY Mellon is a leading investment management and investment services company.

BNY Mellon wanted an integrated approach for its internal Social Business implementation to encourage employees to link up and share ideas from professional concerns to personal interests. It wanted to make sure this integrated community was embedded in the work flow normally used for its 40,000 employees! Named TeamSource, the new integrated community gives employees a forum through which they can share interests or collaborate on business projects among all employees—in one integrated model. Employees, with one view, can see their tweets and internal communities and really become social employees with a single view.

BNY Mellon's Executive Vice President and Chief Information Officer states: "TeamSource is focused on fostering networks between our employees by establishing connections, increasing knowledge awareness, energy, and communication, which equates to higher performing teams. TeamSource is a web-based solution that provides employees an opportunity to establish a Profile Page (including a picture), tweet status updates, build their own internal network, and join communities of interest and practice" (source: BNY Mellon, 2011, http://bnymellon.mediaroom. com/index.php?s=43&item=1517).

In 2011, BNY Mellon received a CIO 100 Award for their TeamSource solution.

CASE STUDY: 1-800-FLOWERS.COM

Chris McMann, the President of 1-800-FLOWERS.COM, discussed at the 2011 IBM Social Business event in Orlando a few of his best practices in becoming a Social Business. His goals were simple but important: integration of his goals and vision throughout all the company's business processes. He never forgot that his clients would be touched by multiple areas: marketing, sales, customer service, and product development.

For instance, in 1-800 remote call centers, they added internal employee communities for keeping in touch with the corporate culture. Chris knew that the employees would reflect the company itself and he wanted to keep it fresh and caring. He ensured that his employees could brainstorm better ways to reach goals and to express themselves.

Externally, the 1-800-FLOWERS.COM employees monitor Twitter and Facebook, especially on special holidays like Mother's Day and Valentine's Day, to address any client needs more quickly. Their competition did not leverage these social tools. While their competitors saw their complaints grow, 1-800-FLOWERS.COM saw positive comments on its responsiveness and care for its customers.

In addition, 1-800-FLOWERS.COM wanted to engage its clients with crowdsourcing new offerings. Using the same engagement philosophy as they did for customer service, they engaged clients to crowdsource a new offering for Mother's Day. With user-generated videos as the source of information, the company created from their client's personal stories a book called "Celebrating Moms" as well as a touching video. Both of these offers are now sold as products for Mother's Day and have become a tradition—part of the relationship between 1-800-FLOWERS.COM and its clients!

And 1-800-FLOWERS.COM has gone further to integrate social techniques for their clients. For example, they integrated Facebook birthday reminders on their website and into emails, merchandised "Likes" on their website, and launched a fully transactional Facebook store. They have even experimented with virtual gifting.

Chris said he is trying to learn even more about his clients and their needs. He is engaged in the dialogue to ensure that he keeps up to speed on what makes people smile. His financial results are growing due to his integrated strategy.

Identify with Emotion and Personal Connection

Never underplay the emotional connection that comes from a personalized experience. The fact that you can identify with customers and their pain, or the way they came to your website, is important. Your company needs all the key elements that make up an exceptional experience that will attract customers. A great customer experience provides detailed personalization based on behavior-driven web analytics.

Personalization is based on the *interests* of an *individual*. It implies that the changes are based on implicit data, such as items purchased or pages viewed. The term *customization* is used instead when the site uses only explicit data such as ratings or preferences. For example, if a user lands on your product page because of an ad they clicked on in Facebook, behavior personalization will profile that user as a "social user," and thus that product page will be customized and offer more social capabilities, communities, or friends of Facebook who also like this page. If a different user lands on the same product page because of an ad they clicked on in YouTube, the behavior personalization will profile that user as a "video user," and thus that product page will be customized and offer more media and video capabilities. In both examples, it is the same product page, but using behavioral-driven personalization based on web analytics, the display can change based on the characteristic of the user and the user's online behavior.

There are a variety of personalization techniques for providing an exceptional experience. Some of the most common techniques are these:

- **Role-based personalization:** Having access to the information that is relevant to my job (or segment).

- **Rule-based personalization:** Showing or sending information based on knowledge we have of the customer controlled by business logic (rules).

- **Behavior-driven personalization:** Showing or sending information based on the user's online browsing behavior.

- **Collaborative filtering:** Making recommendations to the user based on other users' selections.

- **Adaptive web personalization:** Preselecting options based on what this user has selected before.

Personalization is a key in engagement because customers get what they want to see (and keep coming back). The case studies that follow provide some real-world examples of the personalization aspect of engagement.

The case studies in the sections that follow illustrate some of these concepts.

CASE STUDY: FABERGÉ

Fabergé is a Russian-American company that sells luxury goods, one-of-a-kind works of art, and jewelry. The company wanted to revitalize its business model and establish itself as a premiere world luxury brand, and define an online approach to selling its high-value luxury items that avoided the usual mass-market self-service format of the Web. Its primary goal was an experience that would be truly interactive by providing each client a real-life personal sales advisor as they would find in a traditional high-end boutique.

The new site would also become the hub around which all client interactions would be constructed, therefore providing global reach and accessibility without the constraints or cost of a physical store network. The key was to allow the client to choose how, where, and when they purchase. With the new online experience, Fabergé creates the impression of a department store, with a multitude of shops and products accessible to its connoisseur clients backed with the quality of one-on-one VIP experience found in a private salon.

The online experience translates the key elements of the traditional high-end luxury-goods shopping process into an online paradigm that reflects traditional VIP private selling methods based on highly interactive and personal service. Prospective clients are required to pass through a process to access the exclusive "inner sanctum" where they can explore and interact with Fabergé products. As the customer builds trust and explores, more of the product catalog is progressively revealed. Access to a personal agent is provided, avoiding mass-market self-service, and at the client's discretion, these agents can conduct a unique interactive dialogue via the medium of the Web and assist by pushing items to the client's browser and exploring them with the client.

Fabergé did a great job of integrating personal touches of storytelling with stunning behind-the-scenes animations and inspiration storyboards that reveal the sources of some of their designs. The result is an environment of multilayered access, detail, and exploring. Clients can connect to a Fabergé representative 24/7 in 11 different languages via chat, telephone, or video conferencing.

Ordered items are hand delivered and private viewings can be scheduled right from the site. The site gives clients the option to purchase their own personal sales advisor who provides live one-on-one interactive sales service via video, telephone, or live conversation chat. The great example about their site is that Fabergé has integrated an online experience with the offline, and in such a personal manner.

Fabergé set the bar for other luxury brands across the board and at the same time has dramatically turned around its business. Fabergé, the iconic jewelry house, is undergoing a dramatic change of fortune with greatly improved financial results due to this as part of its business strategy.

CASE STUDY: BANK HAPOALIM

Bank Hapoalim is Israel's largest bank, with more than 10,000 employees and many branches in Israel, Asia, Australia, Europe, and Latin and North America. Its large global workforce posed some internal challenges as they needed to establish a better method for information and knowledge management.

They decided to engage their employees with a personalized role-based approach to information, expertise, team projects, forums, and communities. Using a framework for role-based, personalized views, Bank Hapoalim now has more than 28 different professional sites.

Every professional role has a tailored solution, very personalized for its needs. These virtual workspaces support professionals with all the information, applications, access to expertise, and other resources relevant to their work. Each role group takes ownership of its own space, and the professionals themselves are the content authors.

The personalized role-based spaces have become the main communication channel for the bank and gateway to all its employees engagement. It also serves as the bank's effective virtual workspace that provides employees in all different roles with everything they need to do their jobs throughout the day. It is completely user-centric, which has led to this tagline on the professional sites: "Where knowledge works for you."

It is the first thing launched for every employee when they log onto their computers in the morning. How engaging is that!

Conclusion

Engagement is a personal connection, a relationship.

Understanding the new social employee and social client is important to set the right expectations. Recognition that they now exist is the first step!

The principles of engagement direct your company on a set of simple but important goals. These exceptional experiences help your company to bond with your clients, employees, and influencers.

By focusing on engagement based on your goals, engagement can be strengthened with interaction, integration, and identification. Whether you are beginning inside your four walls or outside, the engagement strategy is crucial to your exceptional experience. As we saw with numerous examples, these engagement experiences make your company more relevant in your space.

This is not for the faint of heart but takes resources and a focus on developing a longer-term perspective; however, it is worth the effort with bigger returns than a simple focus on leads. Before you move onto the next chapter, define your engagement strategy, how your clients and employees have changed, and what the key points are that you want to ensure are addressed in your Social Business governance model.

Chapter 5 continues with a look at how the Social Business AGENDA can help you across your business processes.

CHAPTER

5

(Social) Network Your Business Processes

"Business processes
are the 'soul' of your
company—to truly be a
Social Business, you must
embed social into
your soul."

Sandy Carter

"Socially enabling your processes is a key competitive weapon."

Jeremiah Owyang, Altimeter Group

(Social) Network Your Processes

A Social Business embeds social tools and techniques in all processes for greater competitiveness and efficiency. Processes organize the way that businesses are run. Most companies have a process established for events such as on-boarding a new hire, acquiring new capital expenses, changing passwords, completing sales transactions, and the list goes on! In this chapter, I'm going to discuss how and why you should consider reengineering your existing processes or augment them to be more efficient with social tools and techniques.

Even the process of managing business processes is becoming more social. IBM just launched Blueworks Live, a cloud-based business process management (BPM) tool that lets you discover, design, automate, and manage business processes for your organization. Mondial Assistance Group, the worldwide leader in assistance services and travel insurance, used Blueworks Live to increase quality and efficiency of operational processes and has saved several million euros in the first year. This corporate program helps them collaborate on improvement ideas as well as capture and exchange process knowledge with an easy-to-use tool.

In the past, layers in your organization chart dealt with and understood details and information about your company, clients, and partners. According to well-established processes, they passed information up the chain when it was important or needed an exception or approval, as illustrated in Figure 5.1.

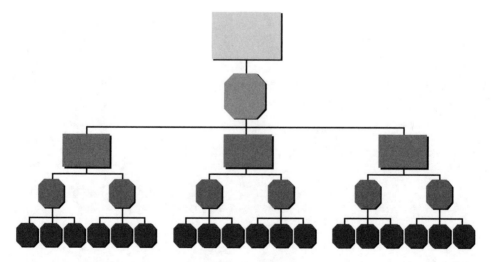

Figure 5.1   Typical organization structure for today's processes

The problem in today's social world is the vast amount of information flooding the organizational chart. It's getting stuck at each node in the chart, where companies are discovering that there aren't enough people, or enough context, or talent, or meaning, or processes, to figure out what to do with the information. Our lack of attention is letting our information fall on the floor unused.

A Social Business approaches this problem very differently. A Social Business has, of course, an organizational chart and an enterprise boundary, as illustrated in Figure 5.2.

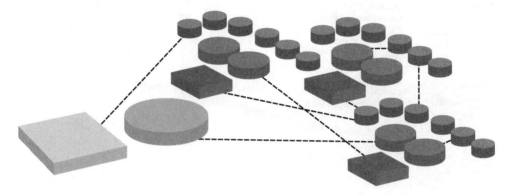

Figure 5.2   Social Business organizational flow

A Social Business doesn't think of that organizational chart and those boundaries as determining how information flows. Using attention-enhancing, social techniques, a Social Business routes information to the people who need it, making sure it applies rules common in business, like compliance or nondisclosures where appropriate.

By obeying those filters and rules, a Social Business engages the right constituents—wherever they are in the hierarchy, or even outside the enterprise. This approach is a very radical social and technological revolution that requires reexamining our business processes. With connections forming and reforming in real time according to the need and conversation, across org chart, organizational, and even enterprise boundaries, Social Business enables the delivery of what we need, when we need it. This is what we call *social networking your business processes,* as illustrated in Figure 5.3.

Let's walk through some different examples to see what this means to different functions, enterprises, and processes. In Figure 5.3, you see that the heaviest focus for most Social Business processes will be on marketing, customer service, product and service development, operational, HR, and talent management.

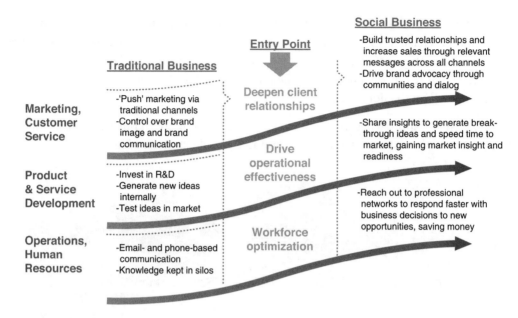

Figure 5.3   Social-empower your processes

Marketing and customer service in a traditional enterprise are control-oriented, pushing out preferred messages and managing customer incidents in a defined and perhaps even secretive way. In a Social Business, marketing and customer service have a different objective—to create customer advocates by building customer relationships. This means engaging customers where they are and proactively resolving their problems, perhaps even openly admitting failure and asking for assistance.

This Social Business process view is a very different approach to marketing and customer service; however, this cultural transformation from "control" to "transparency and openness" is a major theme of a Social Business (and hence this book!). Whether a leadership team likes it or not, businesses, not just marketing, cannot be controlled. A Social Business learns that being open and transparent is a competitive advantage. To embed that into your business, embed that concept into your processes!

Similarly, product development is transformed in a Social Business context. In a traditional business, R & D elaborates an idea into a product in relative isolation, off of a clear plan evolved from product management and from research insights.

In a Social Business, R & D develops these breakthroughs through a process of shared insights—shared across the enterprise, and even across enterprise boundaries with valued customers and partners. The result? Better products, faster. In the technology industry, there is even a movement around social application development. This provides developers direct access to social and collaborative solutions embedded into their application development platform so that they can easily collaborate and search for similar code snippets while writing software code. The users who are responsible for testing new software code can also discover similar problems and solutions that have been shared from other software testers.

Operations and HR processes change also. In a traditional business, we organize people according to fixed structures, and interact with them via email and phone in predefined patterns and times. While groups have goals, they are not typically leveraging talent and expertise outside the four walls the same as inside the four walls of a company.

In a Social Business, the enterprise and its network of partners and customers become a single large network of professionals, working together toward a common goal. As discussed in Chapter 1, "The AGENDA for Social Business Success," more than 80% of Fortune 100 companies leverage LinkedIn and Facebook as recruiting tools today, leveraging outside resources to help judge talent. From IBM's Social Business 2011 Jam report, more insight is shared on employees' views. It shows that a socially enabled HR process needs to embrace the fact that employees have their own personal brands that exist both inside and outside the business, and that it does not own these brands but merely "rents" them while employees are at work. Personal brands need to be measured and rewarded based on how they help your company throughout the social network. As employees transition and become alumni of an organization, it becomes even more important that HR maintains relationships with its alumni network. Social tools can help provide a strong, dynamic way to keep the alumni network active and useful, enabling the organization to keep an invaluable source of knowledge, mentoring, and connections.

In order to take full advantage of the capabilities, HR must work with leadership to expand and instill the use of social technologies in practical and significant ways—a fundamental cultural change. Information can get lost and conversations can taper off when email is the primary form of communication. "I think leaders have a responsibility, where it makes sense, to move people out of email," a participant wrote. "I heard someone once say that 'email is where information goes to die,' implying that we lose something by forcing knowledge into that channel."

Let's look at a great example. BASF is the world's leading chemical company. With about 109,000 employees, and close to 385 production sites worldwide, they serve customers and partners in almost all countries of the world. To improve their internal collaboration, they created connect.BASF, an internal community for their employees. They have socially empowered their HR process so that their employees link socially to form expert networks. This networking among employees and communities across units and regions enables faster and more efficient knowledge sharing and improved collaboration for success. At press time, more than 20,000 employees are active in the community, with 36% joining connect. BASF from another employee's recommendation.

An example that Cordelia Krooss, BASF Senior Enterprise Community Manager, gave to a group of Social Businesses in Berlin showcased the business value of HR being socially empowered. There was a project team with members from four continents that needed to evaluate and select a supplier for a new service. The project team formed a collaboration hub in connect.BASF where all information came together. The project was self-documenting so that new team members could easily orient themselves and actively contribute immediately. The open exchange accelerated project progress so that the time to complete a crucial project step could be shortened by 25%.

Let's look at a couple of businesses that have progressed along the path today. The list that follows outlines how some IBM customers are already leading their organizations toward greater success:

- **Blue Cross and Blue Shield of Massachusetts:** Where they are working to create a better, more transparent healthcare system by integrating collaboration capabilities in their customer service process, providing communities, team rooms, and real-time communication for the service staff. It enabled them to have faster and more transparent access to information and expertise in support of customer claims and health issues. The business benefits were reduced training costs. Also, because they were freed from unproductive processes and outdated tools, they had more time to spend with customers and hence close more sales.

- **Caterpillar:** Where they are gaining customer loyalty by providing individualized, web-based customer experiences through socially empowering their marketing processes of engagement. Their blog was just named by Business 2 Community as one of the Top 10 in the world for the remarkable connection they are creating with their customers.

These organizations have chosen different approaches, and they are changing different parts of their enterprises. Even though these industry leaders all serve different customers, the one common theme running through their stories is that they are all applying social networking in their processes on their path to becoming a Social Business.

Socially Empowered Business

Social networking business processes deliver tremendous ROI and, as shown in Figure 5.4, drive the "next wave" of adoption being integrated into daily activities. This ROI is driven by reduced costs in training, finding experts, increasing revenue with more time for sales calls, and the list goes on. In the recent Social Business Jam run by IBM where more than 2,600 people around the world shared their viewpoints and options around Social Business, 47% of participants stated they would be more encouraged to use more social techniques and tools in their job if it was embedded in the applications they use to do their job.

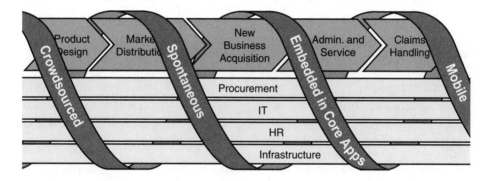

Figure 5.4   Social networking processes drive results.

Let's take a look at some common business processes, and consider how these might change for a Social Business. We will not go through all business processes, but use some for a frame of reference to see the change that social brings.

For each process, we are going to explore engaging customers and employees where they are, with problems as they have them, before they hit their frustration point. For each process, "where they are" will be different. Will it be Twitter or Facebook? Will it be specialized expert networks? Perhaps even in-person venues? A Social Business lives with its customers, without artificial boundaries constraining how customer issues get discovered and addressed.

I am asked a lot by business leaders, such as CMOs, CHROs, CIOs, and others in the C Suite, about where to get started in evaluating the best ROI results for socially empowering business processes. I recommend beginning by reevaluating how to approach the internal processes of collaboration and human resources because this enables experimentation internally and allows for social learning inside the organization with solid ROI. The HR process ROI is typically driven by increased speed in finding the right subject matter expert, and reduced costs in training and communications. The next processes are typically marketing, as this began with roots of social media, and then customer service, product development and innovation, and supply chain.

The sections that follow explore these key processes with a few leadership Social Businesses that have already begun to take those bold first steps. We will go through HR, Marketing, Customer Service, Product Management, and Product Innovation. Then we will proceed to discuss Social Business process maturity. Let's get started!

HR

Human Resources today is faced with three major challenges:

1. How do companies rapidly develop workforce skills and capabilities since new opportunities and competitive threats appear faster than ever? Whether industry, sector, technological, geographic, or social, the need to quickly learn new skills and readjust workers' capabilities is more important than ever.

2. As organizations and their environments become increasingly complex and networked, knowledge is more and more diffuse among larger groups of people. *Shared* information is therefore becoming the new currency, where power is derived not from information scarcity, but from insights gained through sharing.

3. These complex, interconnected environments require a different kind of leader, one who is comfortable with rapidly shifting leadership styles and modes. A one-size-fits-all leadership strategy is increasingly irrelevant in a global mosaic of cultures, styles, technologies, and workers.

Given these challenges, how could socially enabling key HR functions help make your company more competitive?

Let's first look at deploying resources internally. Think about how we all tend to do this today. We find an idea, we create a project, and we assign people to the project. Some are the smartest and best-motivated people for the job. Some aren't. Some insights, perhaps critical to the project's success, are locked away in other people's minds, in other divisions, maybe even in other departments.

A Social Business doesn't do this. A Social Business lets the talent and the problems find each other, letting the network of expertise in the enterprise self-optimize. This is a new, more powerful kind of management, requiring new processes, technologies, and new leaders.

Because of the shifting landscape, where real power comes not from knowledge hoarding but knowledge sharing, it is increasingly in the informal structures and personal relationships of the enterprise's social network where opportunities for innovation and growth lay. The key is in empowering your processes for social collaboration to serve as a catalyst for this type of networking.

This isn't new—great leaders have always leveraged personal relationships, and workers have always leveraged the "softer" business relationships nurtured at the water cooler or business dinners or social outings. What *is* new is that in a globally integrated world, the water cooler is no longer just down the hall, nor is the business dinner just down the street at the club—it's across the world.

Organization charts are not necessarily the best indicator of how work gets done. Top performers are often overlooked or unidentified in formal structures. Senior people are not always central to solving each problem; people at the periphery of formal structures can actually represent a direct line to top management and untapped knowledge. Increasing network visibility by improving social collaboration makes untapped knowledge actionable.

Your employees are already collaborating this way today, regardless of whether your systems and processes acknowledge it. IDC, a global provider of marketing intelligence in the areas of technology and business strategy, estimates that 57% of U.S. workers use social tools for business purposes at least once per week, and 15% use consumer social tools instead of corporate-sponsored sites (source: IDC, "The State of Social Business: 2009 Survey Results," Doc #221383, December 2009). Ironically, IT professionals are the most frequent users of social tools for business. Done the right way, and within the organization's cultural context, extending the support for informal networks can have a market-positive effect on the organization's agility and productivity. Additionally, this support will groom the next generation of leaders who, by working and growing in this net environment, are better able to lead corporations to newer heights.

According to Jacques Bughin and Michael Chui, "The rise of the networked enterprise: Web 2.0 finds its payday," McKinsey Quarterly, www.mckinseyquarterly.com (December, 2010), social-empowered HR processes show real business benefits. Some of the key results are the following:

- 30% median improvement in time to find internal experts and knowledge
- 10% median reduction in costs associated with training and communications

The following sections present three examples of Social Businesses that have taken the bold step with their HR processes. Both Sogeti and IBM are great examples of how to empower your HR processes for social collaboration. In addition, the large U.S. utility company shows with real financial results the potential for competitive advantage by starting with this business process.

CASE STUDY: SOGETI

Sogeti is a leading provider of professional technology services, specializing in application management, infrastructure management, high-tech engineering, and testing. Sogeti brings together more than 20,000 professionals in 15 countries and is present in more than 200 locations in Europe, the U.S., and India. For Sogeti, the challenge was getting these geographically dispersed organizations to all point in the same direction. With many employees working from client sites, home, and small satellite offices, how could Sogeti knit together a stronger sense of a single Sogeti cultural identity that aligns to the same business strategy?

To support innovation and growth that would let it enter new markets, the company decided to find ways of fostering teamwork and peer communication among its multiple business groups and locations. Because Sogeti's people are the company's most valuable asset, a powerful tool was needed to connect Sogeti people all over the world, providing them with a social platform that would allow them to share information and collaborate. To support that goal, Sogeti developed TeamPark, an internal collaborative platform for employees.

TeamPark enables sharing of almost any kind of data, including reports, graphics, white papers, videos, photos, and bookmarked websites. An integrated active profile directory provides a way to identify experts across the company's 200 office locations. This accelerates knowledge transfer, allowing experts to find each other quickly.

Again, the benefits have been tangible. Sogeti was able to greatly improve internal knowledge sharing and collaboration. TeamPark provides a unified entry point to information, ensuring that users will find the latest updates and reducing search time for finding staff expertise. TeamPark also speeds the formation of consulting teams for customer engagements, helping Sogeti more quickly enter new markets, driving new revenue and market-share opportunities.

CASE STUDY: IBM

IBM is a large, highly complex, matrixed organization, with several major business units spanning more than 160 countries and $100 billion in revenues. It provides information technology, software, hardware, and services that address the thorniest problems faced by the most complex of human systems to create smarter cities, smarter water, smarter healthcare, smarter industries, and more.

In such an environment, IBM is in critical need of a new generation of leaders who are comfortable and excited to operate in this fast-moving, complex environment with speed and creativity. The IBM HR leadership team therefore tapped into socially empowering their HR process to develop a from-the-ground-up leadership networking group, to share best practices, education tips, and opportunities to grow and lead new projects, and to strengthen informal networks that are vital to getting things done within a matrixed organization.

The benefits of the Leadership Networking Groups have been tangible. The Leadership Networking Group community was launched, allowing for rapid and organic growth of the community to members from dozens of countries where IBM operates. The community shares best practices for managing and leading teams and projects that span multiple countries, cultures, and business units.

CASE STUDY: LARGE U.S. UTILITY COMPANY

A large electric utility with more than 10,000 employees serving more than 10 million people has a vision of cleaner and smarter energy. To achieve its vision, the utility needed to become more agile and better at managing operational change. Essential to these objectives is the ability to develop and maintain a stable, productive, flexible, and satisfied workforce. At present, workforce productivity suffers because there are few avenues for top performers to share best practices with the rest of the organization. High employee turnover and many planned retirements leave gaps in resources and skills, making it difficult to fill thousands of open positions in the coming years. Seasoned staffers, already busy, are drained from having to train and mentor new hires. There is simply no easy way to reach out to fellow employees or to mine the talent pool for internal job rotations or project teams.

Employee productivity and morale also suffer from reliance on overburdened tools and processes. Employees are overrelying on email, making it hard to discover important information for decision making. Time and manager bandwidth are wasted by a culture of excessive face-to-face meetings to drive consensus and decisions, and a dispersed workforce that must travel to in-person meetings wastes time and energy, raises expenses, and increases safety risk. These and other operational inefficiencies cause poor employee retention, with the highest turnover among those with less than three years on the job.

The utility company wanted to socially empower their HR process with real-time communications, collaboration, and content management. Real-time messaging and improved collaboration would reduce the need for face-to-face meetings and status calls. Team rooms and content libraries would improve sharing of content for projects, teams, and individuals. Profiles, or a place where every employee's expertise would be documented, would help employees find people and make themselves known. Communities of interest would allow employees to share, innovate, and collaborate. And interactive information repositories such as wikis and activity templates would complement and possibly replace formal training.

The financial analysis shows socially empowering this human resource process delivered both direct and indirect financial benefits.

- The expense of travel to face-to-face meetings, and the carbon footprint, were reduced by an estimated US$8 million through online expertise location; project-based commenting, messaging, and status updates; and knowledge management through wikis, blogs, discussion forums, and shared bookmarks.

- Employee training costs were reduced by US$1.6 million, with faster ramp-up of new hires, and with more-engaged and satisfied employees reducing the turnover rate.

- Teleconferencing expenses were reduced by US$700,000.

Top indirect contributors are higher staff productivity, faster employee ramp-up times, and improved employee retention. Total financial benefits from socially empowering this HR process are estimated to be US$28.9 million, with nearly US$1 million occurring during the first year.

Marketing

Marketing executives are focused today on increasing revenue with new markets and opportunities opening up quickly, producing more competitive offerings, and reducing their costs while increasing engagement with clients. Marketing must deliver an experience that is engaging, memorable, and compelling. In addition, they need a way to provide consistency in message everywhere they go and relevant and personalized information customized to customers. A pretty tall order and one for which social tools can excel.

Business imperatives for marketing processes include creating a consistent multichannel experience, delivering relevant interactions that increase customer loyalty and satisfaction, creating brand ambassadors, and integrating across online and face-to-face channels.

Given these challenges, how could socially enabling key marketing functions help make your company more competitive?

Let's first look at marketing in the traditional sense. Think about how we all tend to do this today. We create a message, and push it into the marketplace through traditional channels. The process assumes control over brand image and brand communication. It would take weeks or months to launch a new campaign. Furthermore, marketers would only be able to launch individual promotions.

In the traditional approach, many campaigns are pushed "blindly" with no customer input or feedback and are very call-center and mailing intense. The direct sales teams are challenged to convey values of each new campaign in relevant context to customer.

A Social Business doesn't adopt this approach. A Social Business knows that its marketing department is composed of customers. A Social Business enables creation of new promotions and launches in real time, leveraging multiple campaigns to different targets—end consumers. The Social Business understands customer preferences, and quickly tailors offers and communications to meet their needs. It quickly and reliably gauges the performance of marketing programs to understand when a change is needed. As it socially enables its marketing processes, clients and partners participate at every step. For example, the lead generation process could be socially enabled by adding in communities as a source of high-quality leads, and by analyzing client-stated habits and preferences to "hyper-target" campaigns.

According to Jacques Bughin and Michael Chui, "The rise of the networked enterprise: Web 2.0 finds its payday," McKinsey Quarterly, www.mckinseyquarterly.com (December, 2010), social-enabled marketing processes show real business benefits. Some of the key results are these:

- 20% median improvement in awareness
- 15% median improvement in revenue
- 10% median improvement in effectiveness of conversion

The following sections present two examples of Social Businesses that have taken the bold step with their marketing processes.

CASE STUDY: US OPEN TENNIS

The US Open (http://www.usopen.org/) focused on adding social capabilities into their marketing process both in awareness experience and in lead generation. They focused on personalizing their customer experience to engage their clients. They focused on their website, where most of their business is done. This site is really what a next-generation engaging experience should be—rich in social capabilities, packed with video and interactive media, up-to-date with the latest statistics and analytics, and delivered through mobile devices.

For this year's US Open, an AroundMe iPhone app was created that leverages the GPS features in the phone. When attendees use the augmented reality or interactive ground map features, they can point to a food destination to find out the type of food they can get there, along with other details. Or they can point at a court to see the real-time details of the match and who is playing.

This extended the US Open's reach both geographically and demographically and allowed them to engage fans with innovative technology that delivers differentiated experience. Overall, it increased their advertising and sponsor revenue.

CASE STUDY: IBM

IBM socially empowers its marketing processes. A great example is the way IBM primarily leveraged social in its marketing of "machine" (named Watson) versus man in Jeopardy in 2011. While more than 10 million people watched the challenge, IBM itself relied not on traditional media advertising, but on Social Business techniques. How exactly did it social-enable its marketing process?

Well, it started with a dedicated website on Watson (www.ibm.com/watson). It used engaging videos, and showcased a social media aggregator, compiling all the tweets, searches, and blogs on the subject that are available. IBM set up viewing parties for its documentary on the event, and encouraged tweetups to engage its best clients.

And yes, Watson had a Facebook page and a Twitter id, as well as a YouTube channel with more than 30 videos featured with more than one million viewings before the big TV show. IBM made its company personal by featuring a chief scientist as the spokesperson for the event. And they showcased the engineers who created "Watson" but spoke in easy-to-understand, nontechnical language.

Once the air cover had been achieved, the marketing process began to generate leads on the business side by IBM showcasing in videos the technology's relevance in all industries. As Paul Gillen, author, former editor-in-chief of *Computerworld,* and currently editor of the very popular online B2B publication, wrote,

> "IBMers were active in nooks and crannies of the Internet. The research team chose Reddit, a social news site with a small but enthusiastic membership, to answer the top 10 questions about Watson and the contest. They used TED.com for a live webcast the day after the contest ended."

IBM's marketing process exemplified a socially empowered process in the B2B world. A socially empowered marketing process can provide a significant competitive advantage!

Customer Service

The primary goal of customer service is about serving clients, sometimes in their most frustrated state, as typically they are calling about an issue or a problem. The outcome targeted through listening to the customers and assessing the customers' needs is to help them while leaving them with a pleasant experience. Most are struggling to keep pace with rapidly increasing consumer expectations. High turnover, new communication channels, and budget cuts make the job of client satisfaction even more difficult.

Given these challenges, how could socially empowering key customer service functions help make your company more competitive?

The typical customer service operation today measures customer service in a set of siloed metrics, not looking at the process as a whole. According to Francine Richards, writer for eHow Business, a typical customer service operation measures

> "the average speed of answer of phone calls and the number of calls abandoned before getting to a customer service representative. Additionally, companies may use customer satisfaction surveys and track the number of customer complaints. Setting goals and key performance indicators (KPIs) such as all calls are answered within 10 seconds are critical for success."

Most traditional service centers have limited web self-service and they elevate call levels, especially to support new promotions. With traditional input mechanisms like phone calls, they are challenged to service concerns coming in from Facebook, Twitter, and the other new social channels. More common than not, there is no integration of frequently changing campaigns into frontline sales behavior. For example, if marketing ran a campaign, there is typically not interlock between the campaign and the service center's knowledge when questions come in about the new campaign's offer.

A Social Business doesn't do this. In a socially enabled customer service process, customers interact with each other and directly with relationship managers. They have a rich new community for members that increases trust through interactions with each other and the support team. As an added benefit, their campaigns enhance online communities and relationships.

A Social Business enables a call-center manager with the ability to update web content based on customer behavior—providing critical information when needed, or sharing best practices with blogging, shared bookmarks, shared files, and activities. Those companies that can leverage these new social tools are much fiercer competitors, and more important, understand more about their clients. To further showcase the value of this engagement, the Social Business should also alter the process to provide online services to promote self-service within communities, instant click to chat, and easy access to experts.

In this new world, there is the chance for everyone to complain in many different forums. The new customer service process integrates these social platforms into its strategy as well. According to IDC, there are five areas that enable a Social Business to understand and help clients through social channels (source: Michael Fauscette, IDC Group VP, Software Business Solutions: http://www.mfauscette.com/software_technology_partn/2010/05/the-social-employee-manifesto.html):

- **Acquire knowledge** and ask questions of a community.
- **Share knowledge** with and contribute new ideas to a community.
- **Initiate conversations** about my company's products and services online.
- **Gather feedback** on existing products and services from the community.
- **Manage relationships** with customers and prospects.

According to Jacques Bughin and Michael Chui, "The rise of the networked enterprise: Web 2.0 finds its payday," McKinsey Quarterly, www.mckinseyquarterly.com (December, 2010), social-enabled customer service processes show real business benefits. These are some of the key results:

- 30% median improvement in the speed of access to internal experts
- 30% median improvement in the speed of access to internal knowledge
- 15% median reduction in external communications expense

Zappos.com, IBM, and Southwest have built best-of-class service and support organizations by socially empowering this important client process.

- Zappos.com has world-class customer service and support processes with social insert at many steps in the process: Listening to blogs, tweets, and communities; proactively responding to any issues or opportunities; encouraging collaboration by providing communities for internal employees to chat, and for clients to chat with clients.

- IBM has world-class customer service and support and has been leveraging social tools for many years to ensure that the level of support occurs by sharing client feedback through social networks, celebrating customer success, and using social tools to give customers a view of how committed IBM is to its quality and support.

- Southwest Airlines has embedded its customer support processes with social from start to finish. Their online portal has more than 12 million monthly visits; they have more than 1 million Twitter followers and 1.3 million Facebook Likes, and 29,000 reviewers on their Travel Guide. In addition, their CEO is active on LinkedIn Answers, constantly asking potential business travelers, "What else do you need for Southwest to become your go-to business airline?"

The case studies that follow provide two other examples of how companies are taking this bold step: Sennheiser Electronic GmbH & Co., and Blue Cross and Blue Shield.

CASE STUDY: SENNHEISER ELECTRONIC GMBH & CO. KG

Sennheiser Electronic GmbH & Co. KG, a German-based electronics company, makes high-end microphones, headphones, telephony accessories, and avionics headsets for consumer, professional, and business applications. The company, which has been in business for more than 60 years, currently operates in 90 countries and employs 2,000 people.

Their major challenge was to improve their customer support by socially empowering their process with a deep knowledge base and facilitating online collaboration. To improve client satisfaction, they found that their big competitive differentiator was being able to provide this superior support during live concerts, a big requirement and one with a lot of pressure on those providing the support.

So Sennheiser Electronic GmbH & Co. focused on leveraging social tools to provide strong support and emergency assistance to the audio engineers during live music events. Their key requirement was to give team members instant access to detailed information about the equipment requirements for performers and the technical specifications for a large number of venues.

In order to be successful in this process reengineering, Sennheiser knew they had to foster online collaboration among the Global Relationship Management team, audio engineers, event organizers, and Sennheiser's team of radio frequency experts, who are located around the world. These radio frequency experts might be asked to eliminate radio frequency interference at one venue while solving a problem with the sound system at another venue on the opposite side of the globe. Previously, Sennheiser could only fly these experts to locations or offer phone support, which, in the heat of pressure, was not always the best option for the performing band.

With Sennheiser's process, a community was created online with a number of features. First, any team member can instantly access detailed information about a performer's equipment and a venue's technical specifications through the community's knowledge base. With changes in the process to locate help, the new social-empowered process provides a list of companies and technical experts near a venue to help local engineers resolve problems. If additional assistance is needed, the Global Relationship Management team can use real-time collaboration sessions with Sennheiser radio frequency experts located around the world. In preparing to eliminate as many live-concert situations in the future as possible, Sennheiser Sound Academy has also set up a virtual classroom. A trainer with a webcam explains the use of Sennheiser products to train participants and business partners, leverage best practices, and eliminate as many problems ahead of time as possible.

CASE STUDY: BLUE CROSS AND BLUE SHIELD

Blue Cross and Blue Shield is a leading health-insurance network with millions of members and more than 3,000 employees. Today's healthcare providers are under pressure as never before to improve customer service, boost employee productivity, and increase membership rates. Achieving such results, however, is contingent on effective processes and information technology for communications, collaboration, and knowledge management—areas that this insurer identified as needing dramatic improvement.

Sales staff mired in tedious searches for information and expertise had less time to spend with prospects, reducing their close rates. Similarly, employees isolated in their departments and workplaces found it hard to connect with experts. Duplicate efforts wasted time and money. As one staffer said, "We don't know that similar projects are going on until it's too late." And as in many organizations, employees were pressured to do more with the same resources, a reality captured in the comment: "We can't hire, but our goals are higher." These challenges were exacerbated as the organization overrelied on email to manage these complex interactions and processes for communication and collaboration; according to one employee, "Conversation by email is dizzying!"

For Blue Cross and Blue Shield to socially empower their customer service process, they had to address issues that directly impacted productivity, and they began with an analysis of the financial consequences.

For customer service, they decided to integrate with their current intranet many community features like team rooms and real-time communication so that information would be easier to access from searchable online communities of interest, meeting places, FAQs, and file shares. Employee profiles and profile searches would connect employees with experts and expertise across the organization, as would blogs, self-service forums, and searchable histories of problems solved. Collaboration and messaging would link on-premises and remote employees in real time, raising their productivity in teams and as individuals.

Customer service staff particularly would benefit, thanks to faster and more transparent access to information and expertise in support of customer claims and health issues. This improvement should boost word-of-mouth referrals and retention rates. Sales staff, too, would be more productive through easier access to information and experts, with more dynamic and appropriate collaboration tools. Freed from unproductive processes and outdated tools, they would have more time to spend with customers and hence close more sales.

The enhanced web experience available to staff in sales, customer service, and other departments is estimated to deliver financial benefits over three years.

- Cost savings include lower costs in training, telephone usage, hosted web conferencing, travel to meetings, and hard-copy printing and distribution.
- Additional savings come from membership gains due to higher sales closing rates, and productivity gains from faster information searches and more-effective collaboration.

Product Development and Innovation

Product development and innovation challenges are finding effective methods of identifying and developing breakthrough innovation ideas. Innovation used to be the preserve of a select band of employees (be they designers, engineers, or scientists) whose responsibility it was to generate and pursue new ideas, often in a separate location. That thought process is changing, however. Google now has "20 time." Employees can spend 20% of their time doing what they deem is valuable to think and innovate. Out of this initiative came the RechargeIT project, geared at making the new hybrid cars affordable and efficient for the average consumer.

According to MIT Sloan Management Review, in "The Five Myths of Innovation," innovation has increasingly come to be seen as the responsibility of the entire organization.

Two of the key takeaways of MIT's latest research are the following:

- External innovation forums have access to a broad range of expertise that makes them effective for solving narrow technological problems.
- Internal innovation forums have less breadth but more understanding of context.

Smart companies use their external and internal experts for very different types of problems. The way they socially empower the process for internal and external is taken into account.

Think of the way we all manage products today.

We go out, we listen to customers, then we disappear for a while, and reemerge months later with a prototype, asking, "Is this what you meant?" What if it isn't? What if the requirements have changed? What if what looked right looks less right once you start building it?

A Social Business is different.

A Social Business builds its products with customers and partners. In fact, from IBM's Social Business 2011 Jam report, the 2500-plus people agreed that for innovation to grow in corporations, companies must leverage the experience and connections of their alumni network, and embrace the wisdom of the crowds, while rewarding those employees who take full advantage of those networked ideas.

Product plans are less predictable, but product results are more predictable: Social Businesses have a better chance of building what customers want. According to Jacques Bughin and Michael Chui, "The rise of the networked enterprise: Web 2.0 finds its payday," McKinsey Quarterly, www.mckinseyquarterly.com (December, 2010), social-empowered product development and innovation processes show real business benefits.

Here are some of the key results:

- 25% median improvement in the speed of access to external experts
- 20% median increase in the number of successful innovations
- 20% median reduction in the time-to-market for new products/services

Market-leading organizations have reached out to other parts of the business and to partners and customers for product insights. Market leaders such as Proctor & Gamble have been using crowdsourcing techniques to challenge the best and the brightest (wherever they may reside) to offer up new product ideas or ways existing products can be improved. As a reminder, to crowdsource a product means that you leverage the wisdom of the crowds, usually in the blogosphere to generate new ideas, refine the ideas, and vote on the best idea. Some people also refer to this as collective intelligence.

Because crowdsourcing is leveraging the value gained from multiple people in an online methodology to gain new insights and validate ideas, it can enhance your traditional product development and innovation processes. It ensures that client input is seen in real time, and it enables your development team to garner input from nonclients as well.

In fact, crowdsourcing is growing exponentially. Matt Johnson, leader of UTest's marketing and community management teams, works for a company whose entire business model is built on crowdsourcing, UTest is a venture-funded software testing marketplace based in Massachusetts that crowdsources testing of software for major corporations. Matt Johnson predicts:

> "The line will be drawn clearly between loosely affiliated mobs and highly skilled, well-paid, collaborative communities of experts. In other words, work categories that require greater expertise (for example, software testing and online advertising) will mature from crowdsourcing to expert-sourcing."

Many companies leverage crowdsourcing today. From Snapple and Mountain Dew in the beverage business, to Coach in the luxury space, to IBM and UTest in the software space, and even the National Football League in sports advertising, crowdsourcing is moving from experimentation into mainstream innovation.

But the key here is how you embed this concept into your processes. Stephen King, CEO of Mob4Hire, has built his competitive differentiation on crowdsourcing. Mob4Hire is the only crowdsourced company that provides true mobility testing as well as the ability to conduct market research with the Mob4Hire team of testers. He commented:

> "Crowdsourcing will continue to move from being a source of free/cheap contribution to one where people get compensated for their time. As more and

more mainstream businesses embrace crowdsourcing, we'll also see better systems built to ensure better quality through better processes."

In addition to delivering broader transparency across projects and divisions, these social capabilities have been used to communicate and collaborate with external constituents such as partners and customers. By inviting them into the conversation around product innovation, companies like China Telecom have been able to deliver new and updated products to market faster and with less risk knowing that a market for the new product already existed.

Socially empowering your product development and innovation process enables you to have transparent knowledge sharing by tapping into employee knowledge and creativity across business divisions and time zones to enable an agile and dexterous organization. It enables you to gather more ideas from clients and partners using crowdsourcing and other techniques to deliver compelling offerings to market faster. And finally, a Social Business enables constant product improvement through frequent feedback. The ongoing and responsive conversations with trusted product advisors from top customers keep existing products out in front of the competition.

The sections that follow present two case studies of Social Businesses that have taken the bold step with their product development and innovation processes, both outside the United States: China Telecom and CEMEX.

CASE STUDY: CHINA TELECOM

For China Telecom, socially enabling their product development and innovation processes focused on extending knowledge and idea sharing externally to include customers and partners. And as a result, it brought products to market two times faster with the confidence that its target customers will purchase them (because the product idea came from the target group!).

This approach lowered the risk and the opportunity costs associated with bringing a product to market. Some highlights of social-enabling their development process include the fact that it allowed 554 new "voices" into the development process during the first six months of the platform launch, with the publication of the first idea a mere 10 minutes after launch. The service provider also enabled the organization to gather ideas directly from consumers' entries and launch new services with the proven knowledge that subscriber demand exists. It also reduced its risk by expanding sources for new product ideas.

CASE STUDY: CEMEX

CEMEX, a global industry leader in building materials based in Mexico, has grown through acquisition very quickly over the past couple decades. Within the past year, it became clear that it needed to bring the many worldwide divisions into closer communication and collaboration.

This was both a cultural and a process challenge for them. It launched a social networking platform called Project Shift that has more than 17,000 participating today, with more than 400 communities that have sprung up organically around the world. It has helped with a cultural change to make a big company operate as a small company. Given that the company was so big, the communities brought that entrepreneurial feel to the topics that they focused on. As such, the communities became mini "start-ups" around new, innovative ideas.

One community in particular has become a place where product ideas can be shared across the Atlantic, instantly leading to a better product delivered to both markets faster. This initiative, Project Shift, won the Forrester 2010 Groundswell Award for Best Collaboration System. The Forrester Groundswell Awards are very competitive, and require significant results to have been achieved in order to be named a winner.

The results so far include the following:

- Since January 2010, when Shift was released to a select group of power testers, and after its general release in April, it has gained more than 20,500 users, which represent more than 95% of the company's employees. Furthermore, we have seen exciting results. There are now more than 500 communities where employees can collaborate on topics ranging from everyday work, such as developing commercial practices and improving products, to strategic projects such as the Low Carbon Sustainable strategy for CEMEX.

- More than 700 blogs have been written around best practices and innovative thoughts.

- Nine new "game changing" ideas have been implemented. In fact, one of the communities was responsible for a new global brand in a key product line being delivered in less than 4 months, three times faster than the usual 12 months.

- 1,600 employees are collaborating on global communities to drive innovation, including process improvement, environmental practices, marketing, and product development. Product engineers, previously trapped in their geography silos, are able to share best practices across regions and markets—the engineer in Brazil, for instance, sharing and collaborating with a counterpart in Germany—helping them adapt local products to global markets.

Social Business Maturity

The maturity of your Social Business makes a difference in how you start your journey and how you invest. I work a lot with Altimeter Group. Altimeter Group is a research-based advisory firm that helps companies and industries leverage disruption to their advantage. Altimeter Group was formed in June 2008 by Charlene Li, a veteran technology and business analyst and co-author of the bestselling business book *Groundswell: Living in a World Transformed by Social Technologies*. In addition to Charlene, Jeremiah Owyang, a Partner at Altimeter, is a Social Business expert, well known in the industry.

Altimeter's 2011 report titled "How Corporations Should Prioritize Social Business Budgets" suggests a model for your investment based on your maturity level. A company needs to have a clear idea of where it is on the path to Social Business—whether its business is well-suited to social techniques and how mature its Social Business implementation is.

In Figure 5.5, you can see the results of Altimeter's survey of 140 global corporate social strategists.

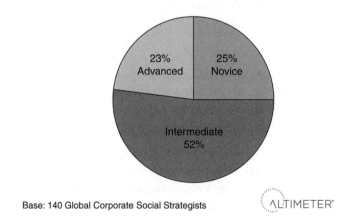

Maturity Level of Corporate Social Business Programs
in 2010 (Self-Assessed)

Base: 140 Global Corporate Social Strategists   ALTIMETER

Figure 5.5   Most corporations are at intermediate levels.

They rated themselves as being one of three stages of Social Business maturity: Novice, Intermediate, and Advanced. The majority of companies consider themselves intermediates in today's world in their pursuit of becoming a Social Business. The most interesting conclusion from the report is how companies progress in their organizational model in their pursuit based on that maturity (see Figure 5.6).

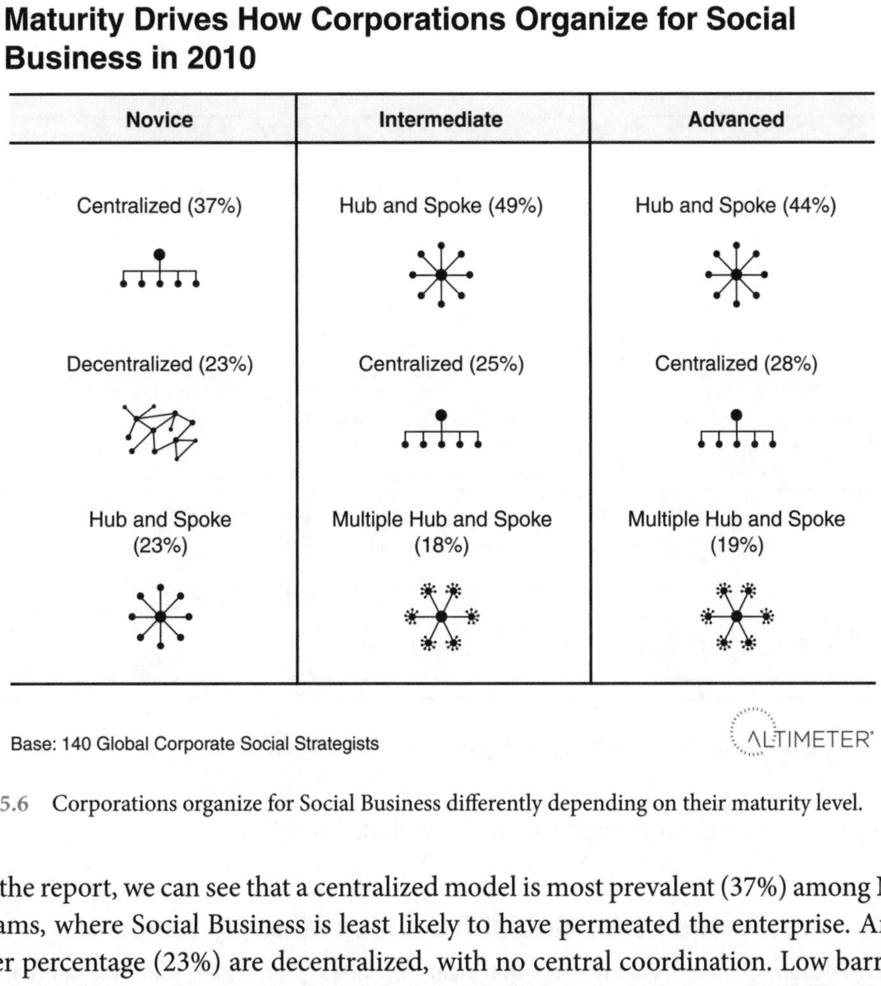

Maturity Drives How Corporations Organize for Social Business in 2010

Novice	Intermediate	Advanced
Centralized (37%)	Hub and Spoke (49%)	Hub and Spoke (44%)
Decentralized (23%)	Centralized (25%)	Centralized (28%)
Hub and Spoke (23%)	Multiple Hub and Spoke (18%)	Multiple Hub and Spoke (19%)

Base: 140 Global Corporate Social Strategists

ALTIMETER

Figure 5.6   Corporations organize for Social Business differently depending on their maturity level.

From the report, we can see that a centralized model is most prevalent (37%) among Novice programs, where Social Business is least likely to have permeated the enterprise. Another quarter percentage (23%) are decentralized, with no central coordination. Low barriers to entry mean that employees adopt social channels before the company formally organizes for Social Business. However, as demands in Social Business compound from customers and internal stakeholders, corporations reorganize and they need their programs to scale. Altimeter found that 67% of Intermediate and 63% of Advanced programs organize into hub and spoke or multiple hub and spoke—models that involve multiple departments and business units outside the corporate function. The shift toward these two models will continue as Social Business programs mature and corporations realize that they cannot manage increasing requests with either a centralized or decentralized model.

The conclusion is that corporations should gauge their own Social Business maturity and prioritize spending decisions. In Figure 5.7, you can see that novice programs must focus on getting their internal teams trained; intermediate programs must scale customer-facing initiatives; and advanced programs must integrate Social Business throughout the enterprise.

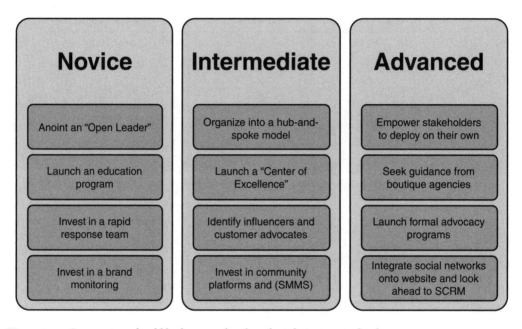

Figure 5.7   Corporations should budget spending based on their maturity level.

Thanks to Altimeter, a sample maturity test is included here!

Assess Your Social Business Maturity Level

For each section, choose the statement that best describes your Social Business program. Give yourself 1 point if you choose "1," 2 points if you choose "2," and 3 points if you choose "3." Add up your total score below to determine your Social Business maturity level.

A. Program

____1.   We are mostly experimenting with social media.

____2.   We've launched long-term initiatives that are part of an overall social strategy.

____3.   Social business permeates the enterprise—it has transcended the Marketing department, and impacts Product, Support, R & D, etc.

B. Leadership and Organizational Model

___1. We do not have a formalized social strategist role or organizational model.

___2. We've organized into a hub and spoke model with a formal social strategist role at the helm.

___3. We've evolved to a multiple hub and spoke or holistic model, and business units can deploy on their own with little guidance from the hub.

C. Processes and Policies

___1. We have not conducted internal audits or established processes or policies for governance.

___2. We've conducted internal audits and established processes and policies across the enterprise.

___3. We've created clear processes and workflow across cross-functional teams.

D. Education

___1. There is no formal education program to train internal associates.

___2. We've launched an education program but it's not rolled out to the entire company.

___3. We've formalized an ongoing education program that serves as a resource for all employees.

E. Measurement

___1. We've tied our social media efforts back to engagement metrics, such as number of clicks, fans, followers, RTs, and check-ins.

___2. We've tied our social media efforts back to social media analytics, such as share of voice, resonation, and word of mouth.

___3. We've tied our social media efforts back to business metrics, such as revenue, reputation, and CSAT.

F. Technology

___1. We've invested in brand monitoring to listen to and develop understanding of our customers.

___2. We've invested in scalable technologies such as community platforms or social media management systems (SMMS).

___3. We've invested in social integration with other digital touch points such as the corporate website, kiosks, and mobile devices, across the entire customer life cycle.

Total score ____

If you scored between 0 and 6 points, your program is at the Novice level.

If you scored between 7 and 12 points, your program is at the Intermediate level.

If you scored between 13-18 points, your program is at the Advanced level.

Your Social Business Maturity Level: _____

Conclusion

A Social Business turns its business processes on their side and ensures that the existing business process flow and the network of people responsible for each stage in the process are able to collaborate. In some cases, new business processes are created.

The power of the Social Business Agenda is in its bold, but systematic approach, with all your company's processes, but at a rate and pace that is acceptable for your risk level. Unlike social media that tends to hone in on marketing only, a Social Business expands its focus to include sales, customer service, product development, product innovation, human resources, and supply chain. The cultural transformations must support these key global processes as Jacques Bughin and Michael Chui, "The rise of the networked enterprise: Web 2.0 finds its payday," McKinsey Quarterly, www.mckinseyquarterly.com (December, 2010), showed us that there is a powerful ROI for this focus:

- 30% increase in speed to knowledge and experts from a focus on HR
- 15% increase in revenue from a focus on Sales and Marketing
- 20% increase in time-to-market and successful innovations from a focus on product innovation

Empowering your processes with social techniques like networking will enable the needed transformation. Multiple disciplines and departments will benefit, and the assembly or adaptation of infrastructure is required to streamline and manage social workflow.

Each of the processes of focus—whether it is human resources, marketing, customer service, product development and innovation, or supply chain—will require a wider scope of active listening and participation across the full spectrum of influence. The recognition that this is people-led, not technology-led, will help to guide each of your processes. Your maturity will impact your starting point, your organizational model, and even your focus.

The next chapter explores how to design for both reputation and risk management.

Design for Reputation and Risk Management

"Your online reputation is your Social Business Currency. Manage it well."

Sandy Carter

"What happens in Vegas might stay in Vegas, but odds are there's footage."

Unknown

Reputation and Risk Management

As I began my research into reputation and risk management, I found many organizations that experienced some sort of crisis in the blogosphere while trying to protect their online reputation. For example, United Airlines had to deal with a crisis with David Carroll's Taylor guitar, which was broken during a flight he took. Because he felt he had not been treated well, he wrote a song about what United had done, and posted it to YouTube (www.youtube.com/watch?v=5YGc4zOqozo). At press time, there were more than 10 million viewings. Taylor Guitars also produced a YouTube video with 500,000 viewings offering support to David, and offering tips to those traveling with Taylor guitars. By the time United did come back and offer to reimburse David, he asked for United to give the money to charity. United Airlines stock plummeted 10%, costing shareholders $180 million dollars, for a $1,200 claim on a guitar! And United isn't the only company faced with these challenges. Consider a few others:

- Dell's support was attacked online with a lead blogger calling it "Dell Hell." Dell handled the situation well, and in fact, listened and created a great solution called IdeaStorm.

- AT&T's poor service for iPhones caused the FCC to step in on a plan from one disgruntled tweeter to shut down AT&T's network.

- Energizer's Night Race 2011, held in Sepang International Circuit, Malaysia, was not well organized. Although the race was only sponsored by Energizer, when negative comments on Facebook appeared, Energizer's brand took a hit by not responding quickly and apologetically, and an alternate site, Boycott Energizer Night Race, took a very aggressive stance against Energizer.

- Honda promoted its Facebook page, seeking input on its new Accord Crosstour design. Most people were critical of the design, although on Facebook a fan seemed to like it, writing *"Interesting design, I would get this car in a heartbeat."* It was later found out that the "fan" was the product planner for the Crosstour. Even though Honda issued an apology, the media did write about the story and of Honda's lack of transparency.

I strongly believe that every Social Business needs to expect the best, but plan for the worst. Planning for your reputation online is a relatively new concept. People have been focused on reputation management offline for a while, but only recently has this focus included the online world. In fact, I discussed this concept with many Fortune 100 HR directors, and they are now hiring many more reputation managers versus risk managers into their companies! A risk manager focuses on what to do when something goes wrong. A reputation manager focuses on protecting the brand, product, or company in a proactive stance.

What is reputation management? It is ensuring that a company knows what is being said about it, building it up through positive actions and having a way to address the negative comments online, and sooner rather than later. Reputation is what others believe to be true about your company, product, or brand. Reputation management is being able to appropriately shape that reputation by

- Listening to know what others think about you
- Countering negative opinions
- Building positive opinions through actions

Much has been said regarding the proliferation of social comments. With so many social tools and such wide scope and content, it is available to everyone and is extremely impactive. What is even worse is that the Internet does not have the same authoritative standards as do traditional media. For example, a newspaper and news channel will often check their facts and do some investigative study before going public. In the blogosphere, you can't count on that level of investigation, and thus it can be difficult to understand whether information is valid or just one person's biased opinion.

But what's different from the media explosion of television and radio some 50 years ago is both the sheer volume, speed, and influence. About 770 million people have visited a social networking site, according to comScore. (comScore is an Internet marketing research company providing marketing data and services to many of the Internet's largest businesses. comScore tracks all Internet data on its surveyed computers in order to study online behavior.) According to Forrester Research, four out of five online U.S. adults use social media in some capacity (source: "Benchmarking Social Marketing Plans For 2011," by Sean Corcoran with Emily Riley, Angie Polanco, October 14, 2010). Furthermore, according to the GlobalWebIndex, over 70% of those in the U.K. leverage social media. It is this power of influence and massive distribution that make social such a potent force in influencing consumer perceptions. In fact, 78% of consumers trust their peer's recommendations—whether good or bad.

It is this volume of content, distribution, and influence that is reshaping how Social Businesses manage their reputation and manage risk that might occur in their relationship to brands, products, services, and issues of the day.

I recently read the "Elements of Reputation" by Arlo Brady. Based on his research, reputation is built from the following:

1. **Knowledge and skills:** A company is only as good as its employees, who are the major determinant of current and future success.

2. **Emotional connections:** Consumers attach emotions to services and products; without this emotional connection many companies would be alike.

3. **Leadership, vision, and desire:** Stakeholders attach a high value to companies that are perceived to be led by a group of people who have vision and desire.

4. **Quality:** This concerns product or service quality, that is, whether a company is seen to be meeting customers' requirements, not just once but consistently.

5. **Financial credibility:** This is the traditional means by which a company's performance is judged. To build credibility, the company should have a strong historical and contemporary record for generating better-than-average returns for shareholders.

6. **Role of the company in the society and community:** People care that you care about bigger things than just profit—that you value helping people.

7. **Environmental credibility:** Given the green movement, companies that focus on the environment tend to have better reputations as citizens value the planet. A Smarter Planet by IBM demonstrated our focus on the planet as much as profit.

These seven items provide a guide for what to watch carefully. Reputation must be managed closely in order to decrease the potential for elements that downgrade the reputation. In fact, if you think about Chapter 5, "(Social) Network Your Business Processes," many of these seven reputation earners are inherent as you socially enable your internal processes. For example, facilitating sharing of talent and subject matter expertise by socially enabling your HR process can impact your knowledge and skills.

Any of the aforementioned seven elements could come under attack at any time, however. In fact, the number one question that I get asked from the C suite is about the "risk" of being so public online. The risk exists even if your company is not proactive online, because clients, influencers, and competitors can write about your company at any time. That is why, despite these risks, IBM's Chief Marketing Officer, Jon Iwata, said the rewards outweigh the risks:

> "We discovered that the risks of *not* encouraging employees to engage in social media and the risks of *not* providing them with the tools and education they need greatly outweigh the risks [of trained participation]. Our assessment has provided

even more evidence that encouraging employees to engage in social media is critical to our future success as a business."

How do you manage risk in the social world? The primary elements in managing risk associated with your reputation are first in knowing you have an issue, and then in addressing it in a speedy and transparent fashion with the right people. This chapter outlines best practices to protect your online reputation and manage the risk associated with the blogosphere.

The rewards of becoming a Social Business far outweigh the risk, however, but not without careful planning and management. In fact, to me, the bigger risk is that your company will create an online presence and no one will come! As with any relationship, it takes work to make it strong. The sections that follow explore how to plan for recovery, while outlining the great rewards that come with a Social Business.

Managing Your Reputation with a "Plan" to Reduce Risk

The goal of your Reputation and Risk Management Plan is to avoid the need for a recovery, but to be ready in case one happens. The following simple 1-2-3 steps can prepare you for the worst but ensure that you are growing and building your online reputation as well:

1. Listen.
2. Create your brand army.
3. Create a response plan.

1. Listen: Do You Know There Is an Issue?

In C. S. Lewis's book *The Lion, the Witch and the Wardrobe,* the light of a lonely lamppost in the forest guides Lucy through the wardrobe into the fantasy world of Narnia. In Social Business, listening acts as a guide, through the vast magical and interesting world of the blogosphere. Listening is about monitoring what is being written (or said or videoed!) about your company, brand, or product. It can even include the category that your product is in, for instance, sports drinks or IT companies.

Listening is mandatory for building your reputation, not just when things go wrong but for understanding about your reputation drivers as well. Listening well can help you avoid any social business disaster from occurring.

The value of proactive listening is that it also assists you in understanding your prospects, clients, and, of course, competitors. It leads to action and awareness of conversations that will compel your company to respond. Because your URL isn't just your website anymore, but everywhere you are on the Web, listening is important to your digital presence. You are building a brand through images and text, and your head is on the "guillotine" everyday if you just rest and don't stay totally tuned in a systemic approach. Business, corporation-related and societal events, and basically everything are simply interconnected and need simultaneous dedicated listening.

There is too much information being processed online for you to listen manually. I would advise you to explore the automated tools that exist. There are many free tools as well as tools for purchase that can help you gather all the data being said on your product, brand, and team.

A tip here is to determine your keywords that are relative to your business. Keywords are those words that are associated with your listening focus. It would be your company, product, or brand. It might include your category, like *ketchup,* as opposed to listening for just *Heinz.* These are words that are key to your success in the marketplace. For example, if you are in the wireless telecommunications industry, those keywords are *dropped calls, 3g, mobile apps, smartphone, data plan,* and so forth. Keywords should reflect what is important to your business. One tool to assist you in the determination of those keywords is Google Keyword Tool. If you type in a term, it shows you the other terms that people are using when they are also searching for your term. For instance, if I type in *Sandra Carter,* it suggests "Sandy Carter." If I type in *SOA,* the Google Keyword Tool shows "flexible architecture."

Another free tool I use is called TweetDeck. I use it to select keywords on brand or category and see all the mentions of that word in any Tweet. It is still a somewhat manual process, but it does provide you a way to listen and respond. You can also use HootSuite, and I know that Twitter itself is trying to make its environment friendlier for searching and listening to these keywords. If you are looking for more sophisticated ways to listen, tools such as IBM's Cognos® Consumer Insight enable you to listen and see sentiment through an automated collection of Social Business and powerful analytics.

Some of the tools in this growing space include these:

- **IBM Cognos Consumer Insight:** A tool to analyze consumer sentiment on publicly available social media sites—blogs, forums, and discussion groups. You can find more information about this tool at www-01.ibm.com/software/analytics/cognos/ analytic-applications/consumer-insight/.

- **Social Mention:** Provides free daily email alerts of your brand, company, CEO, or marketing campaign, or on a developing news story, a competitor, or the latest on a celebrity. You can find more information about this tool at www.socialmention.com/.

- **TweetEffect:** Helps you find out which of your Twitter updates made people follow or leave you. You can find more information about this tool at www.tweeteffect.com.

- **Converseon:** A social media listening agency that listens "for you." This listening is one of the many types that we at IBM leverage. You can find more information about Converseon at www.converseon.com.

- **Spiral16:** Software tool set that provides a fresh approach to social media monitoring based on organization, accuracy, visualization, and analysis. You can find more information about this tool at www.spiral16.com.

- **Google Alerts:** Provides batch or streaming updates of the latest relevant Google results (Web, news, etc.) based on your choice of keywords or topics. You can find more information about this tool at www.google.com/alerts.

- **Insights:** A search tool for Facebook walls to help you identify the traffic around a set of keywords and phrases. You can find more information about this tool at https://developers.facebook.com/docs/insights.

- **TweetDeck:** A free tool that enables you to monitor keywords on your category or brand. You can find more information about this tool at www.tweetdeck.com.

- **HootSuite:** A free tool that enables you to monitor keywords on your category or brand. You can find more information about this tool at http://hootsuite.com/.

- **Samepoint:** A tracker of conversations throughout social media sites. User-generated discussions are typically not indexed by major search engines, such as Google, because they do not reside on static pages. Samepoint.com converts these discussions into web pages, or permalinks, and organizes them within a tag cloud. You can find more information about this tool at www.samepoint.com/.

- **Follower Wonk:** A Twitter application that creates Venn diagrams showing the overlap among followers of up to three different Twitter accounts. You can find more information about this tool at http://followerwonk.com.

- **Alexa.com/siteinfo:** A site that enables you to measure the ranking of your website with the Alexa scoring. You can find more information about this tool at www.alexa.com/siteinfo.

What you want to listen for are items that you have deemed helpful for you to improve your brand or product, as well as negative comments that might be untrue or biased. If you can determine the topics that are important to your business and identify them as potential keywords, those are the words you should search for. Over time, refinement of your listening will enable you to search for new keywords, noting keyword trends.

Some of the things you want to listen for include comments to improve your product, your company, or new trends on the horizon. The way you share the information that you learn from listening will also be a key to your success. Listening is about professional development. Everyone inside of your company should be familiar with what is going on in the marketplace daily. Knowing what is going on makes employees better at their jobs.

Some things that could cause a red alert include employee misuse of the tools, or issues that need to be handled right away, such as quality or safety issues. Of course, complaints and concerns should be explored. Some might require a response and some might not.

Things that I look for include the following:

- **Brandjacking:** Brand hijacking happens when consumers appropriate the brand for themselves and add meaning to it. For instance, one of our Senior Leaders at IBM found that someone was impersonating him on Twitter.
- **Employee or contractor/supplier/agency misuse:** For instance, Chrysler fired their social media agency after they used a Twitter f-bomb.
- **Quality and safety issues:** Think about United's quality issue in handling baggage.
- **Activist protest wave:** Nestlé saw a negative Twitter tsunami when a Forest Activist, one week before the U.S. Easter holiday, put up videos about the supposed destruction of forests by Nestlé. There were more than 1.2 million negative YouTube videos, and 95,000 Facebook fans who saw the negative messages.
- **Trade secrets being shared:** Sharing confidential information is a big issue and is why one of IBM's Social Business guidelines is to not share this type of information.
- **Criminal activity:** Anything that is illegal needs to be immediately addressed.
- **Foul and abusive language:** The previous example of Chrysler illustrates this point.
- **Threats against individuals:** At no time should an individual be targeted. In the David Carroll video about United, he later apologized for calling out one employee by name.

The important element in this first step is to ensure that you know what is happening around your company and brand. To build your reputation, improve it, or avert a crisis, you must understand what is being said, who is saying it, where it is being said, and how impactive it could be. If your PR team or newspaper is telling you about it, it is probably too late. The following list shows the keys to planning for proactive listening:

1. Create search words applicable to your Social Business.

2. Select one or more tools for listening.

3. Train on what to listen for.

Chapter 7, "Analyze Your Data," covers more in-depth ways to listen.

2. Create Your Brand Army

Maggie Fox, CEO and founder of Social Media Group, coined the term "brand army." A brand army is a group of unpaid and paid advocates (that is, your employees!) who engage on behalf of your brand. Your brand army consists of your employees, management, and C suite, and your "friends." Remember that the C suite does not have to be the CEO, but could be a leader in a division or someone influential.

This brand army for your company needs to stay at the forefront of all your brand's news, connections, and actions. In essence, they shape your brand online. They need to embrace transparency while they engage and exchange information with your clients, friends, and fans. They need to be "in the know" and be responsive. Patrick Vogt, writer for Forbes.com, made a great comment on the value they can bring if viewed from a long-term perspective:

> "Topics that do surface have tremendous value for a learning organization, and must be cataloged and reviewed by senior management on a regular basis."

Take the team seriously. You wouldn't put interns in charge of investor relations, so don't put them in charge of your online response! Also, always ensure that legal is part of your brand army. Legal needs to be a full partner in the team.

Your team needs to be in the know—they need to have the information in order to be effective. At IBM, I have my top brand advocates on my brand army, and I communicate to them via private email or more often through phone calls because of the urgency sometimes on the subject so that they have the latest information and can help me shape it. My brand advocates are typically tippers in the area on which I am focused. The number is not important, but what is important is that this is a group of people who love your company, brand, or product and are willing to take a stand because of that passion. This communication needs to occur on a regular basis and especially in times of crisis. Although it seems simple, many companies forget to share this valued information while in the midst of a potential challenge.

This team needs a content activation strategy both for overall reputation management and during a crisis. A content activation strategy is a plan for how content is created, distributed, promoted, and measured. For instance, when your company has a new product announcement, who creates the package of information to share with your top bloggers? In fact, this concept is becoming so important that there is a new role being created, the Chief Content Officer. (Note: LinkedIn has a group just for this new role, at http://www.linkedin. com/groups?home=&gid=2921919&trk=anet_ug_hm !.)

In a noncrisis, making sure that the right content is in the right hands is very important. Things like the following would be important to share:

Quick Cheat Sheet:

Twitter Handle (ID) is: @xxx

Official Twitter Hashtag: #xxx

Shortened URL for the Best Site for Information: xxx

Hot Topics This Week:

Additional recommendations to drive the dialogue: deep content

Learn more and spread the word! Educational topics

Most FAQs:

Question 1:

Question 2:

Suggestions on Communities to Join:

Subscribe to xxx

In the midst of a crisis, sometimes the people who should be creating and distributing content are consumed in putting out the fire. This is too important to miss. A Social Business will often establish a shared services model with a Social Business Reputation and Risk Manager. The role of this individual is to own the responsibility for listening and then filtering information to the correct departments inside the organization. For example, the Social Business Reputation and Risk Manager might pick up a negative sentiment around supporting a product. It is not his or her responsibility to respond, but instead his or her responsibility to notify the appropriate brand army (customer support and advocacy) to handle that situation. The task of making sure you have built the relationships and trust with your brand army includes arming them with strong content.

Finally, I discussed the importance of employee training in Chapter 2, "Align Organizational Goals and Culture." This element is essential in the midst of a crisis. Your first steps should be a Social Business Guideline document and training. Take, for instance, super-market chain Price Chopper. When a client complained in a tweet about the supermarket, the supermarket's public relations team went to the tweeter's employer and asked for disci-plinary action to be taken. (How did they find out his employer? They went to the client's Twitter id and determined his employer from his profile.) It turns out that the customer's friend is a top blogger, and he blogged about the incident, with lots of comments on the situation, and how it was handled (http://pricechopperfail.tumblr.com/post/1156969465/price-chopper-attacks-customers-job-over-negative-tweet). Needless to say, all employees should be trained on how to respond to negative comments.

The following list articulates the key items for your planning with your brand army:

1. Determine your brand army, including brand advocates, legal, executives, subject matter experts, and others critical to your success.

2. Define the roles of Digital Council, Social Business Reputation and Risk Manager, Executive Team, and Brand Advocates.

3. Plan for your "alert system," whether red/yellow/green or number-based.

4. Refine your content activation strategy before, during, and after a crisis.

5. Train everyone.

3. Create a Response Plan

The response plan should be created ahead of any challenge or crisis. It consists of a few items. Think through the following:

- Who flags an issue? To whom does the issue get flagged? PR? Analyst Relations? Legal?

- When should action be taken and who takes the action? Sometimes, communications isn't the way to solve. A rating system helps here. The worse the situation, the higher the response should come!

- Which tool(s) should be used to respond?

- What should the content and overall tone be in the response?

- How do you treat comments? In my opinion, you should treat all social comments as if you were talking to clients, stakeholders, investors, and competitors, because you are!

Who?

The first thing your response plan needs to focus on is clear roles on who will flag when a response is required. Usually the Social Business Reputation and Risk Manager will be the one responsible for this action based on an analytics system (see Chapter 7). This person should be trained and empowered to do this important work. Also, make sure your brand army understands the plan and protocol. Basically, the job description for the Social Business Reputation and Risk Manager is to listen, determine the response and who should respond, contribute to the content activation strategy, and arm the brand army with the facts.

When?

Next, develop a rating system for items that need to be addressed and those will be communicated in an official capacity to the overall team—including your Digital Council. This again should be led by your Social Business Reputation and Risk Manager. That manager should know the Terms of Service for each social tool. For example, YouTube, Twitter, and Facebook all have their own guidelines on unacceptable conduct. I personally contacted YouTube, for instance, when someone commented on a video that violated YouTube's guidelines for posted comments. They took care of the situation right away for me.

I recommend establishing an internal set of terms of service, perhaps in a red or yellow rating on items that you monitor. A great best practice is having a dashboard on these for C suite and for the Social Business Reputation and Risk Manager.

A red rating is one that is a concern to your company—and this does vary by company. Typically, a top executive would address a red-rated item, and given that response time is paramount, plan ahead for which executives are the key communicators. A red-rated item might be a security breach or a tragic product-quality issue. But also know when to take a conversation offline. Sometimes it is best to do a face-to-face or phone call.

A yellow-rated item is a cautionary item of interest. Some of these might be answered and addressed by your community. Again, each company has its own tolerance level. An example of a yellow-rated item would be several comments on a product feature someone doesn't like, or a customer service issue.

Of course, there will be comments in the blogosphere that you will not respond to. Examples would include a client comparing your brand (maybe unfavorably) to another brand, or a minor negative comment on your product. Think through the criteria for those as well.

Make sure you allow for a dialogue. You will need an FAQ wiki so that the details and questions plus your responses are given to the brand army. Don't worry if you don't know the answers to all the questions. As the information becomes available, you will be able to fill in the blanks. But do not publish an external FAQ without the ability to comment and allow for discussion. Use your blog, your Facebook fan page, or your community site to invite discussion.

Which Tools?

Your choice of response tool will be important, too. In some cases, I have seen an issue in Twitter and the company responds on their website. This does not work. As the saying goes, "fight [social] fire with [social] fire," meaning that if the comment was made on Twitter, refute the comment on Twitter. It is critical that you address the issue where the crisis broke out. So if the comment was made on YouTube, address it on YouTube; if it was made on Twitter, then go for Twitter.

What?

Of course the content that you respond with makes a difference. Do your research and make sure you release data in real time even though you might not have all the information complete. If you made a mistake, then apologize. In every relationship an apology opens the door to conversation. Make sure you discuss why the issue happened and what you are doing about it. For example, did you appoint the wrong type of person for handling a complaint, or did you not have the right guidelines in place? Ask your community for their thoughts if appropriate.

How?

Your action should be quick, personal, and direct. Using the internal terms of service will help you decide how. With red ratings that require action from a senior executive, often the appropriate channel for a response is not from any one person, but from the company through an a blog, an online release, or an announcement on your company's website, Facebook page, or Twitter channel. The yellow-rated items probably do not need to go through the same level of review as the red items, and thus a response could be directly from an individual.

At the end, use this opportunity to reflect on what happened. How does this impact the longer term? Collect those issues that are indicative of a larger trend. The list that follows outlines the key items for your response planning:

1. Speed: Get your Digital Council together.
2. Classify into type of issue.
3. Clarify who responds to which issues.
4. Communicate to your "brand army."
5. Activate the plan by updating blogs, tweets, etc.
6. Create a feedback loop for learning.

Learn from Great Examples

As I discussed upfront, there are a lot of examples to learn from, to learn how companies managed through their crises and how some avoided them. The following case studies demonstrate the best of what to do and what not to do! However, please note that the biggest idea to take away is that nothing in this chapter can make up for bad customer service, or a bad product, or—the list goes on. People use the social tools to vent, but having the right product or right customer service processes in place is the real area to address if your company experiences a social disaster. As discussed in Chapter 5, make sure your company is looking at your organization as a whole, and that your culture is willing to be open and transparent. Having the right culture, product, and process is the best way to avoid a disaster!

Richard Branson, CEO and founder of Virgin Atlantic, said in a London keynote,

"Get the product right, put a great brand on it, and then you'll have a great success."

Today, in the blogosphere, they listen and respond to every client comment, whether it is about delayed flights, service treatment, or ideas on their great Twitter offers. They have mastered the art of teaming and engagement both online and offline. But this was not always the case. In 2008, employees on social networks wrote about safety issues. Virgin did the same thing most companies did at that time—found the employees, reprimanded them, and pulled down the comments. Today, they fix those issues that are real, and ensure that the public knows about the actions that they've taken.

CASE STUDY: DOMINO'S PIZZA DEMONSTRATES BOTH "WHAT NOT TO DO" AND HOW TO EXCEL

It all started in North Carolina at a local Domino's pizza location. Employees decided to post YouTube videos of themselves engaging in the unsanitary acts of putting cheese up their noses and sneezing on sandwiches. Millions of people watched the video until it was blocked.

The response from Domino's was slow and done poorly. Forty-eight hours after the video was posted, their president was shown on YouTube with a heavily scripted response. Not quick, personal, or direct. The results showcased this poor response plan. Financially, the stock price dropped 10% the week the video was released. A follow-up study by HCD Research found that 65% of clients (meaning they had previously ordered from Domino's) were now less likely to visit Domino's again. This social incident caused damage to Domino's 50-year-old reputation.

The failures? They didn't see the video until too late, and that caused them to respond too slowly. In addition, they didn't respond transparently. In the end, Domino's reflected on what happened and made changes as they applied social learning. They are an outstanding social company today because they learned (as many of us did) from this incident.

Why do I say outstanding? Today, they have a listening strategy and monitoring plan across Twitter and Facebook. Based on what people are saying, they respond consistently. For instance, during football season, someone complained about the time it took to get a Domino's pizza delivered, so a local Chicago franchisee gave the client a free ticket to the next Chicago football game. Another person had an issue with one of the pizzas they had ordered, so the general manager of the franchise went down to the store and did a video apology. The video went viral around the world and Domino's had a client for life!

And they have innovative ways to get their clients to become brand advocates. For instance, on the menu that is on the pizza box, they locally print their favorite top-10 tweets from local clients each month. Their clients like to see their tweets come into their homes and those of their neighbors! They are innovative in their use of social tools as well. They are leveraging Foursquare, a location-based service covered in Chapter 4, "Engage Through Experiences," and really treat their "mayors" with care. Overall, their plan is a phenomenal combination of global advice and best practices executed in a local fashion. Ramon DeLeon, the managing partner of six Domino's franchises in Chicago, framed it for me:

"Our social strategy is measured on three things: revenue, profit, and fun. And it delivers!"

But their next challenge is upon them! In the second quarter of 2011, they kicked off a campaign with a Twitter hashtag #DPZChicken, asking their clients to comment on their new chicken product. About half of the tweets so far are negative—for instance, "never again...not impressed!" and "still taste the same to me, horrible." Domino's has already responded, thanking the clients for their feedback and articulating how they are going to fix the chicken, but the verdict is out on the change. To their credit, they wanted open and transparent feedback, and responded in the right way when they received it, and they did so quickly. Let's follow their continuing story!

CASE STUDY: FORD MOTOR COMPANY DEMONSTRATES SPEED

Scott Monty, a Ford Motor Company Social Business manager, is a great example of averting a social disaster by listening, and being alert and ready. He consistently listens to Ford activity on Twitter, blogs, and forums, as well as other social tools. When Ford attorneys sent letters of "cease and desist" to users who had altered the Ford logo, he acted quickly and in a personal and direct manner. Everyone could read his tweets, knowing he was on their side: "I'm in active discussions with our legal dept. about resolving it. Pls retweet #ford."

Scott eventually got this issue resolved. It was not an easy task, given that those angry with Ford were also part of his "brand advocates" group. But the quick and direct action diverted a disaster.

What did Ford do right? It had the right listener to know what others thought about this new move, namely Scott. Within 24 hours, Scott countered the comments and built trust and positive responses through the actions that he took. And Ford was flexible in its busines process. It changed!

CASE STUDY: AMAZON.COM FALTERS BY NOT LISTENING

On Amazon.com, an attack group removed all books from Amazon.com written by gay, lesbian, bisexual, and transgender authors. Many people, especially activists, were angry and upset and of course expressed it loudly on Twitter, on Facebook, and in numerous forums. Amazon.com moved slowly to respond because they didn't listen proactively. Therefore, the community assumed that they had removed the content on purpose. This social war continued longer than it should have due to their lack of listening.

CASE STUDY: KENNETH COLE PROVOKES A PUBLIC UPRISING

Designer Kenneth Cole attempted to take advantage of the Egyptian uprising in 2011 to sell his spring collection of clothing. His tweet:

> "Millions are in uproar in #Cairo. Rumor is they heard our spring collection is now available online at http://bit.ly/KCairo - KC."

Within one hour, there were more than 1,500 negative tweets.

Kenneth Cole did delete his first tweet and posted on his Facebook page the following:

> "I apologize to everyone who was offended by my insensitive tweet about the situation in Egypt. I've dedicated my life to raising awareness about serious social issues, and in hindsight my attempt at humor regarding a nation liberating themselves against oppression was poorly timed and absolutely inappropriate."

What went wrong here? This company was trying to use the situation for their own good, not for the good of the brand advocates and clients. This strategy does not work well in the blogosphere. In addition, Kenneth took too long to retract and apologize. Forty-eight hours is just too long. Also, all employees should go to training—including top executives!

Conclusion

The Social Business AGENDA means planning for the worst and expecting the best. Social reputation management is a relatively new concept focusing on people's actions online and converting those negatives into positive articles, blogs, or news stories. Your reputation can sway public opinion positively or negatively, which ultimately will have an impact on the success of any business in which you are involved. Risk management is about planning for those negative moments and being ready to execute. When a crisis brews, the social world dictates the amount of time you have for reaction. It is the worst time to try to develop a plan from scratch. A strong focus from your Digital Council will enable you to have an integrated strategy to get through the crisis, and ideally avoid it. Common patterns and learning from any crisis are valuable for a Social Business and should be reviewed by the C suite on a regular basis.

An action sheet for reputation and risk management is available as a bonus at www.ibm-pressbooks.com/title/9780132618311. Create an account and register your book to gain access. (After you register your book, a link to the additional content will be listed on your Account page, under Registered Products.)

CHAPTER

7

Analyze Your Data

"Social analytics are, in fact, the new black."

Sandy Carter

"No matter how far you have gone on the wrong road, turn back."

Turkish Proverb

ROE: Return on Everything

Every Social Business measures the impact of actions on its results. The process of measuring could be simple or more complex. Today, however, the bottom line for everyone seems to be ROE—return on everything, including social techniques. Because an organization becomes a "Social Business" by empowering all stakeholders in the use of social tools, measuring the result of this empowerment is crucial to showcase competitive advantage.

But how does social work produce value for the business? Efforts to measure actions must go far enough that your company assesses the impact of the actions on the business; anything less is not worth the effort/resources to measure. Your company needs a process and discipline to show there is translation into business results.

Social media has added a degree of complexity into the mix. While you can now measure more things than before, tracking the return of the action has grown more complex. What do you measure? Is it followers or clicks? Is a celebrity's tweet really worth $25,000 for your brand? (At press time, Kim Kardashian was charging $25,000 for her to tweet about a brand!) How do you measure the value of those community members who talk positively about your product? How do you measure soft and hard ROI?

What complicates measuring even more is how you measure incremental gains. Traditionally, companies like hard-dollar savings, or ROI. For example, a web conference can reduce travel costs; or VoIP phones could reduce the expense for desktop phones. With social media, there can be hard ROI. For example, YouTube videos could reduce marketing costs for traditional print advertising. More often, we see a soft ROI that is tougher to measure as social media gets embedded into an existing business process. For example, it is tough to measure the business impact of co-editing documents using a wiki versus emailing attachments around. Using a wiki will likely save you time, but that time savings is difficult for many organizations to accept as hard ROI. The preceding examples are all examples of bottom-line cost savings. When it comes to Social Business as well, much of the ROI will come from top-line revenue upside—for example, the additional revenue from digital coupon click-throughs that are shared through social media techniques.

Aside from tracking, the debate for which measurement methodology to use in today's new social world is even more contentious. Everyone values different things, and that value varies by region. Some regions value the "eyeballs" (or your reach) and some value the impact on ratings (or how your clients rate your product). Whatever you measure, it typically needs to translate into how your company will make more money or how they can save money by working more efficiently. In the next few years, I believe that the sophistication of tools and technology will improve greatly. The relationships of actions to results will become more clear and measurable.

I will share in this chapter the basics of why measuring is important, and provide some simple and more complex metrics for you to review in light of your goals. Analytics applied to the data provide insight into your business and enable you to know what's working and what's not.

First, I'll start out with covering the potential of analytics and then move into some of the types of metrics and tools that are available to assist you in that journey. Then I'll recommend some actions such as creation of a dashboard, a center of excellence, and even a new role in your organization. Again, as a Social Business, choose what fits your goals and culture.

Business Analytics and Social Analytics

Business analytics is the discipline of turning data into insight, and using those insights to drive better business decisions. This process helps to answer the questions of how you are doing, why you are doing well or poorly, what would happen if you changed, and what you should be doing to be more competitive. The output of using analytics is to do the following:

- Enable an evolving workforce to become savvy in making decisions from data
- Expand perspective on the business for a more complete view
- Facilitate collaboration about the information to fuel insight and alignment
- Respond to the growing need for insight to make the right decisions

Now let's add into the picture the concept of social analytics, a subset of business analytics that focuses on the insight gleaned from the social techniques and tools that exist. Social analytics quantifies the role that social initiatives play in influencing engagement, behaviors, and conversions. There was a discussion on Facebook which included IBM, Altimeter, and others on "What Is Social Analytics?" and I like the crowdsourced definition of social analytics. Social analytics is the process of measuring, analyzing, and interpreting a brand's level of engagement, influence, sentiment, and share of voice (mindshare) across earned, paid, and owned digital channels within context of specific business goals and objectives:

- **Earned** is media, content, and channels that are delivered through a third party without exchange of payment. For example, in the traditional world it would be things like public relations generated news, and analyst coverage. In the digital channel, it would be things like tweets, blogs, and product recommendations.
- **Paid** is delivered through a third party or an intermediary in exchange for payment. For example, in the traditional world, it would be things like TV, radio, or print ads. In the digital world, it would be things like sponsored content or display ads.

- **Owned** is media, content, and channels that the company directly delivers, has control over, or owns. For example, in the traditional world it would be things like direct mail, call center, a branch or store, or an ATM or a kiosk. In the digital world, it would be things like a blog, a Facebook page, a community, or a microsite.

The bottom line is that social analytics is a discipline that helps businesses measure and explain the performance of social initiatives in the context of their goals and objectives.

To analyze social data, you must have the ability to tie into broader business metrics and key performance indicators (KPIs) to truly understand the impact. For example, if your broader business metric is improvement in customer satisfaction, then showcasing that your customer satisfaction, through Twitter as a service channel, is improving supports the overall business goal. Social Businesses have the ability to bring together not only the historical perspective but future perspectives based on predictive trends. By drawing actionable conclusions from the information, a Social Business is nimble. For example, the insight could enable a company to come out with a new product due to the data showing a new trend in the market.

Actionable means that you can incorporate the new insight into how you message consumers, perhaps over social media itself, or how to affect employee sentiment to retain your top talent. Strong analysis allows an understanding of the market impact, and assists in making strategic decisions on where to place resources and budget. With internal social techniques, analysis enables your company to gauge how your business is functioning and identify processes that could be improved.

Social analytics can provide an increased aperture of a consumer, a business, or an employee and provides the ability to see new patterns and opportunities. Some examples of leveraging effective social analytics are to do the following:

- Determine target buyers for your products
- Understand future trends and impacts on new products
- Help you understand your customer needs to target new offers and products more cost-effectively—to allow you to grow your business
- Help you make messaging decisions to enhance your reputation among your customers and constituencies
- Strengthen brand preference and loyalty by targeting the right influencers and messages
- Enable you to respond more quickly to customer requests to improve service-level effectiveness to improve customer care

- Understand employees' sentiments by leveraging social networks and forums to augment the existing employee satisfaction and feedback surveys

- Explore changes for employee retention

- Understand how to onboard employees more effectively

- Help you facilitate targeted innovation sessions on new product ideas in specific segments

- Enable you to respond more quickly to top talent employees' need for satisfaction

Finally, a Social Business must leverage this information to drive your business's speed in driving the right decisions and actions. What makes a company stand out from its competition is the ability to use analytics across the end-to-end business model. I'd like to introduce the following four-point strategic plan as part of the bold Social Business AGENDA:

1. Match what you measure to your goals and maturity.

2. Provide easy-to-use reporting and querying.

3. Provide advanced analytics and dashboards for sentiment, affinity relationships, and evolving topics.

4. Create a Social Analytics Center of Excellence. The Center of Excellence will focus on the following:

   a) A dashboard with real-time alerts, notifications, and activity streams to identify critical updates and attention management. This dashboard should include predictive analysis as well.

   b) A Social Analytics Manager who will focus on the digital forms of information for insight (this person complements your Business Intelligence team).

   c) Process sharing and best practice collection.

Match What You Measure to Your Goals and Maturity

Ensuring that what you analyze is aligned to your Social Business goals (discussed in Chapter 2, "Align Organizational Goals and Culture") is crucial. An example is shown in Table 7.1; based on your overall objectives, the areas of metrics will support progress in reaching those goals. The saying, "You get what you measure," is so true. So make sure that your metrics support the business goals that you have set!

Table 7.1   Match Your Goals to Metrics

Overall Goal	How?	Metrics
Effective employee training	Community to increase speed to locate expertise and to onboard new sellers (Per Bauer, T. N., & Erdogan., B. [2011]. *Organizational socialization: The effective onboarding of new employees, onboarding* refers to the mechanism through which new employees acquire the necessary knowledge, skills, and behaviors to become effective organizational members and insiders.)	1. Onboard time 2. Time to find right skill 3. Additional revenue from speed
Better client service	Community for white-glove service to clients	1. Increased conversion rates 2. Stronger trust and engagement 3. Higher revenue from loyalty

If your goal is to speed up the sales process to drive greater revenue, then the social tools you choose and your metrics need to show progress and results around that particular goal. If you wanted to build loyalty in your client base, you would want to measure specific areas of reviews or recommendations from your brand army, or top clients. In addition, you might want to measure feedback results from top innovations suggested by your clients, as well as sentiment improvements.

As Table 7.2 illustrates, you see a Social Business whose goal was a focus on improvements in their marketing process. They wanted to increase conversion rates from marketing campaigns, and lower campaign costs through increased efficiency leveraging social techniques to achieve the results. The business goals are the first step, as shown previously. Then the focus becomes how to reach the goal through social techniques. Finally, the Social Business outcome is illustrated to help you start your business case.

Table 7.2   Metric Alignment

Business Goal	Challenge Area:	Social Business Benefits*
Increase conversion rates from marketing campaigns	Current campaigns are pushed "blindly" with no customer input or feedback.	Community and discussions will provide feedback to improve product alignment. **Increase on lead conversion rate, increased revenue**
Lower campaign costs through increased efficiency	Present campaigns are call-center and mailing intense. Direct sales teams are challenged to convey the values of each new campaign in relevant context to the customer.	**Reduced lead development call time, savings in head count** Campaign promotions in communities and for discussions groups reduce mailings. **Direct cost savings**

*as projected by BVA client

The following list presents a Social Business whose goal was to increase its revenue through a virtual conference. With its Twitter account, they targeted high-quality followers and invited them to their conference. They then wanted to see the revenue generated from those people who attended. This particular small business tracks the revenue per tweet for "new clients."

Tweets: **8**

Followers: **350**

Total # Impressions from Tweets: **2,800**

Clicks from Tweet to Landing Page: **42**

Clicks from Landing Page to Start Registration: **19**

Completed Registrations: **10**

Total Revenue: **$15,000**

Revenue/Tweet: **$5.36**

Revenue/Follower: **$42.86**

The key point of matching your goals to your metrics is clear. You get what you measure, so ensure proper mapping from your goals to your metrics.

Your company's maturity in social analytics will also help to guide your view of what you want to measure and the timeline of capabilities your company will need to get there.

There are four stages of social analytics:

1. The first stage is to monitor and engage. This stage involves identifying your KPIs and using soft means to improve, qualitatively, your overall decisions on processes by listening to the conversations and engaging in the ones that support your brand goals. Typically, this first stage is using data from the blogosphere.

2. The second stage is to quantify and operationalize the analytics approach. This stage involves measuring ROI. It starts to gather insight on the process, like human relations, marketing, or customer service, and operationalizes that insight to the right owner, pulling data not just externally but also internally from CRM systems. This stage moves beyond qualitative means of improvement to more quantifiable means to improve overall socially enabled processes. In addition, differentiation between insight from the masses of networks versus your influencers or tippers begins at this stage.

3. The third stage is to predict and integrate. This stage provides continuous feedback and leverages the insight to optimize decisions across processes. By analyzing the data to understand social conversations and trends, the Social Business can predict behavior and recommend the next best action. It embeds full sentiment, or the way people feel, and geo-spatial analysis, which shapes the insight by geographic region. For example, it could conclude that influencers are positive in London, but negative in New York City. In addition, affinity analysis is added at this stage. Affinity analysis is about the relationships of buyers or buying patterns. For instance, it could enable the discovery that two products are usually purchased together or find the types of people buying a product. The data sources are broadened to internal systems, the blogosphere, and a broader level of partner data.

4. The fourth stage is about the seamless integration of internal, extranet, and public data with a sophisticated governance mechanism. The social analytics are embedded in all decisions, and data is pulled from a complete data set inside, outside, and beyond the company to suppliers and partners.

Provide Easy-to-Use Reporting and Querying

The market today includes a number of tools that generate basic metrics. For those Social Businesses getting started, the basic things that you should measure are focused on the following:

- Social reach and share of voice
- Reputation/influence
- Time
- Engagement

Social Reach and Share of Voice

Your social reach determines the number of overall friends, fans, and brand advocates you have in your domain. It is a simple measure of who is potentially listening to your subject matter expertise or expressing a belief about your company, product, or brand. Social reach is helpful in determining geographic location and the types of people listening to you. It is the measure of total audience (typically represented as some percentage of a total population). For example, my brand has 80% reach for males 18 to 24; or my company has 40% reach for the United Kingdom.

With blogs, sometimes having the most readers isn't the best metric. The long tail, or those blogs that have a smaller but more concentrated and engaged readership, might be the best strategy for your goals. Quality readership is more about the influence. You need to know what drives your business outcome and measure that element—reach or influence.

Share of voice represents the percentage of the conversations for a given topic that include your brand. For example, I have 20% share of voice for topic x (the implication being that for a given topic related to my brand, 20% of the conversations involve my brand and 80% do not). If I am tracking social analytics software topics, I would want my brand to be high in share of voice.

These metrics don't necessarily value the "business" but measure the value to those who are fans/follows of the business. It is a subtle but important distinction.
Some examples of social reach and share of voice metrics include these:

- **Facebook:** Number of fans; number of RSVPs, new fans/removed fans, monthly active users; media consumption: photo views and audio views
- **Twitter:** Number of followers, number of tweets
- **Twitter accounts:** Number of employees who have Twitter accounts
- **YouTube channel:** Number of subscribers, number of unsubscribers
- **LinkedIn:** Number of contacts and the number of people attending your events
- **Communities:** Number of members
- **Website:** Number of unique visitors

Some tools to potentially help you measure the metrics in the aforementioned channels include the following:

- **TweetReach:** Tracks how many potential eyeballs your tweet was in front of.
- **Bitly:** Provides built-in analytics for your shortened URL. When in LinkedIn or Twitter, make sure you use a URL shortener with analytics built in so that you can track the number of clicks, traffic sources, and times of clicks.
- **PitchEngine:** Used primarily to create a social media release and track the number of views.
- **Woopra:** A real-time tool for your website to see where your viewer came from (Facebook, LinkedIn, etc.) and has the capability to segment your visitors based on their demographics, their last action, or a custom criteria that your company wants to explore.

- **TubeMogul:** Provides a complete set of metrics regarding who watched your video, audience geography, referring sites, and so on.

Consider the reach as the number of eyeballs you have on your activity. Just remember, this gives you numbers that are interesting but not complete. Make sure these are not the only metrics that you use to measure success.

Reputation/Influence

Chapter 5, "(Social) Network Your Business Processes," discussed reputation management. Reputation is what others believe to be true about your company, product, or brand. Reputation management is being able to appropriately shape that reputation by doing the following:

- Having the right listening to know what others think about you
- Countering negative opinions
- Building positive opinions through action

Your reputation online matters a great deal, so you need to be able to measure your influence and value in the market. Reputation is not measured by numbers of views, or friends, but by the value they find in your brand, product, or company. Reputation has become so important to both companies and people that there are now many tools that attempt to quantify its value.

Some examples of types of reputation metrics that provide your company insight on your reputation include these:

- Comments on your website, Facebook page, LinkedIn, and so on (neutral, positive, or negative)
- Influence metrics to understand the level of influence they have on with their fans, followers, and friends (will a recommendation or suggestion lead to a purchase?)
- Competitive insights to compare and contrast your reputation against that of your key competitors

Many agencies now specialize in reputation analysis, and your company could consider the value in engaging one. Some tools to help you measure your reputation include the following:

- **SocMetrics:** Measures "real-world" influence as well as online. From its website, SocMetrics evaluates the content people create, as well as the activity their content generates—shares, comments, tweets, and the list goes on. SocMetrics focuses on topical influence—that is, influence on a certain topic or in a certain vertical, as well as how concentrated the followers are within that topic. For example, say your association deals with technology and wants to reach out to moms who are influential on that topic. You can pull a report of influencers in technology who are also moms. I experimented with SocMetrics at SXSW 2011, a social media festival in Austin, Texas (see Figure 7.1).

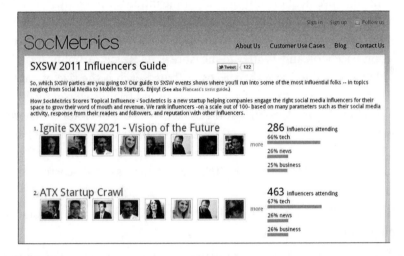

Figure 7.1   SocMetrics example

- **DeepMile's Agent 209™:** Enhances digital and social media efforts by
  - **Predicting influence:** Employs Bayesian models to predict users' likelihood to send a message to their followers or initiate a conversation; looks at frequency and quality of dialogue, not just breadth of reach.
  - **Creating influencers:** Identifies potential influencers within and across communities that lead to message cascades.
  - **Emphasizing relevance:** Analyzes user communications for content and semantics—it's critical to look beyond user profiles to identify influencers based on topical relevance at scale.
  - **Tracking influence of in-market activation:** Once influencers are identified, Agent 209 initiates specific in-market activation and track message cascades to determine which messages/content lead to the most viral activity across segments.

- **Unlimited data sources:** We look at all available social media platforms (Twitter, Flickr, YouTube, LinkedIn, and so on) where there is an API or open access to data.

- **Access to experts**: Human analysts are involved at key points in the process, especially validation. The Agent 209 team is made up of the same people who are analyzing billions of records to track terrorists and other "bad guys" for the CIA and NSA.

- **Klout:** Measures influence, in terms of whether the person can create resonance on Twitter and Facebook. Klout bills itself as the "standard of influence." The Klout Score is the measurement of your overall online influence but only in Facebook and Twitter (a weakness, I think). The scores range from 1 to 100, with higher scores representing a wider and stronger sphere of influence. Klout uses more than 35 variables on Facebook and Twitter to measure True Reach, Amplification Probability, and Network Score. From their website, True Reach is the size of your engaged audience and is based on those of your followers and friends who actively listen and react to your messages. Amplification Probability is the likelihood that your messages will generate actions (retweets, @messages, likes, and comments) and is on a scale of 1 to 100. Network Score indicates how influential your engaged audience is and is also on a scale from 1 to 100. The Klout Score is highly correlated to clicks, comments, and retweets.

- **Vizibility.com:** Showcases all the places with information about your company (and you personally).

- **Soovox:** Soovox is a marketplace or network of top influencers. For an influencer, you get a Social IQ, which is your social influence. According to Soovox, the scoring is done on three attributes: Trust Score, Connections Scores, and Authority Score. The source of the data comes from profiles, the size of the network, and the influencer's content activity. In addition, the quality of the content, and the buzz factor, is weighed in as well. That score can get you rewards from brands that you support.

- **Listorious:** Highlights influencers by domain, not by numerical score. You can go onto Listorious and find the person on Twitter who tweets the most about a topic, region, or profession.

Understanding the reputation of your company as well as the reputation of certain individuals inside and outside of your company will help you better understand where to allocate time and resources. If you find certain people who have a strong reputation across a certain segment of customers, leverage that person. If you identify that there are certain key customer segments where you have little or no reputation, that is where you want to focus time and effort.

YOU SAY YOU WANT A REVOLUTION…

The story has already become the stuff of legend among cyber-activists. On January 25, 2011 an executive in Google's Egypt office named Wael Ghonim sent a 56-character tweet in support of protests that had broken out earlier that day: "Freedom is a bless that deserves fighting for it. #Jan25." Within days, President Mubarak ordered Ghonim's arrest and had all Internet service to the country shut down. After 11 days of interrogation by police, and under enormous international pressure, Ghonim was finally freed. His subsequent interview fueled the flame that, in just two-and-a-half weeks, led to the nearly bloodless revolution that resulted in the toppling of a thirty-year despotic regime. The Western press dubbed Ghonim "The Google Guy" and credited his ability to mobilize the masses through social media as the catalyst that drove the Papyrus Revolution.

As compelling as the public account might be, however, the story of who the real tippers were who set the revolution in motion and how they were identified, reads more like a chapter from a Robert Ludlum novel.

DeepMile Networks is a highly specialized consulting firm located just outside Washington, DC. In addition to their corporate clients, the firm serves a number of government agencies whose chief concerns involve matters of national security. In the days leading up to the Egyptian Revolution, the folks at DeepMile were assigned a singularly interesting mission: Identify the tippers who were the most influential in moving the current events in Egypt.

The DeepMile process was put to work. Beginning with capturing all Twitter traffic for the week leading up to the events of January 25th, the DeepMile team was able to separate the cyber-wheat from the chaff using a set of proprietary filtering algorithms, which allowed them to distill the otherwise-unmanageable mass of data into a much more modest dataset of just 25 million tweets. Although such an enormous volume of messages might daunt even the most ambitious analyst, DeepMile's was able to identify the most relevant semantic clusters within this dataset in near real time, a particularly astonishing feat when one considers that even the most diligent human content coder would take more than a century to process the same amount of information.

Once the relevant conversations were identified, however, DeepMile's work had just begun. The team next identified the communities, sub-communities, and mass influencers engaged in the conversations that were most relevant to real-world activities, and they did so in real-time, as events were still unfolding across Egypt. The goal was not just to find out what was being talked about but also to identify the actual people who were most central to the conversation—and driving the most direct engagement and impact: the tippers.

By way of analogy, here's how their process works: Imagine a large cafeteria—one that can seat, say, 150 million people who are collectively engaged in billions of discussions. Now imagine the nearly unimaginable cacophony of those conversations—a couple over here shouting at their kids, a few people over there talking about sports, and various groups around the room discussing the implications of socio-economic reforms in Egypt. Now imagine having the ability to listen in to all those conversations, all at once. The DeepMile process metaphorically picks up each of the people who are having similar conversations and plops them down so they're all sitting together at the same table. The DeepMile process finds that, like any group of people, whether in real space or cyberspace, those groups tend to exhibit certain human dynamics that can then be identified and quantified. Using the ontological structure of all the analyzed conversations as a starting point—along with a host of calculations grounded in discrete mathematics, graph theory, and nonlinear dynamics—they are able to quantifiably identify the mavens, connectors, and tippers who play the most central role in message initiation, propagation, and amplification. This information allows the DeepMile team to identify the actual individuals who most significantly influence each conversation: the people who cause messages to cascade and even to go viral.

Even after more than a decade in the National Security space, Eric Malawer, the Founder and CEO of DeepMile, still couldn't help but marvel at the identification of these "revolutionary hidden hands"—as did everyone who attended the firm's presentation at the 2011 Department of Defense Intelligence Information Systems conference, an annual event that showcases the hottest new technologies and capabilities in the defense industry: "Imagine being able to listen in on the social media multiverse and then being able to identify who it was that lit the spark for the next big thing—or being able to find out the actual names of the people who can decide whether your mission, message, or new product will be hot, or not. Our solutions provide our clients with insights that would have been unimaginable up til now; it gives them the ability to identify, influence, and measure the effects of mass influencers, at massive scale, and in real time." The unprecedented approaches DeepMile has developed allow them to nearly instantly analyze millions of conversations, isolate the relatively few that are most relevant, and then identify those individuals who are not only central to the discussions but who actually drive others to action.

In the case of the Egyptian Revolution, the DeepMile team did just that. While their analysis confirmed that Wael Ghonim did, in fact, play a pivotal role in influencing the events leading up to Mubarak's resignation, they were also able to identify a small group of mass influencers who had an even greater impact on the momentous events that occurred in Egypt, a group of ordinary people who were able to compel others to engage in activities and actions that resulted in real-world outcomes. What was most astounding was the sheer number of people this small group was able to activate. Think of it as the flip-side of the Kevin Bacon Effect: Rather than looking for the six degrees of separation that connect everyone to a single person, the DeepMile researchers were able to find the folks who were the central axis for six degrees of connection. Here's how it works. Suppose you are closely connected to 100 people, 43 of whom will listen when you speak and take action on what you say. And suppose each of these 43 was similarly connected. Simple multiplication will show that by the time you reach the sixth level of separation, you will have also reached every person on the planet. People who are central to a conversation are important—but those who are connected to people who are also connected tend to have a reach that follows a geometric progression. While no one has perfect reach, the tippers the DeepMile team identified were collectively able to reach—and move—hundreds of thousands of people to action.

Consistent with the new cartography of cyberspace, the tippers DeepMile identified were not constrained by physical geography. They were people few of us had ever heard of before. They came from nowhere, and they came from everywhere. Among the influential eight were citizens of Tehran, Sudan, the Arab Emirates, France, and the United States; in fact, only three of the eight were Egyptians. In a seeming testament to the egalitarianism of cyberspace, half the tippers who most significantly influenced this traditionally patriarchal society were women. And unlike the cyber-savvy Ghonim, the top tippers who served as igniters of the Egyptian flame included relative luddites: an activist, an engineer, an Al Jazeera journalist, and a twenty-something coed. Despite their seemingly benign base, these people engendered a followership that dwarfed that of Ghonim's, or nearly any of the more well known names who orbited around the events in Egypt. They had no official position, but when they spoke, people listened and reacted. They were quoted, retweeted, and moved to the center of conversations that ultimately helped a nation reinvent itself. Collectively, their messages reached millions. And without relying on force, tangible resources, or an official position of any kind, these people proved, unequivocally, that in the cyberworld of social media, a mouse that roars can become a lion—and ignite a revolution.

Time

In a Social Business, time is important. Whether it is time to find a resource, time to solve a problem, or time-to-market with a new product, speed is a competitive advantage. Social techniques like communities or Twitter can assist in this area. For instance, monitoring tweets can help you know about situations that require immediate action. In Chapter 3, "Gain Social Trust," one of the trust builders is the ability to respond responsively.

Here are some examples of time metrics to consider:

- Time to respond to a Twitter concern
- Resource (time to find an expert resource internally)
- Time to onboard a new employee and train them for their job
- Reduction of time-to-market for new products/services

NOTE

There were no tools that I found on the market that measure this as precisely as internal company mechanisms to figure out most of these internal metrics. However, a lot of companies that I am working with are developing SLAs—Service Level Agreements (an agreement between your company and your friends, fans, and brand advocates on the amount of time required to respond). Consider an SLA for your plan!

Engagement

Engagement is critical to your success with people. Engagement is the emotional connection with your client or employee usually created by exceptional experiences that are integrated, interactive, and identifying. This metric gives you a feel for how people associate themselves with your product, company, or brand. Engagement could be someone retweeting your comment (retweeting is when a person takes your tweet and resends it in Twitter), or voting for your article on digg. (digg is a social news site, where content is posted by users and the users vote on the value of the content.) It is really about this interaction with you—sharing content about you. While not all engagement activities are the same, it is important to look at the types of engagement that people have with your company, brand, or products. While we will discuss more advanced metrics such as sentiment in the sections that follow, there are some simple ways to start to see your engagement scores. Different types of engagement have different business value, and, therefore, some types of engagement are more valuable/critical than other types. For example, customer loyalty/retention is a particularly valuable form of engagement. Some examples are given here:

- **Facebook:** Comments, Likes
- **Twitter:** Number of brand mentions, number of retweets
- **YouTube channel:** Comments, virally passing link
- **LinkedIn:** Number of references, number of answers
- **Communities:** Number of members
- **Blogs:** Time spent on site, comments
- **Website:** Number of unique visitors; number of RSS subscribers and your repeat traffic (demonstrates loyalty)
- **Polls:** Number of people who respond and participate

Some tools to potentially help you measure customer engagement in the aforementioned channels include these:

- **Google Analytics:** Measures site engagement goals including mobile.
- **Facebook Insights:** Tracks daily active users, new likes, and referrals, and when you have spikes in comments, it will show you what caused them.
- **SocialToo:** A comprehensive tool for creating social surveys and tracking social stats. It also will send you a daily email describing follows and unfollows on Twitter.
- **YouTube Insights:** Provides views, popularity, content clicked on, and community engagement.
- **ENGAGEMENTdb:** Altimeter has worked on an engagement study exploring the top 100 brands and ranking their engagement with different social media channels—a total of 11. What the study uncovered was that a brand's engagement across multiple social networks significantly impacts its bottom line, but this is preliminary. Keep your eye on this piece of work! http://www.scribd.com/doc/17666696/Engagement-Rankings-Of-The-Worlds-Most-Valuable-Brands.

There is no standard way to measure engagement today. The qualitative aspect of engagement can be estimated by sentiment analysis, which is still an advanced capability.

CASE STUDY: SETON HALL UNIVERSITY

Seton Hall University (SHU) is a major Catholic university located in South Orange, New Jersey. In a diverse and collaborative environment, it focuses on academic and ethical development.

As a private educational institution, Seton Hall University relies on tuition as its primary source of revenue. Prospective students consider degree programs, reputation, location, and many other factors as they "shop" for a college. But a college education encompasses more than tangible product characteristics such as these. Much of the college experience is about the relationships students build once they arrive on campus—in the classroom, in the dorm, and through participation in on-campus events and organizations.

Seton Hall decided to try to increase their revenue by focusing on the relationship aspect of their university and decided to use Facebook as their relationship space. Seton Hall marketers used the capabilities of social analytics in an initiative to increase enrollment for the upcoming academic year. The project involved the launch of the Class of 2014 Facebook page. The goal is to extend the core one-to-one brand attributes of Seton Hall to prospective students, including a sense of community, feeling of home, diversity of experience, and, sometimes, simply fun.

The staff tagged custom Class of 2014 tabs making it possible to identify any www.shu.edu visitors who had also interacted with Facebook. Using social analytics and reporting, marketers could then examine the behavior of these visitors. In addition, the Seton Hall staff began responding to prospective students' requests for help, from orientation, to deposit status, to placement tests, to housing. Soon, "declarations" (posts where prospective students announce a decision such as major, orientation date, or interest in a club or sport) had risen to 47% of all posts. The data showed that visitors who interacted heavily with the Class of 2014 pages demonstrated a high level of engagement with the university website as well. For example, they were more likely to request information and fill out applications than other visitors. The data collected revealed that Facebook was not only important to Seton Hall—but critical.

Prospective students used the Facebook pages to connect with current and prospective students, self-forming groups based on majors, common interests, geographical location, and even residence-hall room number. The "Facebook effect" was unanticipated, but it fit naturally with SHU's historical strengths and proved to be a tangible influence in the decision process. In effect, fence sitters were convinced to attend Seton Hall by other incoming freshmen.

By midsummer (two months before classes were to begin), tuition deposits for the class of 2014 were 25% higher than the previous year at the same time. Moreover, enrollment was tracking at 13% ahead of the previous year's class. By the end of the enrollment period, Seton Hall had its largest freshmen class in 30 years, accounting for an 18% increase in net present revenue of $29 million (USD). These results were particularly staggering given the prevailing trend of lower enrollment for many institutes of higher education. By enabling Seton Hall to capture data on the Facebook interactions and perform a deep level of analysis, social analytics is enabling the university to make more informed decisions regarding their marketing investment.

The overall initiative has eliminated any remaining skepticism about the value of Facebook. The university has embraced Facebook as a vitally important recruitment channel. Seton Hall is now looking at new ways to exploit the power of this new channel. To that end, the online marketing staff regularly shares information on Facebook usage and influence with key stakeholders, including admissions and housing. Together they are working to develop an infrastructure to deal with implications of the changing way today's students expect (and even demand) to interact with the university.

Provide Advanced Analytics and Dashboards for Sentiment, Affinity Relationships, and Evolving Topics

As your Social Business becomes savvy about its use of social techniques, a more advanced look at results is required. For example, while the list of tools in the preceding sections is interesting, it is not aggregated nor does it show the linkage between elements. So for the more advanced user, I recommend looking at tools that aggregate and frame the data into a comprehensive analysis using techniques like predictive analytics and content analytics.

As Figure 7.2 illustrates, data must be gathered from multiple sources. While some of the aforementioned tools look at two or three input parameters, what is needed is a tool that takes real-time data from all the sources available in the Social Business world.

For me, there are four crucial elements that must be viewed:

1. Comprehensive Analysis
2. Evolving Topics
3. Affinity
4. Sentiment

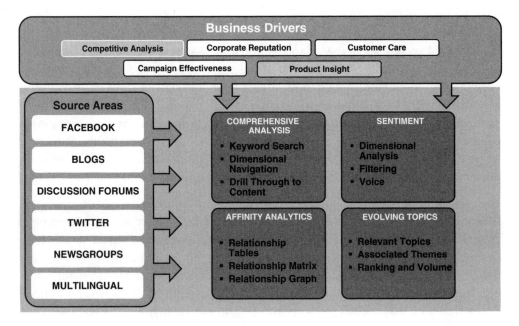

Figure 7.2   Analyze your data.

For Social Businesses, these four elements provide a competitive advantage. The sections that follow examine these four elements in greater detail.

Comprehensive Analysis

One of the first items that you want to be able to focus on is listening to the marketplace or better understanding your internal employees. The key here is to have a comprehensive view of the areas that are of importance to your business. A comprehensive analysis is a view of all that is being written in the blogosphere about your chosen set of keywords, company, brand, or product. Start by defining the set of key topics, regions, timeframes, and brand or product areas that you would like to consistently review for trends.

The ability to analyze billions of blog posts and hundreds of thousands of forums and discussion groups on publicly available websites "on the fly" to measure the effectiveness of your social impact and the sentiment of consumer opinions of your brand and company is invaluable. Companies can get access to publicly available data and data in their own private forums, but not in other private forums. So you need to take some of the metrics with a grain of salt as they measure a subset of the total universe of data.

This comprehensive view of the data provides you with an overall perspective of the topics in relation to the key areas of focus that you determined along with trending.

Evolving Topics

It is important to look at the new topics in the blogosphere and on your internal intranet. A Social Business captures a summary of discussions to determine snippets that share the same terms and related topics above and beyond your analysis of trends and common discussion topics across time.

Evolving topics provide good insight into future products and services. Using content analytics from the crowdsourced data across multiple public and private websites, you can draw relationship to topics around a given keyword. For example, if you sell home entertainment equipment, you might find evolving topics from your customers related to "installations" and "customer service." A Social Business will be able to translate that into an opportunity to do a better job of offering installation services at the point of sale for every home entertainment system.

These evolving topics help you to determine risks and opportunities of related topics to corporate reputation, marketing, product innovation, and customer service.

Analyzing evolving topics enables a Social Business to more effectively target broad adjacent themes and events to link your product, services, and corporate messages while prioritizing and ranking their relevance and applicability for proactive campaigns. In addition, evolving topics provide insight to incorporate other discussion contexts by analyzing evolving topics related to hot word sentiment and by targeting other social media communities or communication channels.

Affinity Analysis

A Social Business needs to understand the relationship between different areas of analysis and view the snippets that are associated with their intersection to gauge impact and identify future messages or innovations among key audiences. Affinity analysis is a process of taking data and seeing the affinity, or relationships, of product purchases. For instance, if a person buys one product, is he more likely to buy another product? Or if someone buys one product, does it make her more likely to *not* buy another product? This level of analysis helps you gain insight into affinity relationships in your marketing, using hot words to modify messaging with more agility and precision. In addition, affinity analysis helps you anticipate new opportunities. Based on this information, a Social Business can engage audiences in specific subject areas with the words and messages that resonate with and are specific to their interests and perspectives.

Finally, a Social Business can better evaluate messaging by analyzing affinity contexts and associations with corporate and brand values to ascertain responsiveness and reaction to reputation, customer service, and corporate social responsibility activities. For example, a Social Business could start to filter down to product categories that they offer and understand how each of those compares against the source to identify whether certain products are more heavily discussed in Twitter than in YouTube.

Sentiment Analysis

Sentiment is the way people view what you are doing, either positively or negatively. You can gain an understanding of how people feel about your company, brand, or category based on what they write. Sentiment defines snippets of social data as positive, negative, or neutral/undefined. Social analytics takes the data into insight about feelings and emotional connections. A Social Business needs to be able to analyze sentiment and filter by concepts, hot words, and media sets to have a complete comparative analysis by comparing positive, negative, neutral, or ambivalent sentiment.

Sentiment analysis helps a Social Business make decisions with analysis into consumer and stakeholder sentiment. It adds value in assessing precise trends and changes in perception of your corporate reputation and reaction to campaigns.

In addition, sentiment analysis can help you identify and target new channels to drive greater advocacy of your products and services with key influencers based on an analysis of sentiment. For example, the effectiveness of your campaigns' messages and their impact on consumers' purchasing decisions, as well as the resonance and believability of their promise, are valuable pieces of information. Internally, sentiment analysis would help a Social Business gain better insight on how employees truly feel about the new travel policy, usage of the CRM solution, or what mobile devices it should support for remote employees.

Establish a Social Analytics Center of Excellence

Social Businesses need social analytics tools and skills. The best way to do this is to staff a skilled set of professionals with an aggregated dashboard that is reviewed and improved upon on a regular basis. The Social Analytics Center of Excellence mission is to expand the company's transformation through the leverage of analysis at the individual, organization, and enterprise levels. Working with leaders across the company, the primary objective is to drive business and client value through the efficient, effective use of tools and data analysis. This Center of Excellence should be linked to the Social Business Digital Council in Chapter 2.

A Center of Excellence could be a full-time staff or could be staffed with individuals on rotational assignments. In addition, your company could leverage external agencies. IBM creates its Center of Excellence with a combination of Market Insights, brand-led Social Business Managers, and external agencies. This approach brings practical experience to the team for a defined period, and then transfers the talent back to the business units after gaining broader experience.

For example, Gatorade, a brand inside of the Pepsi Corporation, set up a Mission Control Center to analyze and more deeply engage with its consumers. This digital hub is a combination of insight analysis with action-oriented changes that are made based on consumer trends. With a combination of tools and four full-time staff, Gatorade uses real-time data and analysis to make changes in their marketing campaigns. Some of their results have been an increase in engagement going from 35% one-on-one interaction about sports performance to over 60% today. Gatorade tracks online discussions, sports landscape, media performance, outreach, brand attributes, and brand buzz. This covers all of the key areas of sentiment, affinity, and evolving topics in their category.

Having a Center of Excellence drives a central focus for your Social Business across internal and external uses. Select a Social Analytics Manager who will focus on the digital forms of information for insight. This person compliments your Business Intelligence team. They can also assist in determining who should have access to analytics and what content should be made available by the process.

The Social Analytics Manager should have experience in analytics, social tools, and understanding of the advanced analytics areas of sentiment, affinity, and predictive models.

In Figure 7.3, I wanted to share some of the top solution areas for the Center of Excellence. As you can see, these are the core areas:

- Customer acquisition, growth, and retention
- Operations management, infrastructure, and security
- Suspicious-behavior detection, risk mitigation, and fraud prevention

In the sections that follow, you will see three examples of the use of social analytics and the value in three processes that cover many of these core areas: customer service, marketing, and human relations.

Acquire Customers	Manage Operations	Detect Suspicious Behavior
• Understand who your best customers are • Connect with them in the right ways • Take the best action to maximize what you sell to them	• Maximize the usage of your assets • Make sure your assets are in the right place at the right time • Identify the impact of investment in various areas of assets	• Identify fraudulent patterns • Reduce false positives • Identity collusive and fraudulent merchants and employees • Identify unanticipated transaction patterns
Grow Customers	**Maintain Infrastructure**	**Mitigate Risk**
• Understand the best mix of things needed by your customers & channels • Maximize the revenue received from your customers & channels • Take the best action every time to interact	• Understand what causes failure in your assets • Maximize uptime of assets • Reduce costs of upkeep	• Identify leaks • Increase compliance • Leverage insights in critical business functions
Retain Customers	**Secure Operations**	**Prevent Fraud**
• Understand what makes your customers leave and what makes them stay • Keep your best customers happy • Take action to prevent them from leaving	• Improve the security of your assets • Identify unanticipated attack patterns on assets • Quickly respond with the best action when security is compromised	• Take action in real time to prevent abuse • Reduce claims handling time • Alert clients of transaction fraud

Figure 7.3   Top solution areas

Sample: IBM Social Analytics for Customer Service

As an example, let's look at social analytics applied to a call center. The call center is the first line of defense in ensuring that customers are happy. If your company understands what drives "happiness," your company can drive more revenue. Chapter 5 discusses how companies are embedding social networking into their customer service processes. Now let's determine the right social analytics that could be used to help your effectiveness.

The goal in the call center is to be more productive by proactively engaging consumers online during the busy season.

In this example, the customer service manager needs to accurately and precisely filter through sources of complaints to engage customers' issues effectively and quickly. In addition, there is a need to assess evolving topics associated with the customer complaints so that the customer service manager can begin to assess and provide feedback to managers on future issues. In a Social Business, the leader of the call center wants to reduce call and email volumes for minor customer complaints by proactively engaging in issues and feedback online through the call center by doing the following:

- Precisely determining the online source of complaints
- Determining the sentiment and filtering down to specifics
- Evaluating and assessing future complaints
- Making the parts of the business causing the dissatisfaction aware of the issues

Social Business analysis requires the review of sentiment in this example. Sentiment analysis across specific consumer discussion boards and blogs will help you reach your goal via a filtered and targeted analysis of online sources of customer complaints.

In addition, evolving topic analysis helps to determine whether there are other problem trending items that you can address before they become too big. In that evolving trending, analysis of the volume of negative and positive feedback, viewed in parallel with call-center statistics, can help you determine any issues ahead of time as demonstrated previously in Chapter 5.

Figure 7.4 shows a consolidation of the metrics that McKinsey found for Social Businesses in the customer service space.

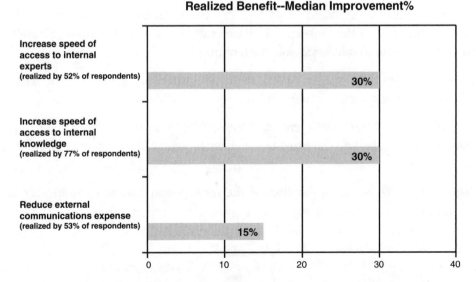

Source: "The rise of the networked enterprise. Web 2.0 finds its payday," McKinsey Global Survey Results, 2010.

Figure 7.4   Value of Social Business for customer service

Sample: IBM and Social Analytics for Marketing

As an example, let's look at social analytics applied to a marketing organization. Applying social analytics to marketing can result in expanded revenue opportunities. For instance, social analytics could assist you in combining attitudinal and survey-based data with social sentiment to anticipate and target new segments, or to predict consumer sentiment through social channels to segment customer behavior and optimize campaign ROI.

The goal in marketing is to make relevant changes to the program strategy or execution. The sample company wants to assess the impact of the company's corporate social responsibility campaign and determine whether it has improved the reputation of the company in the communities it serves. In the corporate social responsibility campaign, the company will need to understand current reputational standing as well as the campaign's effect on either modifying or stabilizing it.

In this example, the marketing team needs to go through 100,000 forums and discussion groups to measure the effectiveness of the social campaign and the sentiment of consumer responses. In addition, they need to gain insight into affinity relationships in search of the campaign's hot words to modify messaging for their campaigns with more agility and precision. They also need a baseline assessment of the company's reputation among stakeholders in communities and to assess the shift in reputation after the campaign.

The Social Business analysis that should be done in this case is sentiment analysis of reputation on community-based blogs and discussion groups. For example, in Figure 7.5, the identification of the most causal variables driving sentiment assists in developing marketing campaigns to maximize positive sentiment.

Social analytics provides the critical baseline to justify engagements with particular stakeholders in your company's community.

With its capacity to assess sentiment regarding attributes associated with the company's reputation, for instance, you can provide management with a clearer picture of the public's reaction to issues.

In Figure 7.6, there is a consolidation of the metrics that McKinsey found for Social Businesses in the marketing process.

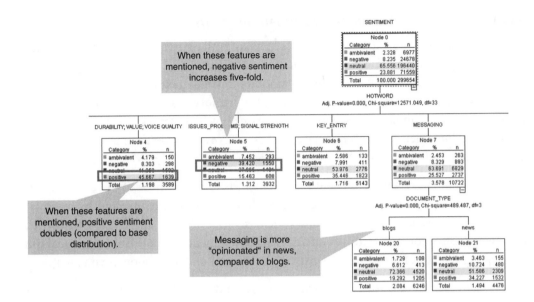

Figure 7.5   Predictive models to drive positive sentiment for marketing campaigns

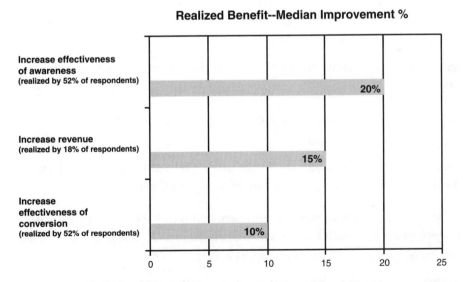

Source: *"The rise of the networked enterprise. Web 2.0 finds its payday," McKinsey Global Survey Results, 2010.*

Figure 7.6   Value of Social Business for marketing management

Sample: IBM Social Analytics for Human Relations

As an example, let's look at social analytics applied to the human relations process. HR is a critical process, where talent management is a competitive advantage for all companies. If through social analytics you can retain more top talent, your company can save money. Gallup says that a 1% improvement in employee turnover saves $1 million (based on a company of 5,000 employees). Chapter 5 discusses how companies are embedding social networking into their customer service processes. Now let's determine the right social analytics that could be used to help our effectiveness.

The goal of human relations in talent management is to retain more of the company's top talent. By understanding employee sentiment through social listening and by leveraging internal and external information sources such as social network and forums, the existing employee satisfaction and feedback surveys can be augmented and even become real time, eliminating the need for the once-a-year view that is out of date as soon as you get it!

In this example, the talent management needs to understand employee sentiment about working at the company by understanding employee sentiment about working at IBM, understanding employee sentiment about IBM's products, services, and clients, and IBM policies/programs. In addition, they need to assess the onboarding experience of new hires, monitor acquired employees assimilation/integration, and identify data/trends that will enable HR to determine whether interventions are necessary to address employee dissatisfaction, especially for critical job roles.

This insight results in improvements across HR's talent management. For instance, they can do the following:

- Identify areas for new/additional training needs (e.g., to sales/delivery teams)
- Obtain insight into employee needs
- Identify whether there is a need for corrective actions related to certain programs (e.g., evaluate the incentive plan to reduce attrition of the sales force)

Social Business analysis requires the review of sentiment in this example. Sentiment analysis across specific employee communities and blogs will help you reach your goal via a filtered and targeted analysis of online sources of employee concerns.

In addition, evolving topic analysis helps to determine whether there are other problems trending by focus area. For instance, filtering and targeted analysis of the source of complaints by geography, business unit, job role, and tenure could help focus the talent management issues on the right areas to have immediate impact.

In Figure 7.7, there is a consolidation of the metrics that McKinsey found for Social Businesses in the human relations space.

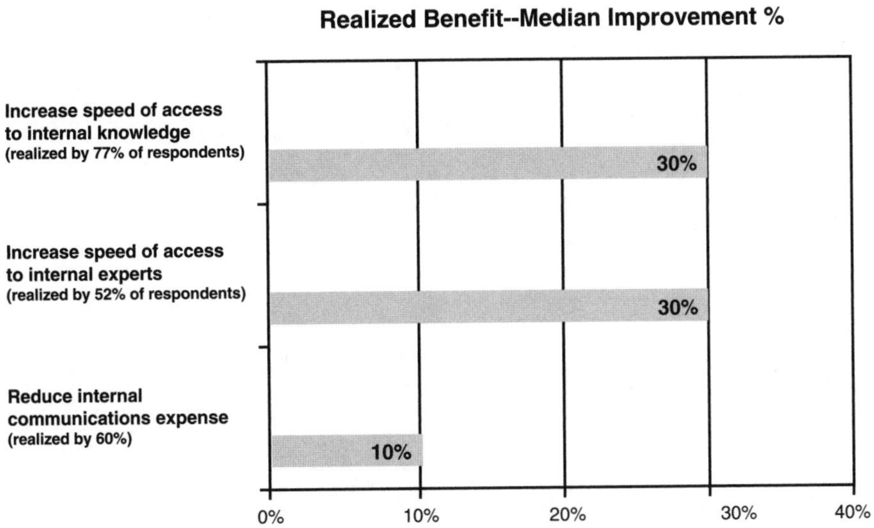

Realized Benefit--Median Improvement %

Increase speed of access to internal knowledge (realized by 77% of respondents)	30%
Increase speed of access to internal experts (realized by 52% of respondents)	30%
Reduce internal communications expense (realized by 60%)	10%

0%   10%   20%   30%   40%

Source: "The rise of the networked enterprise. Web 2.0 finds its payday," McKinsey Global Survey Results, 2010.

Figure 7.7   Value of Social Business for HR

Conclusion

Social analytics are the new black. Black is so popular because it is universally flattering. Social analytics will become popular because these metrics help you understand client needs so that you can target the right offers and products. They drive the evaluation of corporate reputation and help you have the facts to make the right decisions at the right time. In addition, they reduce the response time as they help you predict client requests so that you are ahead of the curve. To use social techniques and media appropriately and to better assess service-level effectiveness and reduce costs, a Center of Excellence with advanced metrics is recommended. Whether you are a small, medium, or large company, the integration of the measurement of your social media strategy into your business and operational processes is the winning play.

Technology as a Competitive Ingredient

"The focus of Social Business is on the business—but new social technologies are the transformative ingredient."

Charlie Hill, IBM Distinguished Engineer, and Chief Technology Officer, Collaboration Solutions

"A Social Business will win or lose based on the competitiveness of their technology platform."

Doug Cox, Vice President, IBM Collaboration Solutions Development and Support

Yes, the Technology Is Important

As a business leader, you'll find that your Social Business will be dependent on technology. Technology is indeed the key ingredient that companies use to transform themselves into Social Businesses and outperform their competition. Clearly, it was Internet technology that broke down many traditional barriers to relationships and formed the foundation for new technologies that enable Social Businesses today. While the Internet has been a catalyst for new unchartered ways for people to collaborate, it is the new social technology capabilities that take these functions and supercharge them for business.

For example, community and forum functions enable relationships to be created, nurtured, and leveraged across boundaries of geography and culture; blogs and managed activity spaces break down barriers of organization and hierarchy even further; file sharing supports collaborative decision making; and instant e-meetings and chat increase the efficiency and speed of processes through timely collaboration. In a nutshell, these new social technology capabilities enable people to operate the way they have always wanted to operate, trading, sharing, developing, rating, discussing, and so on, all without restrictions and barriers that get in the way of productive business relationships.

This chapter is included in the book so that as a business leader you can work hand in hand with your CIO or IT department to select or build the right Social Business platform. Familiarize yourself with some of the core areas that are required. Figure 8.1 shows the key technical capabilities that are essential to a Social Business. This high level diagram illustrates the capabilities required to have a people centric Social Business platform.

As I mentioned in Chapter 5, "(Social) Network Your Business Processes," I'm asked a lot by business leaders how to get started with Social Business, and I mention areas such as HR, marketing, customer service, product development and innovation, and supply chain. This question of where to get started is also common among IT departments.

The good news is this: Getting started with social technology is really no different from getting started with traditional technologies, applications, and platforms. It starts with strategy, planning, design, and an executive champion in most cases.

But there is a difference! Since social technologies are inherently oriented toward the end user, the strategy must embrace the realities of rapid change, unpredictable demand, and unforeseen requirements. As we saw in the example of CEMEX in Chapter 5, once a social platform is made available, it may have enormous uptake in the company, stressing network and storage capacities. The strategy, plan, and design of this system required flexibility and scalability to meet the demands of 17,000 users participating in more than 400 communities.

The need for very dynamic response to unpredictable end-user demand also requires significant consideration for the solution delivery and management capabilities of the IT environment. This is represented as "Change Management" in the diagram shown in Figure 8.1. Most, if not all, companies today are reluctant to spend money based on scenarios of theoretical usage. Instead, they're looking to various virtualization technologies, technologies that allow spikes in usage to take advantage of dormant processing resources, to provide the level of dynamic flexibility required. Many are also leveraging cloud options, with hybrid models integrating cloud and on-premises capabilities becoming an increasingly popular consideration. What does all this mean? Your IT team will need to consider delivery and change management from the beginning of the Social Business implementation. Flexibility must be designed in from the start!

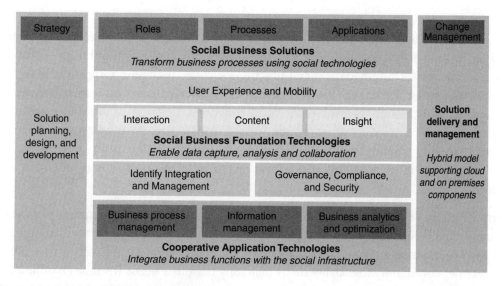

Figure 8.1   Social Business capabilities diagram

What is your IT group's technical strategy and does it map to your overall Social Business strategy? Does the strategy fully anticipate the level of flexibility that will be required to handle unpredictable change?

Social Technologies Extend Existing Systems

While the bold AGENDA of Social Business has the potential to revolutionize business operations, inside and outside the company, the adoption of the Social Business technology must be done in the context of operational systems today. Social Business technologies extend cooperative application technologies to "socially enable" the applications and data they support. In other words, Social Business technologies are evolutionary; they integrate into the fabric of tools already in use; and they extend the ability of end users to more fully collaborate and meet objectives.

SOCIAL BUSINESS TECHNOLOGIES...

- Are evolutionary
- Integrate social capabilities with existing applications and processes
- Extend the ability of end users

Many social strategies simply require the implementation of a platform of capabilities not technically linked or tightly integrated to any specific application or business process. Instead, the platform provides general functions such as discussion forums, blogs, wikis, and communities. The linkage to a given application or business process is then determined by the end user through their use of the social functions. This is great news! Generally, the technical work required to support your Social Business strategy is relatively simple. Of course, there are situations where the degree of technical integration may be more extensive, but the end objective, providing social functions to better connect people, processes, and information, will be the same.

Arrow Enterprise Computing Solutions (Arrow ECS) was looking for a community-based solution that would help increase collaboration within the company's partner community. To meet its business challenges, they created a social collaboration application that allows the partner community to collaborate by matching customer needs with the capabilities of members of the partner community. Using profiles, the community can be used to easily search and find other partners with skills required for a project, issue, or collaboration need. In addition, partners can post their needs. In other words, the community is used for two-way resource identification and engagement. The application did not require extensive technical integration; it was implemented using common social functions of communities, profiles, and so on.

Another example, Cardiff University, has taken an approach that more fully integrates social capabilities into its research, teaching, and administrative processes. Their objective was to stimulate collaboration and learning through distinctive experiences that would attract and retain students, staff, and researchers. The technical approach was to integrate a set of features, including social capabilities such as instant messaging and collaborative workspaces, into a portal environment. Users select from various services and content to create their own portal experiences tailored to their specific interests and needs. Through social communities, users not only collaborate with their colleagues, students, and instructors, but also provide ("crowdsourcing") feedback to the university on new services and content they would like to see added to the available portal site.

Of course, these examples indicate that technical integration required to support a Social Business strategy may vary.

What level of technical integration is required for your solution? The good news is that many Social Business solutions can start quickly with the implementation of a basic platform of social functions (blogs, wikis, communities, and so on) and can evolve to more deeply integrate into specific processes over time. Regardless of the level of technical integration, social technology implementations leverage a core set of capabilities.

Social Technology Core Capabilities

Let's dig a little deeper into the foundational capabilities of social technology: interaction, content, and insight, as shown in Figure 8.2. Many of the case studies like Sogeti, Practicing Law Institute, and Teach for America among others that I have already covered in the previous chapters were based on these foundational capabilities of social technology.

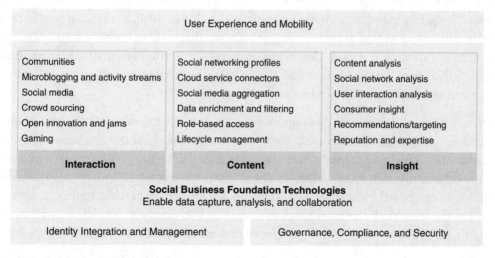

Figure 8.2   User experience and mobility

Interaction capabilities are the heart and soul of social technology; we could even say they are what make social technology social! It is through social interaction that people engage and involve other people in their decisions, actions, and processes. Of course, people have always worked together in these ways, mostly face to face; business has always been a social activity! But with social technologies, the interactions are simpler to make happen, they may be direct or indirect, and they are expedited.

Social interaction capabilities accelerate communication and collaboration across networks of employees, customers, and business partners, thus shortening cycle times, increasing worker productivity, and creating better structured and more transparent management of collaborative processes. Traditionally, email has been used as a primary mechanism for social interaction in business. With the new capabilities of blogs, discussion forums, wikis, communities, and shared project activity spaces, however, social interaction no longer requires the back-and-forth flow of notes; it's no longer dependent on a known distribution list for participation; and it's scaled to a broad group of interested parties, regardless of the formal job title or organizational position.

But how will we cope with an exploding set of options for social interaction? This is a key question. Technical functions are required that help end users organize, filter, and efficiently use the huge amount of information available to them. New capabilities, called *activity streams,* are emerging in many collaboration systems today to address this specific requirement. An *activity stream* is a list of recent activities performed by an individual. Activity streams will enable end users to blend information from internal and external sources, including blogs, wikis, business applications, and so forth, so they can be effectively used in day-to-day work and enable efficient collaboration across a broad network of people. With activity streams, it is likely that many people will shift from an email-centric model of interaction to an activity-centric model that is much more open and dynamic, yet tailored to the end user's specific task needs.

There are, of course, situations that require direct, immediate interaction between a number of people, sometimes one-on-one, sometime one-to-many, and sometimes many-to-many. Social interaction capabilities make these interactions more effective as well. Using integrated instant messaging, "click to chat," instant e-meetings, and so on, individual discussions can be held wherever the two parties are located, even when mobile devices are used for the chat. With the emergence of simple-to-use video capabilities, e-meetings are becoming much more viable for direct, yet virtual, interactions.

Take, for example, a situation that happened to me recently. I hurt my back and was grounded from flying for a period of eight weeks. What was I to do with all my meetings and commitments? Fortunately, I was able to use video e-meetings to successfully present to IBM internal and external audiences. In fact, there were some very interesting lessons learned from these meetings:

- In the case of an external presentation, I was able to respond to audience interest and understanding covering different topics in the presentation by using a hashtag set up in Twitter as a way for the audience to ping me throughout the session.

- I asked IBMers in the room to instant-message indications of audience interest and engagement to me so that I could adjust as the session progressed. While this was not a complete substitute for the ability to sense audience attention in person, it provided me with valuable insight I would not have had without their input.

- Video technology is still emerging, so testing it before the meeting is a must!

> Interaction capabilities integrate social networks with business systems and processes, accelerate communications among experts, and foster collaborative exchanges among employees, partners, and customers.

The power of social interaction is clear, but what about content? *Social content capabilities* allow social data to be captured and managed so it can be used effectively for interaction and insight. For example, in the discussion about activity streams, I indicated a need to filter what flows into the activity stream so the end user is not inundated with too much information. How will the filtering be done? Using profile information. For example, a blog may or may not be included in the stream. Profile information is clearly one form of social data. But, more broadly, what is social data?

Social data is information about people (locations, relationships, expertise, etc.) that is important in engaging them in appropriate networks, processes, and interactions. It is data that, when analyzed, may indicate preferences, affiliations, relationships, and so on that are appropriate for the business to know and to leverage for improved service to employees, partners, or customers. As I just mentioned, often this data is thought of as profile information; however, it is also data that might be derived from internal and external systems. It's the ability to capture and manage this data, integrating it with transaction or process information, that is required for Social Business. Social data can, of course, be seen as an extension to customer data or partner data that is already captured and maintained for many business processes today. But it is an extension that takes into account the broader social context of the relationship the individual has with the company and his or her network, and therefore is an extension that provides the basis for better insight and improved interactions.

To illustrate this, let's take the need for social media aggregation (the collection of social data from social media sources) in the retail industry. All retailers have traditional information about their customers, demographics, transaction histories, payment histories, and so on. This allows the retailer to have a profile indicating who the customer is and what they have done.

But what additional information can help the retailer be more proactive in the relationship? What does the customer really think about the company and how they do business? This is social data indicating the attitude of the customer toward the company. And where is that data? Embedded in the posts on social media sights, Facebook and Twitter for example. Retailers see this data, what customers say about them in the social media, as an indication of their "earned" reputation, and they use it, once it's captured, to perform predictive analytics, to better target individual customers, and to discover new customers from the social media networks of their existing customers.

Social content capabilities also enable the management and use of the growing amount of unstructured information available to meet a particular objective of the company. For example, employee learning can be revolutionized by using community-based methods for aggregating digital instructional content from experts "on the ground," ranking and tagging that content to establish its value and relevance to other users, and ultimately delivering the content on demand to whoever needs it as they go about their jobs. In other words, the best instructors covering a given topic may be a set of practitioners, not in headquarters, but out in the field. These people can quickly and easily create videos, movies, and so on that provide instructional value to others in the company, and with social content capabilities those videos and movies can easily be made directly available to the people who need them.

> Social content capabilities allow social data to be captured and managed so it can be used effectively for interaction and insight.

Social insight capabilities are functions that bring together business analytics and social decision making, as well as social analytics. Working for IBM has given me an opportunity to see the power of this combination in a globally integrated enterprise. Every day, I'm involved in decision-making situations involving sales of software products that involve business leaders all over the world. As large as the organization is, we are empowered to operate with incredible speed because as leaders we leverage a common set of business analytics, and in an open and interactive way, we move forward on business decisions that benefit from the collective assessment of that data.

In May of 2011, it came to my attention, as well as to the attention of my peers, that one of the software products in the portfolio I manage did not have a strong pipeline. Our predictive analytics based on historical data and real-time sales data from our CRM system created a red flag. IBM's social analytics dashboard allowed my team and me to also review recommendations to help correct this issue and provide the highest probability to make our quota in spite of the weak pipeline. Within 4 hours of discovering this issue, the predictive analysis had already made some recommendations. Within 8 hours, my team had met to review and assess the data and situation. Within 24 hours, we had consensus on a solution, and within 48 hours of being notified, we had communicated out to all WW sellers a new sales promotional offering to help close the deals needed to meet the quota.

Social insight capabilities also leverage social data to perform predictive analytics. As indicated in the preceding retail example, retailers use data aggregated from social media sites along with data aggregated from customer website navigation for targeted marketing and customer outreach. Marketing campaigns can be adjusted more quickly when the demographics of various groups cluster and show unexpected interest in a set of products.

Insight capabilities enable businesses to derive enhanced levels of business awareness and decision making by integrating social data and network analysis with transaction and process-oriented data analysis. For example, content analysis, the exploration of structured and unstructured data, enables companies to determine patterns, visualize trends, and predict possible future patterns and trends. When this is combined with social network analysis, it may be possible to determine impacts of relationships, organization affiliation, or other social factors into the patterns and trends. This can be extremely powerful. It can open new ideas for targeted marketing, for market creation, or for new market penetration.

I recently saw an example of the level of insight that can be achieved. I have been working with a large financial institution in the U.K. to determine how they can more effectively analyze and use competitive data. They wanted an efficient dashboard to combine competitive information from various sources with effective tools to enable business leaders to collaborate on specific responses and actions. Using the social media aggregation functions, data analytics, and communities, a prototype was actually created for this social analytics dashboard and built in a matter of weeks.

The dashboard combined graphical representations of trends from website searches; lists of social media posts (Twitter) covering searchable keywords/topics; pie charts and line graphs indicating sentiment and associations (keyword/company); and views of evolving topics ("wealth," "stocks," "Africa," etc.) by keyword. The graphical representations could be modified through selection of various filters, enabling the end user to very quickly focus on specific topic areas. And through the integration of communities into the dashboard, the team was able to establish and complete specific activities, post blogs, have discussions, and so forth. In other words, the competitive team was able to effectively collaborate and take action, working from a common dashboard of key data indicating reputation, sentiment, trends, and the like.

> Insight capabilities and social analytics derive business information and improve business decision making through the analysis and integration of social data with traditional business data.

As you can see from the discussion in this section, there are a number of core technical capabilities that should be considered as you address the technical implementation approach for your Social Business strategy. But the critical factor is alignment—alignment of the strategy and implementation plan of the IT group with the business timing and needs for the Social Business strategy. What degree of social interaction is required? How will social data be aggregated and managed? What capabilities will support the degree of insight required to meet your business objectives? Using these questions can help you effectively align your IT group to your Social Business strategy.

But we're not quite finished yet.

Implications for Underlying Infrastructure

No discussion of Social Business technology can ignore the implications on fundamental infrastructure capabilities. The increased use of social networking and social capabilities will also increase the risks and challenges associated with protecting sensitive company information. Regulatory and company-mandated rules that once applied to tightly controlled company information must now be applied to information that can easily move inside and outside the company. And what about archiving and storage requirements that must be met for legal reasons? What social data must be included?

Clearly, there are a number of risk factors that must be identified, assessed, and woven into social solutions, and imply a need to focus on governance, compliance, and security. In addition, privacy laws, which vary significantly around the world, are critical to consider as well.

When asked how these basic infrastructure issues will be addressed, we fall to the favorite answer of architects: "It depends." Your IT group will need to understand the targeted use cases, users, data, and so on in order to fully determine the requirements and implications on the underlying infrastructure. As I mentioned at the beginning of this chapter, Social Business capabilities are evolutionary. In some cases, the implications will be minor and simple to implement by the technical team. In other cases, they will be more complex.

A final technical topic (of course, this topic could be chapter by itself, but I will just barely touch on it here)—everyone is aware of the mobility explosion that is in progress today. This move to mobile computing is certainly a core element of the technology of a Social Business. Process, transaction, and collaboration functions all need to be available to interested parties whenever and wherever the individual wants access. And while mobility is already being addressed through mobile access to company portals and some internal systems, the shift to Social Business will only accelerate the need for mobile capabilities to be in place.

Conclusion

Social Businesses depend on the implementation of social technology. For the business goals to be reached, business and IT need to join together to create a platform that enables deeper customer and employee relationships, enhances speed to market, and adapts with flexibility to market changes. This chapter provides an introduction to the types of capabilities that your company should begin exploring. Even if you are not a technologist, join with your CIO in the Social Business mission because technology is core to your company's success. These are the questions that we discussed in this chapter that you need to work through:

1. What is your IT group's technical strategy and does it map to your overall Social Business strategy?

2. Does the strategy fully anticipate the level of flexibility that will be required to handle unpredictable change?

3. Does the solution take into account the need for social analytics? Mobile?

4. Does the technology support the regulatory and legal policies of your company and industry?

5. What capabilities will support the degree of insight required to meet your business objectives?

Now let's continue on to draw up your company's Social Business AGENDA!

Special thanks to Bill Hassell for his amazing work with me on this chapter!

9

Draw Up Your AGENDA

"The magic innovation occurs when companies go outside their four walls for ideas, help, and advocacy. The Social Business AGENDA enables you to do just that."

Sandy Carter

"You can't steal second base with your foot still on first."

Ricky Henderson,
NY Yankees

Future-Proofing Your Business

A decade ago the Internet became an important business tool. I remember talking to business leaders about how the Internet would be used in business. On more than one occasion, I had CEOs say the Internet would never be used for anything but hobbies and games. One executive told me that no one would ever do online banking. "Never happening," he said. "I'd stake my career on it."

But the Internet did have a major redefinition and expansion of the value of business. Looking backward, e-business seems so obvious, so inevitable. But back then, adopting e-business was a bold leap forward, one that lots of business leaders just weren't ready for.

In fact, in a way, no one was fully ready for the Internet. As often happens when people predict the impact of new models, the extent of the change was underestimated. No one could envision all of the creative uses that people would find for the technology. There was no blueprint or Internet agenda. Companies embarked on the Internet at their own pace and often through trial and error. There are certain first-of-a-kind technologies where you will have to learn as you go.

Today, another earthshaking model shift is happening and I have the recipe to increase your chances of success. The fusion of current business technologies and the social networking models that have grown up in the consumer world is radiating astonishing business value. In addition, this social model change is happening at an unprecedented velocity.

My own company, IBM, experienced this change when shaking up the world with Watson, a real artificial intelligence machine that competed live on-air with the greatest Jeopardy champions ever in front of 10 million viewers. Jeopardy is a game show where the contestants get the answer and have to come up with the question. IBM leveraged the consumer space of Jeopardy, with the B2B world of selling to Fortune 1000 companies. It also leveraged the bounds of the traditional marketing world with the new Social Business processes, by having a dedicated social site for Watson's creators, creating a Facebook (www.facebook.com/ibmwatson) and Twitter account (@ibmwatsonbot) for Watson, and posting YouTube videos. It goes on with Ted.com talks, and Reddit, a social news site where IBMers can answer questions about Watson, Jeopardy, and more. So the idea of "social" isn't only about Facebook, or YouTube, or Twitter. People connected by smart systems can make better decisions and bring value to business. Those of you who watched Jeopardy recently saw how smart IBM Watson could be when it applied complex analytical ability to a wide range of topics. This model shift has impacted the clients of IBM and IBM in every way possible.

And the shift is not just for big business. Take for instance Richard Scott Salon and Spa, a business based in Westchester County, New York. The owner, Richard Scott, has turned this small but growing business into a social machine. He aggressively markets his services through Facebook, LinkedIn, Twitter, and Foursquare. With changes to his comprehensive integrated marketing process, he embeds trust at every level. Given his social focus, he has done no print advertising for more than 1.5 years, with a tremendous growth in new clients. He is a digital immigrant who has transformed his small business into the next-generation business, taking advantage of the model shift in his backyard.

The global world is primed for the social model shift because they are already digitally native or immigrants, meaning they grew up digital or adapted to it. Social tropes—social ways of thinking, feeling, acting, and being—represent a massive, new aspect of our world. The solutions that have sprung up on the consumer side are only a beginning. The real mass, the real power to transform, is on the business side. Becoming a Social Business is at the stage in life that the Internet was at so many years ago. Leadership companies are acting but not everyone is—yet. Unlike with the Internet, however, I believe time matters much more here, and the advantage goes to those who start early.

Why?

The Internet era was really more about the technology than people. Companies that began to go online were able to make up time by applying more technology and dollars to catch up. Conversely, in Social Business, it is less about technology and more about people and relationships. It is about closed businesses becoming open.

Relationships take time—not just technology. Therefore, I believe that Social Businesses are future-proofing their businesses by adopting early, and creating value by being bold in their usage. Future-proofing means ensuring that your company is anticipating the future in order to seize the opportunity that it represents. As we have discussed throughout the book, at their core, Social Businesses are

- **Engaging:** A Social Business connects people to expertise. It connects individuals (whether customers, partners, or employees) as networks of people to generate new sources of innovation, foster creativity, and establish greater reach and exposure to new business opportunities. It establishes a foundational level of trust across these business networks and thus a willingness to openly share information, developing a deeper sense of loyalty among customers and employees. It empowers these networks with the collaborative, gaming, and analytical tools needed to engage each other and creatively solve business challenges.

- **Transparent:** A Social Business is always learning and therefore believes that there should be no boundaries between experts inside the company and experts in the marketplace. It embraces the tools and leadership models that support capturing knowledge and insight from many sources, allowing it to quickly sense changes in customer mood, employee sentiment, or process efficiencies. It utilizes analytics and social connections inside and outside the company to solve business problems and capture new business opportunities.

- **Nimble:** A Social Business leverages these social networks to speed up business, gaining real-time insight to make quicker and better decisions. It gets information to customers and partners in new ways—faster. Supported by ubiquitous access on mobile devices, new ways of connecting and working together, a Social Business turns time and location from constraints into advantages. Business is free to occur when and where it delivers the greatest value, allowing the organization to adapt quickly to the changing marketplace.

In this book alone, you have seen numerous examples of Social Businesses emerging. For example, IBM crowdsourced (crowdsourcing leverages the collective intelligence of many people to try to solve a problem or generate new ideas; crowdsourcing is also sometimes referred to as "wisdom of the crowd") the nuanced knowledge of its worldwide employees to fine-tune its language-translation engine. KBC, a Belgian bank, totally refreshing its culture, is now getting greatly increased value from organizations that join it. Computer Science Corporation, an IT consulting and managed services company, has transformed itself into a client-focused team by engaging and serving its clients socially. And Blue Cross and Blue Shield is gathering and sharing patients' ratings of healthcare providers, empowering consumers to make more informed choices.

And this applies to governments, too. By the end of 2011, the world population is expected to reach more than seven billion people. The United Nations has a bold idea—they are using social tools and social analytics to illustrate the interconnections of the people behind the number and start a global dialog. A global dialog to advance our collective understanding of how the local, and sometimes individual, decisions we make can have far-reaching impact. The idea is simple: Challenge the world's social networks to host this dialog and catalog more than seven billion posts by capturing these discussions with a common hashtag #7b that can be searched across multiple networks and analyzed for actionable insights.

These Social Businesses know that creating a digital presence can heighten awareness and ultimately bring in new business.

What's often ignored, however, is that without a clear plan and direction in place before a company begins, it can easily fail. A Social Business (or government) needs a bold AGENDA to navigate through the new waters.

The Bold AGENDA

The Social Business AGENDA (Align corporate goals and culture, Gain social trust, Engage through experience, Network your processes, Design for reputation and risk management, Analyze your data) is a way to outline your business plan to capture value and deliver business outcomes. It has been road-tested and is proven to help shape an effective approach. It is **bold** in that Social Business is in its earliest stages of maturity. Bold is the ability to take a risk, manage that risk, and be confident in the outcome.

Your next action upon finishing this book is to develop your AGENDA that is personalized to your goals, culture, and needed outcomes. My experience shows that creating your AGENDA can take as little as a couple days to upwards of a couple weeks. Understand and set the expectations that the AGENDA will change. You will need to be disciplined but nimble to adapt changes and modifications over time. This is a journey and you need to keep an open mind that your Social Business AGENDA will be a perpetual and living strategy that changes as your goals, culture, and needed outcomes change.

Throughout this book, I have highlighted hundreds of clients around the world leveraging social tools and techniques for results; however, I showcased a particular aspect of their journey to emphasize a point. Here is one complete example of an AGENDA from IBM to illustrate their overall Social Business AGENDA so that you can see the end-to-end view of the work and the results to date.

CASE STUDY: IBM GLOBAL FOCUS ON INTERNAL PROCESSES

Align organizational goals & culture: Many of the IBM human resource initiatives, such as work from home and a matrix reporting system, drive new sets of collaboration requirements. With a dispersed workforce in different time zones spread over 170 different countries, and 86 acquisitions in 6 years, IBM needed a new model of retaining knowledge and changing the culture for driving innovation. IBM could no longer just rely solely on a handful of research centers to keep its competitive advantage. Reducing operating costs while growing its leadership as the largest IT company required IBM to bring to bear the "collective intelligence" across different projects and people. Collaboration and technology could not get in the way of that mission.

IBM's senior leadership saw the potential of social technology as the collaboration driver to bridge people and information. In 2007, IBM took a bold step and consolidated some social networking tools being used in research to deploy and support an enterprise social networking solution. With funding and support from the senior leadership, the technology was deployed within months. The majority of the funding was not for the software, hardware, support, or infrastructure costs. Instead, the funding went toward events and programs aimed at a cultural shift to embrace open and public knowledge sharing as the preferred method of communication. IBM established an adoption program, guidelines, training, reward programs, governance process, councils, and more to ensure this journey to become a Social Business was a success.

Along with Social Computing Guidelines and a mature governance process (which was discussed in Chapter 2, "Align Organizational Goals and Culture"), IBM's goals and culture are crucial to its success.

Gain social trust: To generate social trust, two of the biggest traditional obstacles to collaboration were siloed ways of thinking and a traditional hierarchical organization. Driving decisions down into the organization was a mandate. For example, a major focus was decision making done at a country level, allowing business to be done a faster pace than before and showcasing IBM's trust for its employees. Once the organization was flatter, IBMers were able to interact faster at a global level and feel empowered to do business.

Another example of social trust was the removal of moderation processes to contribute knowledge. In early experiments at IBM with social technology, IBM identified some constraints as they moderated creating community sites and content. IBM discovered that users were less likely to contribute content and knowledge if it needed prior approval before publishing. When IBM developed their Social Computing Guidelines in 2005, they opened the door to remove all requirements around moderation. IBM now had in place the appropriate terms of use to hand over authoring rights to all IBM users and trusting them to adhere to the guidelines.

Engage through experiences: The "Social Everyplace" philosophy is to drive the success and adoption of social software by integrating key social services into the existing tools that employees use every day. With this new model, IBM was able to successfully deliver key business initiatives:

- **Human relations**: BlueThx Awards for empowering employees to provide instant rewards to other employees, a community for World Wide First Line Manager to help employees become better managers.

- **Sales:** Best Practice Community used for my sales team globally for keeping the sales force up to date on the latest sales plays and best practices.

- **Marketing:** Access to all key presentations and marketing materials.

- **CIO's office—iPhone community:** IBM does not officially support the iPhone when someone calls the 800 support number. So it used the "wisdom of the crowds" to help support the corporate initiative of "open commuting."

- **Onboarding new employees:** The Women in Europe community with 23,000 members is a way for new employees to feel connected, especially when a team is probably spread across several different countries.

(Social) network your processes: According to IBM's Senior Vice President, Steve Mills, internally embedding social into its processes help to "harness our collective intelligence across IBM and ultimately across our eco-system." This is most prevalent with IBM's global sales force. With IBM's sales force alignment around industries, IBM put a plan in place in 2008 to launch IndustrySpace communities, where employees from hardware, software, and services could come together and have an open dialogue on solutions and trends related to that industry.

In 2009, IBM launched a social networking platform in the cloud for sellers to now better communicate and collaborate with their customers. Sending of email attachments has now been replace with secure communities in the cloud where an IBM seller can have private communications—file sharing, web conferencing, instant messaging, and more—through restricted communities. The best part is that IBM sellers can invite their customers to collaborate in the cloud at no additional cost.

Design for reputation and risk management: IBM's "Corporate Memory" is critical to success and, for a company that just celebrated 100 years, is important for historical measures. In 2010, IBM was preparing for its centennial in June 2011. The charter group was reviewing how to best promote this historic event. They decided that they should leverage the 400,000 plus IBM employees to help spread the news and promote IBM's brand and accomplishments over the last 100 years. The most effective way to do this was through the use of social media and social networks. As you can imagine, there was some hesitance on turning loose the entire IBM employee population on external social media websites like Twitter, Facebook, and YouTube to become brand advocates. For IBM to protect their employees, company, and brand, it needed to update some processes and ensure proper enablement of these external tools. IBM established a **Social Business @ IBM** website for employees to learn how to set up accounts and best leverage external social media websites.

IBM also set up a consumer insights tool that allowed people from marketing, communications, and public relations to monitor all social media related to IBM on these external sites. This allowed them to zone in on certain topics or people to promote positive content or get a plan in place to control the distribution of negative content.

Analyze your data: IBM employees generate one million page views of internal wikis and 40–50 million instant messages per day. And there are more than 73,000 internal blogs and wikis. Three out of four employees each morning open the IBM intranet w3.ibm, which has social elements embedded in it. IBM has all the web analytics and social metrics to monitor the usage of their deployment. What sets IBM aside from many others is their deep content analytics to categorize the information in near real time to better understand more advanced insights, including sentiment analytics, usage patterns by geo/division, emerging topics, and most linked pages, and visualize over time how networks of people are forming and information is flowing throughout IBM.

Now to draw up to your own AGENDA take a moment to review these details of how to establish the strategy in this format.

Align Corporate Goals and Culture

The strategic plan begins with a company's goals. To gain solid business outcomes, start with the end in mind. Rank yourself today in your engagement, nimbleness, and transparency against your competitors and companies you admire.

The key points here are to form your goals based on the business needs. Goals need to be measurable and succinct. These goals should dive into business needs by line of business and across the company as a whole. For example:

- Enhancing your reputation among your customers and constituencies to grow in new markets
- Enabling you to respond more quickly to customer requests to customer care
- Increasing employee retention through employee engagement

Your company's culture matters. Ensure that your plan includes education, Social Business policies, sponsorship from executives, change agents, and celebration of successes. Depending on the size of your company, industry, and objectives, you may want your employees practicing in private networks and experimenting inside your four walls first.

As discussed in Chapter 5, "(Social) Network Your Business Processes," a Social Business Digital Council is a governance body established to ensure that the company is analyzing the reputational effect of employee use of social risks associated with employee use of social outside the firewall. Forming a digital council is a critical element of infusing the right level of focus throughout the organization. A digital council can be made of virtual teammates or those assigned full-time to explore the cross-functional best practices, plans, and direction of your team.

The top elements of your plan to align your company's goals and culture are the following:

- **Measurable goals:** Goals for your business that will guide and direct your Agenda.

- **Social Business guidelines:** A set of guidelines for employees to guide them in their use of social tools outside the firewall.

- **Education, experimentation:** Training for your employees so that they will be ready to experiment with social tools and techniques. This education will enable them to experiment internally first, and then go outside the firewall.

- **Champion at the top:** A Social Business champion is an influential stakeholder at a company that will champion and support the use of social tools and techniques throughout the business and its processes. Usually they are the chairperson of the Digital Council.

- **Governance model with Social Business Digital Council at the heart:** Governance is the structure of relationships and processes to direct and guide the use of Social Techniques in order to achieve the goal of the company. The governance model defines what has to be done to reach the goals, how it is done, who has the authority to do it, and the metrics of success that will be used. Without proper governance, Social Business best practices can be implemented in departmental silos which limit the opportunity for sharing across the entire corporation. The Social Business Digital Council is part of the governance structure established to ensure that the company is analyzing the reputational effect of employee use of social risks associated with employee use of social outside the firewall.

Gain Social Trust

A Social Business is a business with relationships playing the critical role. In this portion of your plan, you need to systematically determine for your corporation who your friends are, and who you want to make friends with. These brand advocates form an important role outside your four walls.

Determining your friends is about listening and selecting based on common interests, knowledge, and other key elements critical for your business. In addition to seeking out your friends, it is important to determine your best friends, or your *tippers*. These are those people who influence your brand online and those whom others listen to about your products. These key influencers have a set of characteristics. Typically, they are people who have strong relationships, and are an expert or authority in a subject. Sometimes influencers are those who get attention, taking an atypical view, or are just loud. I was recently at a virtual conference and heard a speaker talk about an influencer as someone who is honest, trustworthy, and knowledgeable. They have a consistent opinion that is objective and not influenced by someone paying them! These items drive a level of social trust and that trust persuades another person to take action.

Finally, developing social trust is about showcasing care and value. Listen and change where needed. Always be honest, and demonstrate value-add to your clients and the industry. There is a small company in Westchester County, Elegance II, which understands the value of trust. The owner personally develops trust with each client, and her daughter has taken that to social means, like Facebook. You do not have to be a big business to embrace the elements of Social Business.

These are the top elements of your plan to gain friends and fans through social trust:

- **Determination of your friends or brand advocates today:** A friend is a client, a potential client, or an influencer who recommends your brand, company, or product because they like it so much, they feel compelled to discuss it. Determining those who are your friends or brand advocates is important to your overall social trust plan.

- **Determination of your "best friends" or tippers:** These are people who influence the rest of the clients and potential clients online and offline, usually about 5% to 10% of your product's or category's population. These tippers are important people for your overall strategy and your company will pay extra attention to them.

- **Brand army (advocacy) strategy:** A brand army (advocacy) strategy is a plan to determine those actions your company can take to build brand advocates, or people who are passionate about your brand and reference you as a normal course of business. Part of this strategy could be in the content that you share, your shared vision of a point of view in the market, or even support of a common cause that is outside the primary goal of making profit—for example, making the planet a better place.

- **Content activation plan:** This is a plan to create content, distribute content, promote content, and measure its success. This content activation plan is usually determined in the Social Business Digital Council. The goal of the content is to showcase your company's subject matter expertise or point of view (POV). It is critical when starting a community, and for guarding your reputation.

- **Determination of key methods to establish social trust in your space:** Based on your company's goals, a trust plan is formed to create and protect trust through online experiences and dialogues with a company, product, or brand.

Engage Through Experience

Engagement is about reaching your audience in a way that compels, inspires, and drives transparency. Research shows that engagement is highest when connection is made interactive and identifying or personal. An integrated approach is also essential in being consistent to your client. For example, at IBM we have a Social Business manager for a particular category or brand who orchestrates the multiple channels and messages for a consistent and coherent brand image. A Social Business manager is a person whose role it is to lead a company's transformational initiatives which empower employees to deliver business value through sharing their expertise across the social web. The Social Business manager plays an active role in the community, engaging with all audiences on an ongoing basis, working to continually grow the network and improve the experience.

Key responsibilities include the following:

- Nurture and grow the network (on- and offline)
- Steward the network conversation
- Seek out streams of utterances and brief conversations
- Provide valuable content and experiences designed to spur conversation/viral sharing
- Offer a POV as a brand or knowledgeable network expert
- Ensure that input/feedback gets channeled to the appropriate internal functional group and expert
- Manage related platforms and content
- Remain responsible to the network first
- Monitor network health
- Evangelize social media best practices

The most engaging techniques for interactivity include the use of mobile, gaming, virtual gifts, other virtual and interactive cool concepts, video, location-based services, communities, micro-blogging, and more. The technique needs to fit the goal, culture, and brand, as well as the needs of your brand advocates, friends, and tippers. It should reinforce trust.

These are the top elements of your plan to engage through experience:

- **Creation of an engagement plan and methods:** Because engagement is your emotional connection with your client or employee, it can be enhanced by exceptional experiences that are integrated, interactive, and identifying. By connecting people to expertise, it generates new sources of innovation, fosters creativity, and establishes greater reach and exposure to new business opportunities. It establishes a foundational level of trust across these business networks and thus a willingness to openly share information, developing a deeper sense of loyalty among customers and employees. It empowers these networks with the collaborative, gaming, and analytical tools needed to engage each other and creatively solve business challenges. This plan should be built with the help of your own teams, including your Social Business manager and community manager, as well as your brand advocates. The right set of metrics based on your choice of engagement methods will be critical to know if you are successful.

- **Selection of Social Business manager and/or community manager:** Select the right team to evaluate your engagement plans. A Social Business manager is a person whose role it is to lead a company's transformational initiatives which empower employees to deliver business value through sharing their expertise across the social web. They understand the social tools and techniques and should be able to offer choices to the Social Business Digital Council. A community manager is a person who manages an online community. This person's role is to keep the community members active and engaged by setting the strategy, gaining trust of the members, and ensuring the appropriate content activation plan. Given that they know the community best, they are best suited to speak on behalf of your brand advocates and help in testing and evaluating the right engagement methods.

- **Evaluation of social tools for both internal and external use:** Technology enables exceptional experiences. Through the appropriate use of mobile, gaming, video, virtual gifting, location-based services, and the new social tools, your engagement can be more competitive and of more value to your clients.

(Social) Network Your Processes

As your Social Business becomes savvy about its use of social techniques, a more advanced look at overall process efficiency is the next step. Today, the most common process with embedded social aspects is marketing. Other processes usually followed are human resources, customer service and support, product innovation, and supply chain.

In your Social Business AGENDA, explore ways that embedding social techniques could improve your process or allow you to explore new markets and thus create new processes. From IBM's 2011 CIO study, nearly three out of four CIOs expect changes to their internal collaboration processes with high transformational potential for their organizations. For example, our workplaces encompass global teams connected by the Internet, whether we're in our home offices, in the car pool line, or at the airport. At IBM, our 400,000 employees work in more than 170 countries. We bring new employees into our company on a regular basis, with more than 70 acquisitions in the past decade. Most of our employees work away from traditional offices, and 73% of our managers have remote employees. Our "follow the sun" work environment operates 24 hours a day, 7 days a week, 365 days a year. Inside IBM, we are working smarter, unlocking innovation, and building relationships using the same types of social tools *inside* our company network. Individuals and teams gain productivity, and they retain an appropriate level of confidentiality for our business.

Examples include ways to improve the following processes:

- Customer service process, by adding social self-service to the company's community and blogs
- Public relations process, by enabling them to leverage a virtual press room with interactive demos

The top elements of your plan to (social) network your processes are these:

- **Define your core process focus:** Selection of your first business process to which to add social techniques will enable you to gain support across the organization in becoming a Social Business. I would encourage you to look at human relations, product innovation, and marketing or public relations first, but plan to phase in customer service and other operational processes.
- **Select champions and teams:** Carefully match the IT and business talents of your team to the tasks at hand. For instance, if you choose to start with HR, make sure that your HR leader is engaged and championing the effort.

- **Set metrics:** Your company won't know if it is successful if you do not measure your process improvements. Whether you use ROI or increases in new innovations, revenue, or access to experts, you need to make sure you have agreement on the right set of metrics.

- **Benchmark with other companies:** From "The Rise of the Networked Enterprise: Web 2.0 Finds Its Payday" (McKinsey Global Survey Results, 2010), I shared that on average 30% of those that social-enabled their HR and talent management process increased their speed to knowledge and experts and that 20% of those companies that socially enabled their product innovation process increased time-to-market and successful innovation. Make sure you are comparing yourselves across other bold companies!

Design for Reputation and Risk Management

Risk management is a top subject for every company management team that I have spoken with this year. Recently, a CEO told me that the company had chosen not to leverage social in their business to protect their brand. I showed him that regardless of whether they allowed their brand and employees to participate, their brand was still out there. In the social world today, your clients, tippers, and influencers are your new marketing department, so managing your reputation and risk is a top priority. Having a risk management plan is smart business.

To begin, you need to define your "go-to" team for reputation and risk management and create your plan before a small incident or even a disaster occurs. A disaster could be as minor as someone tweeting about your product in a negative tone, or as serious as a full-out digital attack from an activist group on your supply-chain process. Success comes to those who are prepared. Speed and being proactive are the currency for success so make sure that you are nimble. With the right team and plan in place, your listening tools will alert you to issues. Your response should be transparent.

I often see this "go-to" team as a shared service across multiple lines of business. Because not all issues are equal, having a rating system on the seriousness of the situation will make the response appropriate to the issue. As these issues arise, the "go-to" team will engage the appropriate business owner or stakeholders to take action. For example, the team listening may route some issues to marketing or communications while other issues may be routed to HR or Legal departments.

These are the top elements of your plan to design for reputation and risk management:

- **Run a premortem:** I went to Harvard Business School, and the professors there used to teach us about "prospective hindsight," or imagining that an event has already occurred. This hindsight increases the ability to correctly identify reasons for future outcomes by 30%. If your company conducts a premortem on the worst thing that could happen to your company, brand, and product from your Social Business plan, you can assess risks at the outset. This premortem will prepare you for success. Take it seriously! Guy Kawasaki highlighted premortems in his new book, *Enchantment*.

- **Select the appropriate listening tool(s):** Listening enables you to gather and analyze conversations about your company, brand, and product. Because there are conversations about your brand going on all the time, you need an automated way to gather up the information about your brand. Gathering is one part of the equation; analyzing it to build or protect your reputation is equally important. With the amount of data in the blogosphere, you need tools to assist you in doing this.

- **Classify the types of issues requiring response, and the speed needed in each case:** Determining your system of warning is important. This enables you to have categories of issues—for instance, a single tweet about your brand that you need to address quickly to avoid damage to your reputation versus an entire organized attack online against your company. This categorization could be as simple as red, yellow, green, but regardless of what the system is, you need to have one for your company, and know the speed with which you have to respond based on the category of issue.

- **Select a Social Business Reputation and Risk manager:** The role of this individual is to own the responsibility for listening and then filtering information to the correct departments inside the organization. For example, the Social Reputation and Risk manager might pick up a negative sentiment around supporting a product. It is not the manager's responsibility to respond, but instead it's his or her responsibility to notify the appropriate brand army (customer support and advocacy) to handle that situation.

- **Create a reputation and risk management plan:** This plan needs to define how your company will organize the response, create an activation plan for the crisis, and select the right team to handle before the crisis occurs. In addition, they will define the reputation elements of your brand and proactively build and protect your company, brand, and product.

- **Refine through postmortem:** A postmortem enables your company to learn and get better each time. Most of the Fortune 100s have had some crisis, learned from their mistakes, and gotten better at addressing and avoiding future issues.

Analyze Your Data

Turning data into insight is essential for any Social Business. Analytics enables a company to make decisions and to leverage predictive tools to get ahead of the next big trend so that they can better satisfy their clients. Social analytics can provide an increased aperture of the consumer and the ability to see new patterns and opportunities.

Social analytics is a new area of focus, but I advise clients to jump into a set of metrics and learn from the best practices of others. Even if it is in small steps. For example, Morning Report is an IBM research project that showcases a simple but valuable use of analytics.

This solution focuses on the ritual of waking up in the morning and wanting to know immediately the latest news applicable to you, meetings you need to attend, and how the business is going. Morning Report is more than just a dashboard of content. It uses analytics to generate what content is surfaced in the report. The report allows customers to aggregate content and social feeds into our user experience.

While your first set of selected metrics will have to be refined, over time you will see what the best predictors of your success are. For instance, business goals might be these:

1. Brand advocacy, community engagement—marketing and PR
2. Reputation management—customer service and PR
3. Innovation—product development
4. Demand generation—marketing and sales
5. Employee advocacy—HR

These are the top elements of your plan to analyze your date:

- **Set up your command center:** Your command center could be virtual on people's desktops or in a room, but you need to have a dashboard that has real-time data collection and generates insights through feedback collection by connecting to social networks.

- **Chose keywords or topics, categories, and segments:** Your company needs to select the right words to search and listen to. Keywords are those that are associated with your listening focus. It would be your company, product or brand. It might include your category, like ketchup, as opposed to listening for just Heinz. These are words that are key to your success in the marketplace.

- Define core metrics: Overall, metrics include engagement, influence sentiment, and mindshare. But you need to go deeper. In this book, we also discussed these topics:

  - **Comprehensive analysis view based on chosen keywords:** These metrics look at overall statistics about your company, brand, or product, or keywords.

  - **Affinity analysis:** This involves the connection between people. In this tracking, this metric explores the relationship of the follower or friend to your company.

  - **Sentiment view:** This metric helps you understand how people feel about your company, brand, or category based on what they write. Sentiment defines snippets of social data as positive, negative, or neutral/undefined. Social analytics takes the data into insight about feelings and emotional connections.

  - **Trending topics:** This metric is about predictive trends that are occurring in the blogosphere that impact your company, brand, product ,or keywords. Tools help you build models to predict behavior and recommend the next best action.

  - **Earned:** This metric looks at the media, content, and channels that are delivered through a third party without exchange of payment—for example, traditional (public-relations-generated news, analyst coverage, or digital), Twitter, blogs, and product reviews.

- **Determine what data and sites you want to analyze:** Your company might just want to review sentiment from your employee community as a way to gauge employee satisfaction, or go after all the sources in the blogosphere to have a full view of all sources. Make sure you determine what data sources you want to leverage.

- **Select tool or tools for advanced analytics:** Given that there are many free and fee tools in the marketplace, you need to have a selection process for the right one. Automation is required in this space due to the sheer amount of data.

- **Create feedback loop to make changes:** Because this is a new space, there needs to be a systematic way to determine what is working and to modify as you move forward. Make sure you have a feedback loop in place to capture and learn.

- **Benchmark with other companies:** Learning from others is always crucial for success. Make sure you are constantly learning from others on their social analytics best practices.

Sample AGENDAS from Around the World

A journey to become a Social Business is never over. One of the best ways to learn is through others. Social Business is also not a North America phenomenon. It is truly global, opening up more doors for competitive advantage. As you approach the Global Market, make sure you learn about the adoption practices in that area of the world!

Here I've included additional sample AGENDAs for your reference from companies around the world.

SAMPLE AGENDA: AVERY DENNISON

Avery Dennison is a diversified manufacturing and consumer products company whose pioneering technologies are an integral part of products found in virtually every major industry around the globe. It has more than 30,000 employees in 60 countries. Avery Dennison began to introduce internal social networking in the fall of 2009, shortly before launching the company's first employee intranet portal and an expanded set of internal social tools in January 2010.

Align corporate goals and culture: Early in 2010, Avery Dennison announced a new vision for the company: to make every brand more inspiring and the world more intelligent. To make this vision a reality, employees around the world needed better ways to share information and ideas and collaborate more easily across geographic, business, and functional boundaries. This provided a strong business case for investing in the portal and social tools.

Gain social trust: Before launch, a team of social networking advocates developed a set of internal social networking guidelines that connected how to use these tools with the company's values. The guidelines were written in plain English to make it easy for employees to understand the "rules of the road." The company was committed to providing guidance and trusting employees to do the right thing.

Avery Dennison continued to build social trust in a couple of ways. First, employees control the content on the social tools themselves with very few restrictions. Any employee can start a community or a blog, comment on content, upload, download, and share information. The employee is in the driver's seat. Second, the social networking guidelines do not limit employees to work-related activities. This allows them to build more collaborative work relationships by getting to know each other in a more personal way, as long as they follow the guidelines and relevant policies.

For Avery Dennison employees, social isn't just social anymore; the social tools are becoming part of how people do their jobs. Through the online collaborative tools, they can create virtual workspaces to connect with colleagues and information anytime, anywhere.

Avery Dennison Chief Information Officer Rich Hoffman is a strong proponent: "Employees are talking among themselves. They're sharing and offering ideas, and debating them across time zones, functions, and business boundaries. When they talk about 'nonwork' subjects, it's mainly about health—which is highly relevant to work."

Engage through experience: In order to get employees to use these new tools, Avery Dennison focused on building personal experiences for employees related to the work they have to do. At launch, in addition to a series of electronic communications and traditional print methods, a global team of advocates helped introduce the tools to their colleagues in building-specific events. This provided much-needed one-on-one encouragement and support for initial login.

Many employees were intimidated by the new tools and not sure how, why, or when to use them. To combat this initial reluctance, the company offered in-depth training sessions to key user groups (admins, project teams, leaders, etc.) and developed a series of self-help and marketing materials based on real-life use cases and best practices from within the company. Employees continue to share tips, questions, and success stories online, making the transition to these tools even easier for others and providing valuable feedback for improvements to the user experience.

By seeding initial content and providing encouragement and guidance to those people already eager to use the tools, Avery Dennison has seen use of the tools increase steadily.

(Social) network your processes: One key to increasing use of the internal social tools was to ensure that employees would find valuable information and contacts. All internal documentation and processes can now have a social component, allowing for the best and most current information and ideas to be shared, updates to happen when they're needed, and employees to always have access to the most up-to-date version.

For example, a profile tool goes beyond the employee directory, helping employees find others who have a specific expertise using a tagging feature. Wikis make policy manuals easy to update and easy for employees to search. The Dictionary of Abbreviations and Acronyms wiki takes the mystery out of the company's "unique language." One of the most popular communities gives employees a place to share best practices and success stories on LEAN manufacturing and Six Sigma. There, they also ask questions and discuss key topics in a discussion forum.

Design for reputation and risk management: Avery Dennison has a clear set of guidelines in place for using internal social tools, and requires that employees read and acknowledge these guidelines and relevant policies before they can use the tools. Feedback and "inappropriate content" options ensure that employees can flag any issues, and the company has a process in place to manage any issues. At this time, the intranet portal and social tools are restricted to employees only, minimizing risk to the company's confidential information.

Analyze your data: Because the tools are so new to the organization, a weekly email summarizes the latest news, dramatically increasing readership of key stories after each distribution. Direct user feedback, focus groups, and periodic survey work also contribute to drawing a clear picture of how useful the tools have become to the organization. This analysis directs focus areas for improvement.

In addition, the company looks beyond the basic usage statistics to measure adoption. The social tools themselves offer easy access to what's on employees' minds via their blogs, comments, and other public activity; provide insight to trends; help identify internal brand advocates; and help measure communication outcomes.

Results to date: In a very short time, Avery Dennison has transformed how it communicates with employees. In tandem with sharing more consistent and clear messages with employees via the portal, the company is using the social tools to elevate employees' voices and enable collaboration, excellence, and innovation. Communication has shifted from one- and two-way to fully networked.

Within 12 months, about 90% of employees with PCs had signed on to the portal, and more than two-thirds of users had used one or more of the social tools. Activity continues strong with more than 500 blogs, 850 different communities, and thousands of bookmarked sites, among the most impressive statistics.

Employee feedback has been passionate and strong in support of continued improvements to the tools and minimizing any barriers to their use. According to Avery Dennison Chairman, President, and CEO Dean Scarborough,

> "These tools are truly empowering employees. With the combination of the new vision and strategy and these tools, we're seeing higher levels of employee engagement. We are empowering our employees, unleashing their creativity and supporting their desire to make a difference for our customers."

SAMPLE AGENDA: BASF GERMANY

BASF is the world's leading chemical company. With about 109,000 employees, six Verbund sites, and close to 385 production sites worldwide, they serve customers and partners in almost all countries of the world. In 2010, BASF did over €63 million in sales.

Align corporate goals and culture: BASF goals and culture are focused on achieving value-adding growth. Four strategic goals (see Figure 9.1) are the foundation for their goals:

- We earn a premium on our cost of capital
- We help our customers to be more successful
- We form the best team in the industry
- We ensure sustainable development

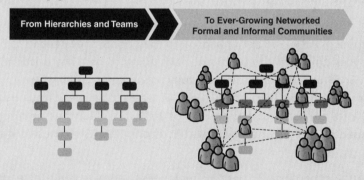

Dr. C.C. Liew and the team (BASF SE) K. Torts & T. DeSchufther (BASF, IT Services), September 10, 2010, Amsterdam.

Figure 9.1   BASF goals and cultural change

At BASF they carefully focused on their culture to ensure that these goals were possible in the transformation beginning with their Social Business Governance model (see Figure 9.2).

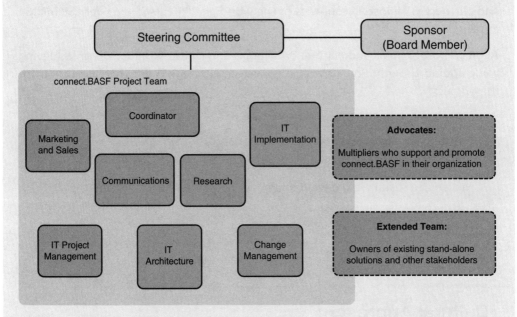

Figure 9.2   BASF Social Business Governance board

Gain social trust: For BASF to better align with their goals, they needed to build upon their employees' trust. Trust in each other was going to be a key driver in achieving these goals. BASF was working toward a fully connected company by trying to move away from the traditional hierarchical mode of teams to an ever-growing network of formal and informal communities. In May of 2010, they launched an internal social platform based on IBM technology they called connect.BASF to network employees across units regions.

Engage through experience: To get the employees to engage while increasing knowledge sharing and collaboration, connect.BASF offered a variety of easy-to-use and initiative social capabilities including these:

- **Profiles:** Employees could present themselves and be visible.
- **Communities:** Employees could build up and strengthen network ties.
- **Tags and Search:** Employees could find experts and information.

- **Blogs, Bookmarks, Forums:** Employees could share knowledge and experiences.
- **Files:** Employees could work together across units.
- **Wikis:** Employees could collaborate and gain access to collective knowledge.

(Social) network your processes: For connect.BASF to launch, there was a series of processes that need to be created and updated. The three main processes that had to be reviewed were the legal provisions, workers' councils, and some existing workflows. BASF had to create a registration process where employees would have to agree to Terms of Usage and then request that a profile be created. A deregistration process was also created for users who wanted to be removed.

Design for reputation and risk management: BASF developed a steering committee prior to the launch made up of members from Marketing, Sales, Communications, Research, IT Implementation, IT Project Management, IT Architecture, and Change Management. Since they went live in May, BASF has an ongoing team to support connect.BASF that they call the Sounding Board. The Sounding Board consists of a global community issue manager, North American community manager, Asia Pacific community manager, South American community manager, governance manager, application owner, and global community content manager.

Analyze your data: Since connect.BASF requires users to register to gain access to the social platform, a good measurement for them was keeping track of the number of users. In the first two months, connect.BASF had more than 8,000 users, of which about 2,000 had already uploaded a photo. After only eight months, there were more than 18,000 registered users. North America has the largest percentage of users at about 30%, followed by Ludwigshafen at about 22%. There have been more than 1,200 total communities created in the first eight months (see Figure 9.3).

Results to date: BASF has been conducting interviews and collecting internal case studies to understand the value of connect.BASF to their corporate goals. In one example, a marketing manager had posted a status update on his profile stating, "Evaluating market information on detergents." An information professional saw the status update and posted a response on his board to a new study. Not only did the marketing manager find it helpful, but one of their colleagues, a key account manager, then discovered it.

Another example of connect.BASF success in connecting people and sharing information was a blog that complemented the communication on BASF's employee donation campaign for Pakistan flood relief. The blog allowed employees to follow the amount of donations collected. The general manager of BASF Pakistan commented on the blog, which triggered an overwhelming response. As a result, BASF was the second-largest corporate donor to the Central Emergency Response Fund.

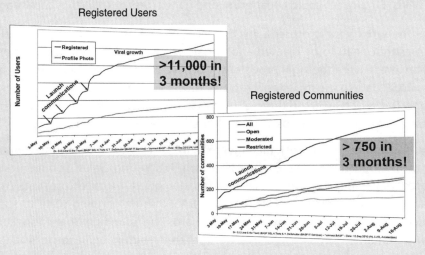

Figure 9.3   BASF progress

SAMPLE AGENDA: CARS.COM

Cars.com is a top destination for automotive that delivers a comprehensive suite of tools and information to help buyers form opinions on what to buy, where to buy, and how much to pay for a car, and to help sellers connect with in-market car shoppers. They are a $400 million business and they began their Social Business journey a few years ago.

Align corporate goals and culture: Cars.com developed a set of social media guidelines to free their employees to be brand advocates for the Cars.com brand. Their liberal Social Business policy was designed to encourage employee participation. As a pure-play Internet site for automotive shopping content and classifieds, a Social Business AGENDA seems like second nature at Cars.com and the attitude and culture reflect a belief in its power.

Gain social trust: At Cars.com, they focused on social trust in a few ways. They focused on understanding their clients and fans and learned that buyers wanted someone to advise them on what to buy, both trusted editorial experts and peer opinions. This understanding led to a focus on professional reviews, blogs, reader conversations, and consumer vehicle reviews. Since their goal was to engage in the world of word of mouth, which is one of the top influencers of automotive purchase decisions, their trust strategy is less about promotion and more about enabling consumers to leverage social networks at the same time they're using Cars.com (see Figure 9.4).

Figure 9.4   Cars.com leveraging social networks and promoting their own site

Engage through experience: Cars.com has a number of interactive engagement techniques. One example that fit with their goals and their social trust focus was to engage dealers. They proposed to allow consumers to review their dealership experiences on the site, an undertaking not without risk since dealers drive a large portion of the site's ad revenue. While the benefit was clear to car shoppers, Cars.com was able to demonstrate dealer opportunity as well. The interactive dealer review system encourages high engagement with dealer customers who now use the site to manage their online reputation. In addition to helping consumers find dealers, these reviews also help Cars.com dealers address potential problems in their sales processes.

In addition, Cars.com has watched other companies in their space experiment with direct Facebook applications and features, but results so far have been marginal. They have found that community is a limited concept in the mainstream automovtive vspace. In-market car shoppers are not looking for persistent relationships around a shopping process that usually happens once every three years or so. Cars.com's culture has encouraged experimentation and the capturing of learning.

According to Bill Swislow, Cars.com's CIO and Senior Vice President of Product, they are still working on their integrated approach to Social Business. Today, Cars.com has a collection of strategies and tactics that are very well-suited for certain purposes and certain audiences, but not for everything and not one size fits all. This is a journey.

(Social) network your processes: Cars.com is leveraging social internally to collaborate for innovation. They have Cars Connections, a platform of blogs, wikis, and communities that facilitates social connection within the company. The most popular of these include communities around business intelligence, agile development, and sales success. Teams rely on these collaboration tools on a daily basis to manage projects and share best practices.

Design for reputation and risk management: Cars.com monitors its reputation and prepares for issues that come up in the blogosphere.

Analyze your data: Cars.com has included social analytics with their existing analytics. This additional source of insight into user interests and behavior brought new tools into their portfolio and leveraged existing platforms that include Omniture, proprietary logging, Net Promoter surveys, online user testing, SEO, and internal search analysis to understand interests, and comprehensive inventory keywords helped to guide Cars.com's focus.

Results to date: While Cars.com is still in the early phases of social adoption and tracking, the company's exploratory approach and willingness to embrace social content and collaboration are driving positive results. Internally, employees are empowered to share opinions and build knowledge. Cars Connections is effectively driving knowledge sharing across teams and geographies, and building a culture where all employees have a voice and a platform on which to share knowledge and expertise.

Consumer-generated content in the form of vehicle and dealer reviews is also being embraced. In the case of Dealer Reviews, more than 30% of Cars.com's dealer base opted-in for the product's beta period, the site is steadily building its review base, and traffic to consumer-review content is increasing.

The site also has an active social following. With more than 40,000 Facebook fans and more than 10,000 Twitter followers across the company's handles, the site has the largest social following in its category. Through these channels, the company is effectively driving opinions of key influencers and better engaging automotive enthusiasts and brand advocates.

SAMPLE AGENDA: CELESTICA

Celestica is a Toronto, Canada–based global electronics manufacturer and end-to-end product life-cycle services provider with over $6.5 billion in revenue and 35,000 employees around the world. It provides design, manufacturing, logistics, supply chain, and after-market services to a wide range of customers in enterprise computing, communications, aerospace and defense, industrial and green technology, communications, and healthcare. Celestica started its Social Business journey in 2009.

When I went to their headquarters in Canada, the first thing I noticed was all the banners around the corporation on going social with their new Social Business Platform.

Align corporate goals and culture: Celestica is highly regarded for its engineering and supply-chain excellence, and its business strategy is to become the undisputed leader in the electronics manufacturing services industry. To achieve its goal, the company must effectively leverage innovation and best practices created at each of its 30-plus locations and share them across a vast global operating network. To do this, Celestica realized that it needed to provide employees with the right collaborative tools to communicate with each other and drive innovation across multiple locations, functions, and businesses.

In support of this goal, Celestica launched Operations Central in 2009, which enables shop-floor employees with self-service capability to exchange ideas and connect with experts to share solutions and ideas. In early 2010, Celestica established a Collaboration Council, with the goal of driving more collaborative behaviors across the organization, realizing that effective collaboration tools need to be supported by processes that also encourage a collaborative culture. Inspired by the success of Operations Central, Celestica then launched Connections in 2011, which links employees across the entire organization to drive collaboration from within.

Sometimes referred to internally as the "Facebook for business," Connections is a collaboration tool that allows employees to more easily connect with each other across the company's 30-plus locations in 14 countries. Employees use Connections to collaborate on global projects by using wikis to share requirements and project plans, greatly reducing the need for lengthy conference calls across time zones. Connections is also credited with speeding up development cycles and increasing product release frequencies.

Gain social trust: Celestica recognized that the key to social media momentum in a business setting is to build trust, whether it's sharing best practices openly within the enterprise or creating communities for people with common interests.

Engage through experience: Operations Central is a repository for engineers and production-line operators worldwide to share best practices and learn from one another. It was quickly embraced by employees, and within a couple of weeks, there were already 100 best practices shared.

For Connections, engagement goes beyond day-to-day business. For example, the devastating earthquake and tsunami that struck the northern region of Japan in March 2011 affected Celestica's operations. A Connections community, called "Lending a Hand to Japan," was established for employees across Celestica's global network to leave words of encouragement and support for affected co-workers. Employees from all levels of the organization visited the community often. Ten days after the disaster had struck, a local employee posted a note to the forum: "Today, all employees are able to come to the site. Many thanks for your ongoing wishes of support." The company's CEO quickly replied to the posting: "We celebrate today as a new beginning in our journey together."

(Social) network your processes: Celestica focused first on the process of collaboration across the lines of business and across the globe. This process of ideation, or of idea generation, is the first place that social has been embedded into the workflow of the company.

Design for reputation and risk management: Members of Celestica's Collaboration Council, as well as the company's compliance team, regularly monitor the Connections and Operations Central communities globally to ensure that they are being leveraged for business purposes and are within the boundaries of the company's Business Conduct Governance policies.

Analyze your data: Celestica tracks the most active locations and communities to understand what topics and actions drive the most activity.

Results to date: Celestica has connected a majority of its 20,000-plus production employees since the launch of Operations Central. The Connections tool is also gaining momentum as employees across the organization build their personal profiles and begin sharing ideas and solutions with their colleagues. Between the two collaboration tools, thousands of best practices have been shared and adopted that have resulted in significant cost benefits.

SAMPLE AGENDA: GLOBAL COMPANY—IBM INDIA

India is forecasted to have the fourth-largest number of social networking users after China, the U.S., and Brazil by 2014 (source: Datamonitor). Seventy-nine percent of online users were blog readers and 78% had created and managed a social network profile in 2009. In addition, technology products ranked in the top-three products researched and purchased online (source: eMarketer.com). Indian bloggers are the most prolific, posting new material more than five times a week on average, compared to three times a week overall (source: Pulse Group).

Align corporate goals and culture: IBM Software Group, India/South Asia, decided to capitalize on these trends and its access to the local India Software Lab Experts to launch a digital influence program to increase mindshare and conversations about IBM Software. The objective was threefold:

1. To monitor, capture, and analyze relevant conversations taking place in online social media communities to glean actionable insights around Software

2. To make the "Smarter Software for a Smarter Planet" campaign messaging more relevant and impactful for the Indian audience

3. To gather evidence, analysis, and insights about topics, domains, influencers, and events to draw a sustainable digital influence strategy

Engage through experience: Instead of treating this as a one-time tactic, we launched an "always-on" digital listening and influence framework with the following steps:

1. Conducted a 30-day brand audit/listening exercise to understand the brand perception of the IBM software brands among the target audience.

2. Shared the findings of the listening report with the Senior IBM Software Lab Leadership team and identified a set of subject matter experts (SME) from the Lab who would be trained and motivated to participate and contribute in relevant forums/media to increase share of voice for IBM Software and its brands.

3. "Unleashed" the Lab SMEs to serve as brand "ambassadors" and reputation managers. Some of them would ultimately end up as "go-to experts" to interact with media, write articles, and so on.

4. Continuously monitored the brand through follow-up listening exercises and brand audits.

The listening exercise was an eye-opener for us because most conversations were neutral to IBM and were mostly centered around individual software brands, which meant that specific audiences associated with specific brands and not IBM Software overall. A few of these brand conversations primarily related to technical aspects of the products, practice tests or exams, certifications and jobs rather than overall brand benefits, capabilities, and attributes. Two of the largest IBM Software sub-brands surprisingly had hardly any conversations. Further analysis of the quality of influencers and content revealed an absence of posts related to IT managers, CIOs, and senior developers/architects. Finally, there were only a handful of existing technology bloggers with a prominent following in the Indian context.

Engage through experience: We then set out to enable, empower, and engage our digital brand ambassadors through a series of "blogferences." A blogference is a conference where the participants learn by doing—in this case, learn by blogging! We armed them with specific keywords where we needed them to generate some thought leadership through new blogs and also drove them to specific forums where there were already conversations about their area of expertise. We monitored the frequency of postings and held quarterly recognition for the most active bloggers.

(Social) network your processes: This example in the IBM India plan is about socially enabling the marketing process. The team changed the way they showcased their subject matter expertise, the way they created new leads through leveraging these communities in their local events in the regions, and the way they progressed the marketing leads by leveraging word of mouth to build trust in the IBM product set and its applicability in the Indian market. The next step will be to socially enable their sales process, with a pilot already in place around LinkedIn.

Design for reputation and risk management: Virginia Sharma, the Vice President of Marketing for IBM India, commented, "Recognizing that the clients of India were now my marketing department, I decided to get them 'on my team' from day one and include them in my strategy and execution." Her focus throughout was on IBM's reputation. The design of the "Unleash" the Lab subject matter experts was to raise IBM's reputation in the region. These SMEs served as brand ambassadors and reputation managers. The value of this focus on reputation management enabled the team to be the "go-to experts" to interact with media, write articles, and beyond.

In addition, the team had developed a plan ahead of time in case any issues came up that threatened IBM's reputation. This proactive planning enabled them to be nimble in their response.

Analyze your data: We recruited more than 60 SMEs from the IBM Software Group to participate in social media. They produced more than 200 blog entries in 2010. These SMEs helped IBM India to gain share of voice from 0% to 14% around software conversations in digital social spaces. We set a worldwide best practice for managing these SMEs with team leads and then recognizing and rewarding the SMEs for their contributions:

- From an average of 84 mentions of the brand (or sub-brands) to an average of roughly 2,010 between June and December 2010.

- From IBM being ranked #3 to being ranked #2 in India-specific content created and brand mentioned or discussed in the social space

- From having no communities to having 10 communities that are India-specific across social media channels.

- From having no business members (only IT) to having more than 300!

- From having no C-level executive contacts to having more than 300 C Suite members of communities.

SAMPLE AGENDA: GLOBAL COMPANY—SOGETI, FRANCE

Sogeti is an IT service provider with more than 20,000 people in 15 countries based in France. They embraced social media in many small steps, with local initiatives going back as far as the late 1990s.

Align corporate goals and culture: In 2007, the Sogeti board of directors initiated a broad initiative to stimulate bottom-up innovation, the exchange of ideas, and increased bonding between employees. For Sogeti as a service provider with many employees spending their days working from clients' offices, bonding and knowledge exchange are both important and challenging. Responding quickly to clients' requests is part of Sogeti's core business.

After starting with strategic discussions, an innovation jam was held—a massive brainstorm where all employees were invited to share their ideas and opinions. Not surprisingly, many of the ideas revolved around applying social media inside Sogeti. The innovation jam kicked off broader discussions about culture, innovation, and the balance between top-down and bottom-up initiatives. Also, a Sogeti internal social collaborative space was launched.

Gain social trust: The whole initiative was one of transparency: all workshops, activities, and progress were made visible and open for discussion. The workspace was called TeamPark.

Once the social collaborative space was made available, the people who were already most active in the public social media space (see Figure 9.5) were invited to become VIP early adopters. They served as the catalysts for change, bringing content, ideas, and, through networking, broader adoption.

Figure 9.5 A sample set of public communities: TeamPark

The corporate social space was one where private topics were explicitly allowed: the content was in no way restricted or steered and anyone has total freedom to create. Besides the business communities, more personal communities were started on topics ranging from "Japanese language" to "diving" and "vacations."

Engage through experience: There were almost no straightforward training sessions to teach these new tools, but instead there were "life hacking" workshops, where participants were encouraged to look for ways to optimize their workday: how to move activities out of email to a more productive and engaging environment, how to save time by finding the right resource/person quickly, new ways to deliver something to a client. A lot of experimentation was encouraged. The support team highlights initiatives that have good potential and helps to make connections where they aren't made organically.

(Social) network your processes: People from across the company are finding each other using the network to work on a proposal or find the solution to a problem. More interestingly, peers who are interested in similar innovations also start to connect, first casually, but over time they evolve into true solution development teams, crafting new commercial solutions for the company. The fact that for the first time people from, for example, U.S., France, Netherlands, and Sweden could collaborate in the same space was extremely valuable in itself. After initial hesitation, the functional entities such as HR, Finance, Legal, or even Sales are now starting to find that being connected to their (international) peers makes sense, both for the company *and* for personal efficiency.

Design for reputation and risk management: The legal team was involved early in the process to think through both the international dimensions of social media (try creating a legal framework for privacy that works across Europe, the U.S., and Asia). Also, the company ethics team was engaged to act as the review board for escalations: Whenever someone reports something that happens in the social space, it is reviewed against the code of conduct. The code of conduct allows for much, but tells people to "act smart."

Analyze your data: Sogeti is tracking progress on many levels, with critical followers at all levels reviewing progress and continuously questioning every new investment for expected value. Primary measurements are around adoption (number and type of users), activities (what kind of content is created), and trends. On top of that is the qualitative review, tracking examples of success: a new service that was defined, a client request that was quickly addressed, or an expert who could be located quickly when needed. Finally, after more time has passed, the yearly employee survey should show improvement in how employees experience the Sogeti culture: hopefully with increased transparency, employee engagement, and better retention.

Results to date: New services have been defined and created, functional communities have seen a decline in email and improved exchange of information, and blogs are starting to share the hard-to-capture knowledge of the professionals. Without a doubt, the results are positive, though in many discussions it still proves extremely hard to translate this back into dollars: A culture of bottom-up innovation and knowledge exchange? Priceless!

New Roles Created by Social Business

With all this change, Social Business has now started to grow the types of jobs that are available in the marketplace. Just like the Internet, which transformed the company's focus and brought with it new jobs, Social Business is our fifth era of change looking to do the same. During the Internet era, new job types were created in abundance. In fact, according to the McKinsey Global Institute's report "The Net's Sweeping Impact," the Internet had a significant impact on growth and prosperity of the economy, and created more than two new jobs for each lost job (for instance, a brick-and-mortar company moving online). Social Business is doing the same.

What are some of the new job types that the Social era is producing? We have been discussing them throughout the book, but I wanted to consolidate them in one place to make it easy for your consideration:

- **Community manager:** A person responsible for building, maintaining, and activating members in an online location around certain topics. The key skills required for this role include the ability to be transparent, to drive sharing among members, and to listen and shape conversations. This role has become so popular that a day honoring it was created!

- **Social business risk manager:** A person who is focused on managing the risk associated with the orchestration of your brand value online. The role entails building a risk management plan, selecting a listening tool for ensuring that risk is assessed, and ensuring that groups of people can rally around a recovery. The key skills required for this role include the ability to understand new Social Business tools and techniques, public relations knowledge, and grace under fire in a crisis.

- **Social business reputation manager:** A person responsible for building, maintaining, and protecting a company's reputation. Reputation is what clients and potential clients believe to be true about your company. The key skills required for this role include the ability to understand new Social Business tools and techniques, marketing, and the ability to position a brand, company, or product in a positive light. This role has now outpaced the risk manager role, showing that the industry has moved to being much more proactive.

- **Social analytics manager:** A person who monitors, listens, and analyzes the sentiment (or feelings of people online), and turns the massive amounts of data into insight. This role will become increasingly important as more automated tools are coming into the market. The key skills required for this role include the ability to understand new Social Business tools and techniques, business intelligence, and the ability to make recommendations on incomplete data.

- **Social curator:** A person at your company who is responsible for information quality and quantity. Just as a curator at a museum is responsible for placing information and displaying it, this person is responsible for the content activation plan. A content activation plan is a plan to create content, distribute content, promote content, and measure its success.

- **Social customer support manager:** A person responsible for scouring the blogosphere for customer concerns, insights, and statements. This person's role will have to extend through multiple channels of input—including social tools like Twitter and Facebook, as well as traditional channels of phone, which has now become one of many places where listening and turning data into insight will occur. Key skills for this role include the ability to understand new Social Business tools and techniques, customer service, and CRM.

- **Social product innovation manager:** A person who can generate ideas, refine ideas, and solicit valid "votes" on the best ideas that customers will actually buy into. With the increase in crowdsourcing or the ability of using crowds in the blogosphere to create and vote on new product concepts, this person becomes crucial to your company's innovation engine. Key skills for this role include the ability to understand new Social Business tools and techniques, product management, and product development.

With the growth of Social Business on a global scale, companies exploring these new job categories will be those with the most future success.

My advice? As you start your journey to become a Social Business, make sure you are looking at the training you need to provide to your current employees, as well as the new job types that will help you succeed in today's competitive landscape.

Conclusion

Today, more than two billion people use the Internet. By the end of this year, Generation Y will outnumber baby boomers, and already over 96% of them have joined a social network. In fact, according to comScore, Inc., a leader in measuring the digital world, in "The State of the Internet," social networking now accounts for over 22% of all time spent online.

As we explored the impact of these numbers, the speed was notable. This adoption has happened at an incredible pace. If you look at the amount of time it took for radio or TV to reach 50 million users (nearly 40 years for radio and 14 for TV), the Internet has far outstripped them, reaching that number in only *4 years*. And to put even that number in perspective, Facebook added 100 million users in less than 9 months, while iPhone applications hit one billion downloads in 9 months.

It's clear we are now in the midst of a revolution. And companies are not being left out. According to a survey of nearly 1,700 executives by McKinsey,

- 74% are integrating Web 2.0 with customer interaction, and
- 75% are integrating Web 2.0 into employee day-to-day activities.

And these companies are seeing results: 69% report they have delivered measurable business benefits. The Social Business AGENDA is an innovative, breakthrough approach to guide you to defining your approach in this collaborative world. The sample AGENDA, references, and guidance templates provide a quick-start way for you to get started today. Get bold! Start on your Social Business journey today!

I wrote this book to share my best practices and those of other leading companies so that you and your company can drive competitive advantage and great client values. I have no doubt that more social avenues will emerge over time. I hope you will continue to learn with me by following my blog (http://socialmediasandy.wordpress.com/) and Twitter account (http://twitter.com/sandy_carter).

I wish you the best of success in your Social Business endeavor.

Glossary of Social Business Terms

Active Participant   A person who sometimes comments while acquiring information and knowledge. Engagement with your active participants will be based on how to pull them into more active involvement with your brand. An active participant is someone who comments, rates, or authors content in a social networking system on a regular basis.

Activity Streams   An *activity stream* is a list of recent activities performed by an individual. These enable end users to blend information from internal and external sources, including blogs, wikis, business applications, and so on, so that information can be effectively used in day-to-day work and enable efficient collaboration across a broad network of people.

Affinity Analysis   A process of taking data and seeing the affinity, or relationships, of product purchases. For instance, if a person buys one product, are they more likely to buy another product? Or if they buy one product, does it make them more likely to *not* buy another product?

Authentic   Genuine. In the context of Social Business engagement, it is the act of being open and true to the actions and words online.

Blog   A type of website used to enhance the communication and culture in a corporation or externally for marketing, branding, or public relations purposes. Blogs are online journals that you can use to share information with the rest of your organization. A blog is a great way to communicate your latest news and views in an efficient, dynamic style. By posting regular entries on a specific subject or theme, you can make sure people are kept up-to-date with the latest developments in a particular area.

Blogosphere   A connected community of all blogs and their interconnections, including microblogs, LinkedIn, Facebook, and so on. Essentially all social tools online.

Bold   The ability to take a risk, manage the risk, and be confident in the outcome.

Brand Advocate   A person who is passionate about your brand and references you in the normal course of business.

Brand Army   A group of unpaid and paid advocates (that is, your employees!) who engage on behalf of your brand.

Brand Hijacking   Happens when consumers appropriate the brand for themselves and add meaning to it.

Business Analytics   The discipline of turning data into insight, and using those insights to drive better business decisions.

Cloud Computing   Software and/or hardware services provided through an online computer network.

Communities   A group of people interacting in an online space about shared interests, topics, or material. They are not brought together because of hierarchy or authority, but rather just shared common interest. Communities provide an excellent way to connect members of a team and help them to stay in touch and share information. Communities can be public or restricted, allowing community owners to control who can join the community and access community content.

Community Manager—A person who manages an online community. This person's role is to keep the community members active and engaged by setting the strategy, gaining the trust of the members, and ensuring that the appropriate content activation plan is followed.

Comprehensive Analysis   A view of all that is being written about in the blogosphere about your chosen set of keywords, company, brand, or product.

Content Activation Strategy   A plan to create content, distribute content, promote content, and measure its success.

Crowdsourcing   Leveraging the wisdom of the crowd to generate new ideas and to refine ideas that exist, as well as vote on the "best" idea. Crowdsourcing leverages the collective intelligence of many people to try to solve a problem or generate new ideas. Crowdsourcing is also sometimes referred to as "wisdom of the crowd" or "collective intelligence."

Culture   Consists of learned ways of acting, feeling, and thinking.

Digg   A social news site where content is posted by users, and the users vote on the value of the content.

Digital Citizen   Someone who leverages social tools in everyday use.

Digital Council   A cross-organizational body (marketing, HR, product development, supply chain, customer service, and more). In the most successful cases, it is cochaired by a line of business and IT. The mission is to explore best practices to share and replicate in the company. In addition, the Council should help craft the Social Computing Guidelines, set up a content activation strategy, create a Risk Management and Reputation Management plan, and provide guidance. It is not set up to be a blocker of social tools and techniques but rather a promoter of Social Business for competitive advantage.

Digital Immigrant   Someone who was not raised with digital tools but has adapted to them quite naturally.

Digital Native   Someone who grew up with digital tools and techniques.

e-Business   A purely Internet business or part of a business that focuses on selling goods and services through the Internet

Earned   Refers to media, content, and channels that are delivered through a third party without exchange of payment. For example, in the traditional world it would be things like public relations–generated news, and analyst coverage. In the digital channel it would be things like Twitter, blogs, and product recommendations.

Engaged Clients Clients who are attentive, interested, and active in their support for your brand, product, or company. The depth of their conversations online showcases their knowledge and care. They recommend and passionately advocate on your behalf in the blogosphere.

Engaged Employees Those who know the company's values and are empowered to leverage those values with their partners and clients. They know their role and understand how to reach out to the right expert. These new social employees are about commitment and success.

Engagement Your emotional connection with your client or employee, usually created by exceptional experiences that are integrated, interactive, and identifying. A Social Business connects people to expertise. It connects individuals—whether customers, partners, or employees—as networks of people to generate new sources of innovation, foster creativity, and establish greater reach and exposure to new business opportunities. It establishes a foundational level of trust across these business networks and thus a willingness to openly share information, developing a deeper sense of loyalty among customers and employees. It empowers these networks with the collaborative, gaming, and analytical tools needed to engage each other and creatively solve business challenges.

Expert Sourcing Leveraging the wisdom of the experts. Like crowdsourcing, but because of the level of knowledge required, experts must be used.

Feed A feed or news feed such as Atom or RSS allows users to subscribe to content on a web page or part of a web page.

Firestorm In social media, a firestorm is a large number of people twitting or blogging about something they have a strong opinion about. For example, in 2011, when Netflix proposed price increases, clients protested with many tweets and blogs about the issue.

Friend/Fan A client or potential client who recommends your brand, company, or product because they like it so much that they feel compelled to discuss it. Someone who would recommend you, your brand, your product, or your company publicly on a social networking site.

Future-proofing Ensuring that your company is anticipating the future in order to seize the opportunity that it represents.

Gamification Research into human behavior demonstrates that people are motivated by challenges that feel inherently worthwhile. Both the scholarly literature on games and the real-world experience of game designers demonstrate that people will compete for extraordinarily low-value prizes, or no prizes at all, when the experience itself is the reward. Companies and governments are beginning to use the elements of games and competitions to motivate employees, customers, and communities. This phenomenon has become known as *gamification*.

Generation Y Group of people born in the 1980s who are familiar with and in some cases, dependent upon, the Internet and electronic devices. They are sometimes called Millennials.

Geo-spatial Analysis Part of social analytics, it enables the insight to be shaped by geographic region. For example, it could conclude that influencers are positive in London, but negative in New York City.

Hashtag   A # sign placed in a tweet to signal a topic. For instance, #ls11 was used for IBM's Lotus-phere conference in 2011.

Ideation   The process of creating new ideas. It is essentially idea generation.

Identification   To personalize the experience with your clients or employees while engaging with them.

Interact   The act of presenting your online presence and your offline presence as a single experience.

Integrate   The act of having your clients or employees become active participants, not spectators.

Jam   An Internet-based platform for conducting conversations through brainstorming. It con-nects diverse populations of individuals to gain new perspectives on problems and challenges and to develop actionable ideas centered on business-critical societal issues.

Keywords   Words that are associated with your listening focus. It would be your company, product, or brand. It might include your category, like ketchup, as opposed to listening for just Heinz. These are words that are key to your success in the marketplace.

KPI   Key performance indicator. A measure of performance.

Location-Based Service (LBS)   A service that uses a GPS (global positioning system) feature of a mobile device to engage at the geographic location. It allows you to find out where your clients or friends are, to learn where their favorite places in cities or stores are, and to locate others in a com-mon location. Common LBS services are Foursquare, Gowalla, and Jiepang.

Micro-blog   A shorter form of a blog. Typically no more than 140 characters.

Mobile Computing   Software design and implementation tailored for mobile devices.

Multimedia   Most often associated with video, audio, and animated images.

Onboard   The process of bringing a new employee into the company. Per Bauer, T. N., & Erdogan., B. (2011) in the book *Organizational socialization: The effective onboarding of new employees,* onboard-ing refers to the mechanism through which new employees acquire the necessary knowledge, skills, and behaviors to become effective organizational members and insiders. Usually includes training, discussion of culture, and insiders.

Owned   Refers to media, content, and channels that the company directly delivers, has control over, or owns. For example, in the traditional world it would be things like direct mail; a call center, branch, or store; or an ATM or a kiosk. In the digital world it would be things like a blog, Facebook page, community, or microsite.

P2P   People to people. The market is no longer about business-to-business (B2B) or business-to-consumer (B2C) communication, but is about people talking to people.

Paid Media   Media delivered through a third party or an intermediary in exchange for payment. For example, in the traditional world it would be things like TV, radio, or print ads. In the digital world it would be things like sponsored content or display ads.

Passive Participant   Someone who uses social tools only to acquire information and knowledge. They do not comment or share their thoughts and opinions. Some articles call these folks "lurkers." They lurk around the information but do not take an active part in it.

Personalization   Personalization is about making your service targeted to the individual interests. It is based on the interests of an individual. It implies that the changes are based on implicit data, such as items purchased or pages viewed.

Podcast   A prerecorded audio playback.

Reach   The number of overall friends, fans, and brand advocates you have in your domain; the number of eyeballs on your company, product, or brand.

Reputation Management   What others believe to be true about your company, product, or brand. Reputation management is being able to appropriately shape that reputation by

- Having the right listening to know what others think about you
- Countering negative opinions
- Building positive opinions through actions

Retweet   To take a tweet and resend it in Twitter.

Risk Management   A plan to manage the risks of having your brand, company, or product in the blogosphere. Your brand is out there today, the major question being how to manage the brand without controlling it.

ROE   Return on Everything. Return on everything that you do, including the social techniques.

ROI   Return on Investment. A common measure to evaluate benefits achieved versus the cost to operate.

Sentiment   Understanding how people feel about your company, brand, or category based on what they write. Sentiment defines snippets of social data as positive, negative, or neutral/undefined. Social analytics turns data into insight about feelings and emotional connections.

Service Level Agreement   An agreement between your company and your friends, fans, and brand advocates on the amount of time required to respond. Commonly known as an *SLA*.

Share of Voice   Represents the percentage of the conversations for a given topic that include your brand. For example, I might have 20% share of voice for topic x (the implication being that for a given topic related to my brand, 20% of the conversations involve my brand and 80% do not).

Social Analytics   The practice of being able to understand customers and predict trends using data from the social web. Social analytics is the process of measuring, analyzing, and interpreting a brand's level of engagement, influence, sentiment, and share of voice (mindshare) across earned, paid, and owned digital channels within the context of specific business goals and objectives.

Social Analytics Manager   A person who focuses on social analytics inside of an organization. This person monitors, listens, and analyzes the sentiment (or feelings of people online), and turns the massive amounts of data into insight. This role will become increasingly important as more automated tools are coming into the market. Key skills required: Ability to understand new Social Business tools and techniques, business intelligence, and ability to make recommendations on incomplete data.

Social Business   A business that embeds "social" in all of its processes, connecting people to people, people to information, and data to insight. It is a company that engages its employees and clients in a two-way dialogue with social tools, is transparent in sharing its expertise beyond its four walls, and is nimble in its use of insight to change on a dime, It is different from social media in that social media primarily addresses or focuses on marketing and public relations. (That's where the media comes from.)

Social Business AGENDA   A framework built from the experiences of other companies on a set of workstreams to guide the Social Business journey along: Align, Gain, Engage, Network, Design, Analyze (AGENDA).

Social Business Champion   An influential stakeholder at a company that will champion and support the use of social tools and techniques throughout the business and its processes. Usually this is the chairperson of the Digital Council.

Social Business Digital Council   A cross-organizational body (marketing, HR, product development, supply chain, customer service, and more). In the most successful cases, it is cochaired by a line of business and IT. The mission is to explore best practices to share and replicate in the company. In addition, the Council should help to craft the Social Computing Guidelines, set up a content activation strategy, create a Risk Management and Reputation Management plan, and provide guidance. It is not set up to be a blocker of social tools and techniques but rather a promoter of Social Business for competitive advantage.

Social Business Governance   The structure of relationships and processes to direct and guide the use of social techniques in order to achieve the goal of the company. The governance model defines what has to be done to reach the goals, how it is done, who has the authority to do it, and the metrics of success that will be used. Without proper governance, Social Business best practices can be implemented in departmental silos which limit the opportunity for sharing across the entire corporation.

Social Business Guidelines or Social Computing Guidelines   A set of guidelines for employees to guide them in their use of social tools outside the firewall.

Social Business Manager   A person whose role it is to lead a company's transformational initiatives which empower employees to deliver business value through sharing their expertise across the social web. The Social Business manager plays an active role in the community, engaging with all audiences on an ongoing basis, working to continually grow the network and improve the experience.

Social Business Platform   The technology platform that underpins a Social Business and drives its competitiveness.

Social Business Reputation and Risk Manager   Someone whose role is to own the responsibility for listening and then filter information to the correct departments inside the organization. For example, the social reputation and risk manager may pick up a negative sentiment around supporting a product. It is not the manager's responsibility to respond, but instead it is his or her responsibility to notify the appropriate brand army (customer support and advocacy) to handle that situation.

Social Business Technologies   Extend cooperative application technologies to "socially enable" the applications and data they support. In other words, Social Business technologies are evolutionary; they integrate into the fabric of tools already in use; and they extend the ability of end users to more fully collaborate and meet objectives.

Social Capital   Connectedness of relationships people have with others, companies, and societies and the benefits these relationships bring to the individual.

Social CEO   A CEO who is active in the blogosphere. According to Forrester, by 2015, 50% of corporate boards will recruit only social CEOs.

Social Client   A client who has grown up in the digital world with gaming, mobile phones, and videos. Social clients expect customer service teams to be customer-friendly and knowledgeable about what they tweet. If your company doesn't have a great reputation, they probably won't consider your brand, and if they do decide to go with your product or offering, your teams need to be available at any time in all channels. And they expect your company to provide an experience that is like none other. On top of all that, they expect you to be able to anticipate needs before they are demanded.

Social Curator   A person at your company who is responsible for information quality and quantity.

Social Data   Information about people (locations, relationships, expertise, etc.) that is important to engage them in appropriate networks, processes, and interactions.

Social Employee   An employee who has grown up in the digital world of gaming, mobile phones, and Facebook. Social employees expect to be social and online. And they want a leadership team that is open and involves them in the decisions. Brainstorming and ad hoc teams to solve key problems are expected and required in order for this new employee to remain with your company. Millennials, those born between 1977 and 1997, expect you to use the new social tools, and 94% of them in 2011 will use online methods like LinkedIn and Facebook to find a job with your company, according to the new study by Elance, a leader in online employment and millennials. These new employees are networked 24/7 and expect the company to accommodate pervasive connectivity and collaboration.

Social-Enabled Process   A business process that becomes engaging and transparent through groups of people contributing and impacting the process. The collective actions of the group impact the success of the process. An example would be inserting a community voice into the product innovation process to brainstorm and refine new ideas.

Social Reach   Your social reach determines the number of overall friends, fans, and brand advocates you have in your domain. It is a simple measure of who is potentially listening to your subject matter expertise or expressing a belief about your company, product, or brand. Social reach is the measure of total audience (typically represented as some percentage of a total population). For example, my brand has 80% reach for males 18 to 24.

Social Techniques   A technique used to facilitate social interactions. For example, polling, jams, and discussion threads are all examples of social techniques.

Social Tool   A technology tool used by people to facilitate social interactions. For example, Facebook, Sing, MySpace, LinkedIn, and Twitter are all examples of social tools.

Social Tropes   Social ways of thinking, feeling, acting, and being.

Social Trust   Trust that is formed through online experiences and dialogues with a company, product, or brand.

Subject Matter Expert (SME)   Someone whose role is knowledge leadership and understanding a subject at an expert level. This ability is viewed as extremely valuable in today's digital world.

Swarm   A term in Foursquare, a location-based service, that signifies that more than 50 people are at a location and have "checked in" with their mobile device.

Tag   A keyword or term assigned to a piece of information that helps describe an item and allows it to be found again by browsing or searching.

Tag Cloud   A collection of tags that are visually displayed. The bigger and bolder the tag, the more often it is used.

Tipper   Someone who influences the rest of the clients and potential clients online and offline, usually about 5% to 10% of your product's or category's population.

Transparent   Open and with a propensity to freely share skills, knowledge, and talent, and always learning. One who is transparent therefore believes that there should be no boundaries between experts inside the company and experts in the marketplace. Transparency embraces the tools and leadership models that support capturing knowledge and insight from many sources, allowing for quick sensing of changes in customer mood, employee sentiment, or process efficiencies. It utilizes analytics and social connections inside and outside the company to solve business problems and capture new business opportunities.

Trending   Predictive trends that are occurring in the blogosphere that impact your company, brand, product, or keywords. Tools help you build models to predict behavior and recommend the next best action.

Tweet   A post or status update on Twitter of 140 characters or fewer.

Twitter   A website which offers a social networking and micro-blogging service.

User Experience   Software design elements that affect how a user navigates an application or a website.

Virtual Gift   An online image or picture of an object that your company or an employee might give to someone. It is not a real item or object but exists only in the virtual world.

Wiki   A collection of web pages about a particular topic. Wikis are a great way to share information centrally and encourage collaboration within your project team. Wiki members can add their own pages, and edit and comment on existing pages, thereby ensuring that information is always kept up-to-date.

Index

C

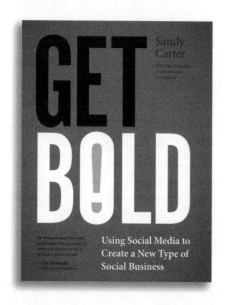

 **FREE Online Edition**

Your purchase of **Get Bold** includes access to a free online edition for 120 days through the Safari Books Online subscription service. Nearly every IBM Press book is available online through Safari Books Online, along with more than 5,000 other technical books and videos from publishers such as Addison-Wesley Professional, Cisco Press, Exam Cram, O'Reilly, Prentice Hall, Que, and Sams.

SAFARI BOOKS ONLINE allows you to search for a specific answer, cut and paste code, download chapters, and stay current with emerging technologies.

Activate your FREE Online Edition at www.informit.com/safarifree

> **STEP 1:** Enter the coupon code: HNRLOGA.

> **STEP 2:** New Safari users, complete the brief registration form.
> Safari subscribers, just log in.

If you have difficulty registering on Safari or accessing the online edition, please e-mail customer-service@safaribooksonline.com